What Women Want Next

What Women Want Next

In my twenties, I thought sex and career would solve everything.
At thirty, I thought marriage would. Later I tried motherhood, therapy,
and then divorce. At forty, I decided to renovate.

Susan Maushart

BLOOMSBURY

Published by Bloomsbury USA, New York
Distributed to the trade by Holtzbrinck Publishers

All papers used by Bloomsbury USA are natural, recyclable products made from wood grown in well-managed forests. The manufacturing processes conform to the environmental regulations of the country of origin.

Library of Congress Cataloging-in-Publication Data has been applied for.

ISBN-10 1-59691-352-5
ISBN-13 978-1-59691-352-3

First published in Australia in 2005 by The Text Publishing Company
First U.S. Edition 2007

10 9 8 7 6 5 4 3 2 1

Typeset by J&M Typesetting
Printed in the United States of America by Quebecor World Fairfield

For my daughters

'There are two tragedies in life.
One is to lose our heart's desire. The other is to gain it.'
GEORGE BERNARD SHAW

contents

as good as a feast

'You've done *what*?!' my mother thundered down the phone. I'd just confessed the news I'd been concealing for months now: that the 'temporary separation' my husband and I had been 'trialling' was over. We were no longer separated. In fact, we never really had been. When we broke up, we broke up like a hurled mirror—irrevocably and in pieces sharp enough to draw blood.

'Divorce? But on what grounds?' she pressed. I tried to explain about no-fault divorce, about how you didn't need 'grounds' anymore—didn't this happen back in the '70s, for heaven's sake?—but I could tell I was just digging myself in deeper.

'I was just really, really unhappy, Mom. Can't we just leave it at that?' No, evidently, we couldn't. Once, years before, when I'd hinted at a problem with domestic violence, she'd responded crisply, 'Well, you *can* be very annoying, you know.'

'Insufficient happiness? That's your grounds for divorce?' she snorted. 'Listen to me, young lady: happiness is where you find it.'

I sighed. How often had I heard that one over the years? What was she going to tell me next? To lie back and think of England?

'He didn't drink. He didn't fool around. He paid the bills. Where's the unhappiness in that?'

It was hard to know how to respond. 'It's different now' just didn't seem to cut it—or to reflect the immensity of the generational change since her marriage and my own. What made me happy—for example, holding down a demanding job even when I didn't 'have to'—only succeeded in puzzling her. What made her happy only succeeded in making me crazy.

No wonder talk of 'happiness', whether as a social or even an individual aim, makes so many people nervous. We tend to dismiss it as unachievable or even immature—a cottony mouthful of conceptual fairy floss, airy, insubstantial and prone to evaporate without cause. Happiness, it is widely believed, cannot be measured or analysed, let alone predicted or politicised. Aristotle considered happiness to be 'vulgar'. Wittgenstein thought it irrelevant. Freud rejected it as therapeutically untenable. Why, even the very word *happy* comes from a root meaning 'chance'. We assume that happiness, like the proverbial bluebird, either alights on your shoulder or it doesn't. That you can't 'plan' to be happy any more than you can 'plan' to fall in love or win the lottery.

For women especially, happiness seems more elusive than ever—quaint, almost. Like my friend Charlie, a single mum who told me she loved her partner but didn't have time to live with him, it's almost as if we regard happiness as an indulgence we can't really afford. Women with families tend to think of happiness as something to be given to others, like clean underwear. In the dog-days of motherhood, with partners often working long hours and small children not yet in preschool, even a woman's most basic needs may be sacrificed for the good of her family. Aspiring to anything more psychologically exalted than a few hours' sleep, or even the proverbial five minutes alone in the bathroom, may seem the stuff of fantasy.

When I started to consider the question, 'What do women want?' I was a fugitive from my second failed marriage, twelve thousand miles from a family support network, unemployed and solely responsible for the care of three children aged four, two and six months. And—despite that awful phone call to my mother—I'd never been happier in my life. I felt so happy I was almost ashamed of myself. Like Ebenezer Scrooge on Christmas morning, I was sure I had done nothing to *deserve* such happiness. But I simply couldn't help myself. (*Happiness Lesson No. 1: Joy is sometimes an unearned gift.*)

So many of the things I'd been taught—or had I just assumed?—were the staple ingredients of a woman's happiness were turning out to be strangely irrelevant. It was as if life had handed me a bag of mismatched groceries—a jar of peanut butter, some lasagne sheets, a bottle of washing-up liquid and a six-pack of beer, say—and asked me to cook dinner with them. In my marriage, I'd had a husband willing to work long hours to support us all, a beautiful, big house, nice clothes, plenty of money, the perfect family car. Once I'd fallen pregnant with my second child, I'd taken long-term leave from my university job. My husband's earnings were such that I didn't have to work for pay anymore, and this, I kept reminding myself, was a great privilege. Indeed, the whole set-up was a great privilege: from the sparkling pool (complete with its own pre-programmed bottom-feeder) to the ironing lady, whose arrival was like a perfectly chosen birthday present that came every week.

I learned the hard way that ducted vacuuming, an SUV and a third bathroom do not a family make. That a 'lifestyle' without a 'life' is, to paraphrase Socrates, not worth living. Somewhere along the line, I'd gotten mixed up. I'd mistaken 'being supported by my partner' for being...well, supported by my partner. I bought into the perks of a single-breadwinner family lifestyle and never reckoned on any of the costs—which in my case (though certainly not in all cases) translated into a steep decline in personal autonomy. The unwritten contract of traditional family life cast me in a role I was suited neither by temperament, training nor conviction to pursue. I missed my work more than I ever could have predicted. I missed having colleagues. I missed having lunch. I missed my *friends*. I missed plenty of stuff that other new mums miss almost by definition: long walks on the beach, an uninterrupted phone call, my old body. Yet more than anything, I missed the formerly taken-for-granted privilege of knowing that my life—my destiny, if you will—was my own.

Call it a control issue. I prefer the term 'meaning issue'.

I know now—and suspected even then—that few women feel even remotely elated when a relationship breaks down. Becoming a single parent at any stage of life, and especially when children are so young and dependent, is not some secret recipe for happiness; on the contrary, it is a risk factor for clinical depression. Despite its familiar trappings, in other words, my marriage was not a typical one. Nevertheless, the experience of stepping out of its frame gave me an unusual opportunity to ponder the sources of my own wellbeing, Before and After. It also enabled me to separate out what I used to think of as the 'mother stuff'—the normal abnormal state of suspended personal animation we call new motherhood—from the 'other stuff'.

The clean break enabled me to look at my life closely, even clinically. While I was still in the marriage, it was so easy to locate all the unhappiness in 'the relationship' (i.e. him). My initial euphoria temporarily encouraged me in this delusion. Eventually, and inevitably, the break-up dust cleared. And when it did I had no one left to blame for my frustrations and bad moods, my frequent struggles with guilt and occasional bouts of exhaustion and despair. He was not 'making me unhappy' anymore now. As much as I hated to admit it, my dissatisfactions were my own affair. So too were my gratifications.

I was 37 when my marriage imploded, taking a whole lifetime of assumptions along with it—especially the ones about living 'happily ever after'. (Even my four-year-old knew that marriage was where all the story books *ended*.) So now what? Until this time, I had never taken seriously the question of what *I* wanted, let alone begun to consider what other women might want. I knew what my mother wanted for me. I knew what my husband had assumed I wanted. I knew what the mainstream culture was telling me to want. And I knew too what my politically correct feminist friends insisted I 'really' wanted. I knew what everybody else wanted. It was just *me* I didn't get.

At around this time, I watched a Borsht-belt style comedy sketch on TV that made me laugh so hard I started choking and scared the kids. It was about a mother who blames her son for absolutely everything—from spilling his milk at dinner to the extinction of the dinosaurs. The punchline, repeated by the mother like a refrain, was, 'Are you happy now?' ('...Thanks to your carelessness, I now have a big stain on my best tablecloth. Congratulations. Are you happy now?...And let's not forget what happened during the Ice Age. Hah? You had to be a big shot and get involved, didn't you? And now look what happened. Are you happy now?') With the recitation of each new disaster, the punch line just seemed to get funnier and funnier. At the end, I could only roll around on the couch gasping and squeaking and crying, a circle of very worried children gathered around me.

At the time, I couldn't have explained what it was about this routine that set me off. The tension between guilt and gratification? The absurdity of blaming a child for global disasters? Or was it something about the refrain, 'Are you happy now?' Heaven knows I remembered it vividly from my own childhood, as unmistakably New York as the smell of hot tar or the taste of sauerkraut. Today the answer seems obvious. I laughed so hard because I understood so well. Like the kid in the sketch, I too was carrying an outrageous burden of responsibility for the wellbeing of everyone around me...except me.

I spent the next decade not so much examining the building blocks of personal happiness as stumbling over them. (It was only much later, in doing the research for this book, that I realised how closely my own experiences as a woman, wife, mother and friend, paralleled 'the literature'.) One of the first things I noticed was a weird relationship between money and wellbeing: that having a large income was nowhere near as important as having a dependable income, and one I felt empowered to control and manage. As a result, the transition from doctor's wife to sole-parent pensioner was much less traumatic than I'd anticipated. The day I went in to Centrelink to apply, the lady behind the counter seemed more upset than I was.

But after years of financial bi-polar disorder, with the housekeeping money either lavishly laid on or withheld altogether, I found comfort in the sheer consistency of my new income. It was small, but it was mine, and I knew I could manage on it. I know now that the relationship between money and happiness is surprisingly weak not just for newly separated middle-class mothers, but for nearly all human beings. This is why international studies show that the world's happiest people dwell in some of the world's most deprived circumstances—in countries like Nigeria, Mexico and Venezuela. (Other research has found per-capita wealth and wellbeing to be more strongly correlated, but only when affluence is linked to human rights.) International studies also show that most people, no matter how large or how small their income, say they would be happier still with just a little bit more. This is why job satisfaction is more closely linked to *changes* in pay than it is to *levels* of pay. Yet overall, average happiness is greatest in countries where wealth is widely dispersed, and social mobility—keeping up with the Joneses, or the Garcias, or the Ukazus—low.

When it comes to personal wellbeing, an adequate income—not a large one—is the key. Enough really *is* as good as a feast.

How obvious. How trite, even. Yet for me, this insight was a real breakthrough. For, despite the lip service most of us pay, the simple fact that money matters so much less than we think was a message I'd never gotten from *anybody*. Certainly not from my upwardly mobile middle-class parents, whose Depression-era childhoods had left an indelible (and understandable) mark of economic anxiety. God knows not from my husband, whose own sense of self-worth was disastrously tied up with his earning potential. Even my feminist frame of reference—with its insistent emphasis on the importance of paid work—had failed to prepare me for the upscaled joys of a downsized lifestyle.

A woman was supposed to want a rich husband to support her in as lavish a style as possible. Alternatively, she was supposed to work full-time at a high paying job and become her own rich husband. Getting by on a mix of social security benefits, eked out by the occasional freelance gig, was supposed to spell failure in anybody's ideological language.

When I wasn't thinking about money, I was thinking about sex. As you do, when you find yourself single for the first time in your life since the age of fifteen. And yet, for the previous few years, I'd made a special effort *not* to think about sex. As you do, when you've got three kids under four. For us, as for so many married couples with preschool-aged children, sex had degenerated into yet another contest of wills. In our brief time together as a childless couple, making love had been our most successful form of communication. But once the babies started arriving, my appetite for sex diminished almost as abruptly and absolutely as my craving for cigarettes had done. We still had sex— probably more often than most couples in our phase of life. But it wasn't the same. Deep down, I felt I'd 'kicked the habit' of needing sex…or even, if truth be known, of wanting it.

My feelings about all this were ambivalent. You could say that I didn't miss actually having sex. But I definitely missed having had sex. On the one hand, I was happy to offload the tensions and uncertainties of sexual intimacy: the who-initiates-what thing, the am-I-doing-this-OK thing, the why-isn't-he-doing-that thing. It was the closeness one felt afterwards that I missed—not the cuddling, exactly (I loved nothing better than sleeping alone, starfished in the middle of bed) but the sense of oneness, the connection. More than anything, perhaps, I was worried about what my rapacious lack of interest might *mean*. Going off sex was a bit like losing your appetite for lunch. It was either an unexpected bonus—or a sign of terrifying ill-health.

Since that time, I have gone from being a postpartum survivor to a peri-menopausal one. I have gone back 'on' sex—rather spectacularly, if I do say so myself—and 'off' again several times in succession. I've sometimes wondered whether, for me, sex is less like an appetite and more like a stage or a cycle or (at the risk of sounding like a complete bitch) a season. I know that whatever phase of the sexual moon I've been in, I've worried that what I'm wanting (or not wanting) is the wrong thing.

That is my experience. My reflections on that experience—including an extensive review of the literature on contemporary female sexuality—confirm that many women share these anxieties. Many of us feel as guilty and wrong about our sexuality as we imagine our grandmothers did. That much has remained a constant. What has shifted is the locus of our guilt. Few women today worry about being seen as brazen hussies. But a surprising number worry about not being brazen enough. In a world in which lack of interest in sex is regarded, both clinically and otherwise, as a form of sexual dysfunction, it's not hard to see why.

As a child of the sexual revolution, I came of age in the belief that what women really wanted sexually was to fuck as men did: as freely, as frequently, and as unfettered by complicating strings. I believed this implicitly. The fact that I was never able to put this belief into practice was a mere detail, I told myself. As a child of the middle class, growing up in the decades just before the nuclear family detonated, 'sexuality' wasn't even a *word* yet. Nice girls wore cotton underpants under their flannel nighties. So did their mothers. There was no MTV, or raunchy girl bands, or billboards featuring the enhanced genitalia of male models. There were no single mothers in those days, only 'divorcees', and the priest at our church preached regularly on the mortal sin of abortion. I was fourteen before I saw my first M-rated movie, *The Prime of Miss Jean Brodie*, and even then endured my mother's hand clamped over my eyes during the nude scene. A year before my first marriage, my parents were horrified to discover that my fiancé and I—aged 36 and 26, respectively—had slept together 'under their roof', as they put it. So much for fucking as men did. Hell, in my family, not even my *dad* was allowed to do that.

Twenty years on, many parents tolerate 'sexual sleepovers' by the time their kids are in high school, and adding a live-in boyfriend or girlfriend to the family circle is increasingly accepted middle-class practice. The mixed messages about female sexuality which my generation struggled womanfully to reconcile have not entirely disappeared, and I don't care how many journalists cite 'Sex and the City' as proof positive to the contrary. (They should try eavesdropping on a group of thirteen-year-olds discussing the 'skanks' who are already Doing It in middle school.)

There are still contradictions, but they are less pointed, less polarised. One of the first songs my daughter learned in her Montessori preschool was 'I have a body, a very special body. It belongs to me!' which she never tired of singing lustily to her bewildered grandparents. Our local high school teaches tenth-graders how to put a condom on a banana. Eight-year-olds don't wear singlets anymore, but 'crop tops' and bikini underwear. And don't try calling them 'little girls', either. They are 'tweens' now, advertisers insist, and they've got the purchasing power to prove it.

All the evidence suggests that the onset of sexual activity is occurring earlier and earlier among today's young women. Yet the flipside of that trend is a correspondingly early onset of sexual apathy.

Determining what women want sexually *now*—postfeminism, post-pill, post-AIDS, post-*Rules*, post-HRT—is a question not even the most arrogant of observers, myself included, could presume to answer definitively. Yet a number of tentative observations can be made.

The first, and most subversive, thing today's women want sexually is to decide for *themselves* what they want sexually. Perhaps even to decide for themselves what sexuality *is*: how it will be defined and measured, practised and assessed. Until extraordinarily recently, women's sexuality has been men's business. Even our impressive successes in achieving sexual liberation have been mostly about winning the privilege—if that's what you want to call it—to behave as men do. The destruction of the double standard has left us with a single standard…but it is not really ours. It is theirs. Now it is time to go beyond the freedom to be sexual as men are, and to work out what it means to be sexual as women are. Playing by the same rulebook was a big step up. On the next level, we get to write our own rules.

Sexually, as well as in every other dimension of life, the big shift for women is away from demanding equality, roughly defined as 'what men have', and towards self-determining wholeness, roughly defined as 'what women can be'. In a sense, what our feminist foremothers fought for, and largely achieved, was a policy of assimilation. Yet, now that women have been more or less successfully mainstreamed, the achievement feels unexpectedly hollow. For one thing, we are tired. If doing what men do on top of doing what women have always done is Having it All, most of us have decided we'd prefer a smaller portion, thanks very much. After all, the goal was to multiply women's options—not divide our wellbeing.

Figuring out what women want next from sex, marriage, motherhood and work is an absurdly tall order. That's OK. I don't even come close to fulfilling it. No one—not even me—would be presumptuous enough to provide definitive answers to these questions. And anyway, haven't you had a gutful of people telling you what you 'really' want? From feminist critics to Family Firsters to the writers of fairytales, there is no shortage of people shouting orders at women about how to lead their lives. Marry late, marry early, don't marry at all. Have kids now or you'll regret it. Have a career now or you'll regret it. Express yourself sexually. Respect yourself sexually. Work part time, or you'll be exploited. Work full time, or you won't be taken seriously. Get out there and compete! Get in there and cocoon! Put your relationship first. Put yourself first. Put your kids first.

And above all else, achieve work/life balance—godammit!—or fall off your perch trying.

Don't worry. This isn't just another book telling you what you 'really' want or what will 'really' make you happy. It's less a sermon, I hope, than a survey—or a series of probes, perhaps—into the heart of what we mean by happiness, both as women and as human beings. Along the way, we'll be examining the hugely expanded range of possibilities with which our postfeminist world confronts us, and discovering the wonderful news there are an astounding number of ways to get it right.

At the same time, we'll observe that achieving authentic happiness in an affluent age is a lot harder than it looks—not because we lack for options, but because we have more than we can handle. This 'paradox of choice', as sociologist Barry Schwartz calls it, is at present particularly acute for women. There is just so much good stuff on the menu right now. No wonder we display a schizy tendency to splurge (by insisting on Having it All) or purge (by Opting Out Altogether).

'Women!' goes the familiar refrain. 'They're never satisfied!' I'm the first to admit how true that is. But I also think it's important to acknowledge how *fortunate* that is. The unquenchable desire of womankind to make a good thing better is one of humanity's greatest evolutionary assets. Our insistence that near enough is not, as a matter of fact, good enough is what makes our families flourish and our businesses boom. It is also the driving force reinvigorating our relationships—all of them. (Learning how to leave well enough alone, on the other hand, is arguably a life skill many of us could use some brushing up on—but there's no reason we can't put that one on the wishlist too!)

Would it be easier to write a book about what women *don't* want next? Probably. But it wouldn't be nearly as much fun.

are we having fun yet?

'If I can't dance, I don't want to be part of your revolution.'
Emma Goldman

'The idea that the continuing feminist revolution was and is about making individual women happy and fulfilled is a continuing error,' writes leading US pro-choice activist Merle Hoffman in an article titled—improbably, as it turns out—'Happiness and the Feminist Mind'.

And we wonder why so many young women are continuing to dodge the feminist draft.

Yet Hoffman has a point. 'Feminism' and 'happiness' have not exactly proved natural bedfellows. For many of us, male and female alike, the notion of a 'happy feminist' is vaguely oxymoronic. Feminists are supposed to be people who specialise in outrage. Almost by definition, a feminist is someone who is dissatisfied with life as we know it—who has a knack for stirring things up, for causing what my mother used to call 'upsetment'.

If the key to happiness is acceptance, and the key to feminism is resistance…what's a woman to do? Especially a woman who wants to have her options, as it were, and eat them too?

To attain personal happiness—in relationships, in family life, in meaningful work—within the context of a more just social order is what most women want next, whether they call themselves feminists or not. And if this is some sort of ideological 'error', then I think most of us would be happy to flunk out now. Ironically, the warning that women's desire for personal happiness is somehow missing the mark—that it is misguided or immature or even dangerous—is one of patriarchy's oldest tales. It's the same old story of female self-sacrifice in an excruciatingly 'correct' cover: Women should be selfless. Women should be 'good'. Women should think about the happiness of *others*.

Plato had a similar attitude problem when it came to happiness. His belief that one had to conquer pleasure in order to be happy may have been philosophically defensible. But it hardly made him the life of the party.

The same complaint could be made about diehard feminists. In fact, the same complaint *is* being made, though often by women who are more inclined to vote with their feet than to write manifestos about it. Feminism, like Platonism, has been afflicted by the same po-faced suspicion of pleasure for its own sake. And the perception that feminists are not particularly happy people—and, even worse, do not entirely *approve* of happiness—has resulted in backlash from both genders, particularly among young people. To me this is entirely understandable. A feminism that is seen as rejecting playfulness (think dressing up and wearing make-up), laughter (remember the old lightbulb joke? Q: How many feminists does it take to screw in a lightbulb? A: That's not funny), and carnal pleasures (for fear of 'sleeping with the enemy') has as much appeal as a pair of pre-loved Birkenstocks. No wonder fewer and fewer women want to go there.

When even the mammalian joys of motherhood come under suspicion of 'false consciousness'—when pregnancy is something to be 'powered through', as if it were a bad cold, breastfeeding an activity you do with a pump, and parenting a hobby you dabble in during maternity leave—then feminism really has lost touch with what women want. Personally, I believe that the perception that feminism and happiness are irreconcilable is just that: a perception. On the other hand, it is not an entirely baseless perception. The onus of disproof— rhetorically, yes, but also in the way we lead our lives—rests squarely on the shoulders of whoever still considers herself a feminist. I suspect F. Scott Fitzgerald didn't take it far enough. Living well is not only the best revenge. It's PR to die for.

Like the traditional medical model defining 'health' as the absence of illness, feminism's early waves focused on what was *wrong* with women's lives. Heaven knows there was no shortage of raw material. Women did not have the vote. Women could not control their fertility. Women faced discrimination in the workforce. Women suffered sexual and physical abuse in relationships. These were among the major social ills that first- and second-wave feminism sought, largely successfully, to cure. You might say that early feminism adopted an illness model for social change. The challenge today is to create a feminist wellness movement, in which women dare to ask not only what the world needs, but what we ourselves desire.

Whatever it is women want, it seems doubtful we are getting it. Maybe it was never feminism's aim to make us happy. But was it really supposed to make us anxious and confused and plagued with self-doubt? Was it supposed to send divorce rates through the roof and fertility down the gurgler? Was it supposed to turn parenting into a battlefield, or to strip the dignity from unpaid labour? Was it supposed to alienate us from our mothers, or create a time drought, or a sleep drought, or an intimacy drought? Was it supposed to turn women's depression into a global epidemic? Was it supposed to divide mothers from non-mothers, or breastfeeders from bottle-feeders? Was it supposed to decimate our leisure time (if we work for pay), or our self-esteem (if we don't work for pay)—and paralyse us with guilt no matter which choice we make?

It was anger that started the feminist ball rolling: anger at injustice and abuse, at missed opportunities and wasted resources. Anger that was explosive, self-righteous and as taut with energy as a drawn hunting bow. Without women's anger, expressed and channelled into action, there would be no feminism to question. There would be no progress to analyse. Yet anger—like lust—has a predictable psychological running time. No matter how fired up we may feel at the outset, sooner or later our passion cools. It is the same for any social movement predicated on 'maintaining the rage'. You might as well try to maintain an orgasm.

In a world where more and more young women regard the 'f' word with suspicion and even dread, feminism can no longer afford to fall back on its big fat assumptions. Or perhaps I should say its big fat unexamined assumptions. 'Equality', for example, which is so self-evidently a good thing. Men and women are 'equal' and should be treated 'equally'. On that we have all agreed. What we still can't figure out is when 'equal' should mean 'identical', and when it should mean 'equivalent'. Is 'equality' the same as 'fairness'? (This is a question with particular relevance for those of us engaged in studying or—heaven help us—actually doing the housework.)

Feminism's second stage was largely concerned with fighting the good fight for equal opportunity in the workplace—the assumption being that once the barriers to women's participation were toppled, or at least nudged aside, we would take to breadwinning like a duck to water, or a man to a sixty-hour-a-week job. And we did, too. At first.

From the 1960s to well into the '90s, women's participation in the paid workforce swelled from a trickle to a tsunami. By the late '80s, the old bumper stickers reminding us that Every Mother Is a Working Mother had taken on an entirely unintended meaning, as the majority of mothers of even very young children were now working for pay.

Home, it was widely if tacitly agreed, was at best nowheresville, at worst a spiritual quicksand waiting to suck the unwary to the depths of domestic tedium.

By the early 1990s, the disenchantment of the home, as Australian sociologist Kerreen Reiger called it, had reached its nadir. The moment was epitomised by Arlie Hochschild's classic 1997 work *The Time Bind*, whose subtitle—'When Work Becomes Home, and Home Becomes Work'—seemed to say it all. Four years earlier, in *The Second Shift* (surely one of the most widely cited sociological works *ever*) Hochschild had demonstrated that women in dual-earner families were beginning to sag under the weight of the 'second shift'—the childcare and domestic chores for which they were still dismayingly and overwhelmingly responsible.

Something, clearly, was going to have to give. In *The Time Bind*, Hochschild argued that that something was the concept of 'home' itself. For women as well as for men, she declared, work was now officially where the heart was.

Or was it?

Four years later, in 2001, Nigella Lawson's spectacularly successful *How to Be a Domestic Goddess* kickstarted the kitchen counter-revolution. (Or did it simply reflect a growing nostalgia for cosier times and places, a yearning to look homeward once more?) Industry goss had it that the sexy celebrity chef's unlikely bestseller was being snapped up by second-shifters too busy to do more than salivate over the photos—a younger slice of the same demographic that the stalwart but hopelessly unhip Martha Stewart had been hogging for more than a decade. One thing was as clear as aspic: a new publishing sub-genre had been born. Domestic voyeurism.

At the same time, Laura Doyle's international bestseller *The Surrendered Wife*—think *The Taming of the Shrew* meets *Who Moved My Cheese?*—urged women to recapture the lost magic of a Ralph and Alice Kramden-style marriage. Doyle's thesis—that women could resuscitate the institution of marriage by rolling over, playing dead, and faking orgasm—was pure fantasy. Even the author herself admitted as much. Yet *The Surrendered Wife* was one of those books everybody made fun of, but nobody could resist buying. Laura Doyle, at least, could afford to surrender.

Four years later, US talkback queen Dr Laura Schlessinger recycled the same themes in *The Proper Care and Feeding of Husbands*. The chief reason for marriage breakdown, she argued, was women's 'self-centredness', a vice encouraged by years of feminist brainwashing. The subtext was as shrill as a fishwife on AM radio: women who insist on considering their own needs in marriage risk Losing it All, bigtime. '"I have a right to be happy, don't I?" is a not infrequent comment from callers frustrated that their marriages haven't put them in a perpetual Valium-drip state,' Dr Laura practically sneered. 'And this focus on happiness helps them to rationalise their virtual abandonment of marriage and family.' The book took a caning from the critics—and fairly flew off the shelves.

Just the opposite fate awaited Sylvia Ann Hewlett's 2002 book *Baby Hunger* (originally published in the US as *Creating a Life*), a critical triumph that proceeded straight from the talk show circuit to the remainder bin without passing Go. Hewlett addressed herself to the 'Omigosh! I forgot to have kids!' generation, issuing a stern call to women to look to their biological shelf-lives before planning careers and relationships. As a first-time mum who shimmied under the reproductive wire at the age of 45, Hewlett spoke from bitter personal experience of the topsy-turvy priorities that equated personal fulfilment with professional success. Hewlett reminded frightened singletons of a truism no one particularly wanted to hear: that age, like gender itself, was more than just a state of mind, especially where fertility was concerned. Anatomy was not exactly destiny, but nor was a woman's use-by date just a piece of patriarchal propaganda.

Books specifically addressed to the women 'feminism forgot'—the ones for whom relationship goals (marriage and motherhood) had always loomed larger than professional ambitions—began to appear in growing numbers from the mid '90s. Among the first of these was Maureen Freely's *What About Us?: An Open Letter to the Mothers Feminism Forgot*, published in 1995. My own book, *The Mask of Motherhood* (1997) and Naomi Wolf's *Misconceptions* (2001), among a swag of others, argued that feminism had failed to prepare young women—i.e. ourselves—for the onslaught of motherhood. Or, for that matter, for its exquisite rewards.

Older feminists (perhaps predictably) denied that feminism had ever 'forgotten' about motherhood in the first place—for hadn't most of them had families of their own? Some cried 'backlash!' Others diagnosed the new wave as 'solipsisters' or simply accused them of suffering from 'feminist amnesia'.

By decade's end, conservative commentators were going even further. Feminism had not only failed to prepare women for their roles as mothers and caregivers, they insisted, it had sold them a bill of goods about the whole package of adult life. With its emphasis on paid work, on enshrining the rights of women to live life as men did—which is what Having it All was supposed to signify—what feminism 'forgot' wasn't simply motherhood, or marriage, or the value of domesticity. It forgot what made life worth living in the first place. It forgot, in short, about happiness. A considerable oversight, by anybody's reckoning.

Among the most incisive (and annoying) critiques of the postfeminist predicament was neocon poster girl Danielle Crittenden's 1999 polemic *What Our Mothers Didn't Tell Us*. Crittenden, a journalist, founding editor of *Women's Quarterly* and mother of two, set out to explain, in the words of her subtitle, 'why happiness eludes the modern woman'—starting with the observation that the price of feminism was an eternity of bellyaching.

Crittenden argued that women experienced greater freedom thanks to feminism. But at the same time (and maybe even for the same reasons) that they also 'enjoy less happiness, less fulfilment, less dignity'—not to mention more confusion, more guilt, more anxiety, and many, many more divorces. The baby boom feminists may assure us that their own, often fiercely independent lives, have been rich and full and rewarding. 'Yet everything about the way their lives turned out,' Crittenden observed with full-throttle bitchery, 'contradicts them.' In brief, What Our Mothers Didn't Tell Us is that a life without what Faulkner Fox calls the house/man/baby package is not worth living. And a life with that package, if it is to be lived fully and according to the manufacturer's instructions, means turning one's back on the illusion of egalitarianism firmly and forever.

Danielle Crittenden is no social scientist. Her idea of a data set is the latest Gallup poll, and her methodology little more than participatory scorn. Yet her critique of second-wave feminism raises a host of uncomfortable issues with which most observers, including the present 'baby boom feminist', would probably agree.

'If there has been one legacy of modern feminism,' Crittenden writes, 'it has been to teach women to think of themselves as a victimised subset of humanity and not as active participants in a free and democratic society.' Much as I hate to admit it, she's right—and the evidence, like a veritable glass wall, is all around us. Feminism *has* encouraged a victim mentality. Too many of us do suffer from an almost congenital discontent. And we have allowed our whingeing to become a substitute for analysis or, even worse, for action.

It may be argued that women feel victimised for the simple reason that they often have been victims, and at times continue to be. Yet understanding the motivations for a behaviour is one thing. Endorsing it is quite another. The fact is, a victim mentality never got anybody anything—except a higher rate of victimage.

Like many other critics, Crittenden saves her sharpest rebukes for the mythology of Having it All, the second-wave's most trod-upon Achilles heel and one of the most avidly debunked (and debunkable) artefacts of late-twentieth-century life. With all the ink spilled, and all the research funding squandered, if we don't know by now that women can't have it all, after all—that, more to the point, *no one can*—it's hard to imagine what anybody can know.

Crittenden's own eulogy for Supermom stresses a dust-to-dust theme, arguing that over the past forty years, 'women have come full circle, back to experiencing the busy but spiritually empty lives from which we hoped work would emancipate us'. A similar point is made by an elderly informant in social researcher Hugh Mackay's *Generations*, a study of intergenerational change in Australian society. 'Our daughters think we've had a dreadful life,' this woman confided to researchers. 'Mine thinks I was a doormat to her father. But I simply don't feel like that. Although I admire what she's achieved, I think my daughter is a bit of a doormat to her children and her job, so perhaps no generation gets it quite right.'

One can't help but admire her generosity of spirit. It's a virtue we daughters of the revolution seem to have discarded along with the frilly aprons and the bedjackets.

Our pre-feminist mothers and grandmothers never thought of themselves as victims—let alone as doormats—though we, their daughters, have a hard time understanding why. Today, baby boomers regard the housewives of the '50s and '60s with 'a mixture of pity, outrage on their behalf, and gently mocking humor', as Caitlin Flanagan notes in the *Atlantic Monthly*—our collective horror of degenerating into our own mildly depressed mothers celebrated in greeting cards, tea towels and fridge magnets ('Marjorie could mix a gin sling in her sleep and still leave the kitchen spotless'). Flanagan argues that this 'narrative of boredom, oppression and uselessness' is a key literary device of the feminist success story. Feminism, she observes, *needs* oppression…the way a vampire needs fresh blood.

At the remove of a single generation, the Housewife inspired horror. Two generations on, she is being picked up and dusted off—

renovated, if you will—like an antique doll or a nineteenth-century worker's cottage. Caitlin Flanagan herself—an 'at home' mother assisted by a full-time live-in nanny—confesses to a weakness for Erma Bombeck and stain removal. She is evidently in increasingly good company.

The 'Opt-Out Generation', as *New York Times* journalist Lisa Belkin dubbed them, are facing a new kind of workplace barrier: the DIY variety. The most affluent and the most highly qualified (i.e. the ones who can afford to do so) are 'rejecting the workplace' in significant numbers. In the US, the percentage of new mothers who went back to work after their first child fell from 59 percent in 1998 to 55 percent in 2000, and the number of kids being cared for by full-time mums at home has increased by nearly 13 percent in the last decade.

Among female parents, it is professional women who appear to be leading the charge. One recent survey by research firm Catalyst found that 26 percent of women on the brink of senior management don't actually *want* to be promoted. Almost one in five female executives who made it to *Fortune* magazine's 'Fifty Most Powerful Women' list in recent years have left their desks, most of them voluntarily, for lives that are 'less intense' and 'more fulfilling'.

'Why don't women run the world?' Belkin asks. 'Maybe it's because they don't want to.'

The new radicalism (if that's what you want to call it) isn't confined to American high-flyers. Australian data compiled by Sydney-based market research firm Heartbeat Trends lends support to Belkin's hypothesis. In a 2004 report based on focus-group research with 1000 Australian mothers aged 30 to 45, Heartbeat found a growing backlash against the 'compartmentalisation of life' experienced by women in the workforce.

'Women don't feel at all restricted now,' maintains Heartbeat director Neer Korn. 'What they've said is the price for corporate success is too big.' For young women today, Korn's research found, the

Homemaker has shifted decisively from cringe-making cultural cartoon to trouvé role model. Granted, the gulf between what we say and what we do may be wide enough to drive an SUV through. Yet even among dads, the belief that 'there's nothing more worthwhile than spending time with the kids' is trendy to the point of truism. So much for disarming the nuclear family.

In other recent Australian research, the 2003 Relationship Indicators survey, nine out of ten respondents believed the trend toward dual careers was 'putting relationships in jeopardy'; 93 percent described 'being a good husband or wife' as the most important aspect of their personal identity. (A bit odd, perhaps, when you consider that 40 percent of men in their early thirties are single—and the proportion that are married has slumped almost 20 percentage points since 1986.) Ninety-one percent also nominated parenthood as their central concern—yet, overall, less than one in five rated paid maternity leave or better childcare as high priorities.

Our fertility rates may be falling, but our enthusiasm for—some would say fetishising of—parenthood has never been more extreme. As the *Guardian*'s Mary Kenny notes in a 2004 article titled 'The Strange Rebirth of the Family', 'the passion for babies is everywhere'. Even gay families, many of whom have gone to extraordinary bureaucratic or biological lengths to acquire offspring, are increasingly adopting a sole breadwinner model. In the US, census data show that among male same-sex couples with children, more than a quarter now include a stay-at-home parent. That's a higher rate than among heterosexual couples.

In London, according to the *Sunday Times*, 'Yummy mummydom has suddenly become aspirational', with urban parks purportedly teeming with 'thirtysomethings who have thrown off the shackles of the bar or the trading floor to look after their toddlers'.

'We were the daughters of working mothers and we expected the same lives for ourselves,' explains one highly educated young mum.

'Now my generation is saying, "Hang on a minute." We've seen what life did to our mothers and we don't want it for ourselves.' According to other recent UK research, only one in seven women regard their jobs as 'central to their lives'.

At the same time, the 'protirement' movement is gaining momentum among both sexes. According to some estimates, one in fifteen under-35s has already dropped out of paid work to pursue 'self-improvement'—and nearly half have plans to do so in the near future. Even weirder, having kids is evidently regarded as a means of achieving this!

One can't help but wonder: for how many women is 'protirement' simply a sexy new word for financial dependence? A survey published in 2003 by UK teen magazine *CosmoGirl* involving more than 5000 teenage girls found that nine out of ten believe it is a husband's job to provide for his wife—and 85 percent would rather depend on that support than achieve their own financial independence.

In the US a decade ago, the participation of women in the full-time workforce, especially women with dependent children, was widely regarded as the jewel in the feminist crown. Today, that same success story is being reframed as a kind of new-look white woman's burden. The problem now is not the underemployment of women. It's our 'overemployment', and the psychological scarring inflicted by competing obligations to relationships, self and home.

'Working moms battle feelings of guilt over leaving their children and powerlessness over the stress in frenetic careers,' notes a typical article on the trend, this one from *Business Week*. It features one thirty-year-old woman who has won the battle—or has she just gone AWOL?—by abandoning the workforce altogether. (She is 'lucky she and her husband can afford to forgo the income she made in sales', notes a photo caption.) This woman feels good about her decision, and cites a friend's children who are 'fat, TV-addicted disasters' as evidence for her belief that being a full-time mum at home is 'the best thing for the child'. The 'narrative of oppression' is old already. The new happy ending is staying home.

The question whether women are qualitatively less happy today than their mothers or grandmothers—or simply more apt to tell the truth—is likely to remain contentious. But there is not the slenderest shred of evidence to suggest we are any more happy. Between the longer hours we work, the shorter hours we sleep, and the burden of the guilt that we seem inevitably to carry regardless of the life choices we have made, most of us feel less exalted than we do exhausted.

Someone asked me recently if I was old enough to recall the famous Helen Reddy song from the '70s. 'Sure,' I replied. '"I Am Woman: Hear Me Yawn".' It wasn't until everybody started laughing that I realised my mistake. 'Yes, we've paid the price, but look how much we've gained!' were the words our foremothers were singing in the '70s. Thirty years on, women are more likely to turn that sentiment on its head. 'Yes, we gained a lot—but look how much we've paid.' If what women want next is more value for money, who can blame us?

stalking the bluebird

The perception that the world is full of whingeing women is impossible to refute. But it must be fuller still of whingeing men. The evidence is clear: 'All around the world, in rich nations and poor ones, women are happier with their lives than men are,' in the words of one recent, and typical, international survey. That's the good news (provided you happen to be female). The bad news is that the 'happiness gap' is getting smaller all the time. This is especially true for women in developed countries—precisely those nations in which women have benefited from feminism's enormous gains.

Women acknowledge that their lives have changed for the better—according to a 2003 study of 38,000 individuals in 44 countries, women were significantly more likely to say they had seen progress in their lives, compared to five years ago. At the same time, however, women were less optimistic about the future. (Partly this was owing to women's relative lack of faith in the improving power of technology. For instance, men in almost every country surveyed believed cell phones made life better. Women were much more equivocal. In Japan, two out of three women stated that cell phones had made life worse— and so did one out of three in Canada and the UK.) More and more, women's public lives are resembling those of men. So too, apparently, are our inner lives. Now how's that for a scary thought?

My own personal epiphany on this one came a couple of years ago. I was just getting back into dating in the aftermath of a relationship breakdown. I had met a man I liked very much and found devastatingly attractive, and the feeling seemed to be mutual. There was only one problem. (Trust me to turn this into a moral dilemma.) As much as I wanted to sleep with him, I knew that I didn't want to actually *sleep* with him.

Now, at this point in my life, after two marriages, two long-term de facto relationships and assorted shorter-term couplings, I would have thought the days were long over when I could shock myself. If only. Realising how much I wanted the sex but dreaded the sleepover (which would have entailed a set of complications I wanted no part of at that point in my life) was a real wake-up call for me. I didn't know whether to be impressed with my own maturity, or appalled that I was behaving exactly like a man.

'Gosh!' I remember thinking to myself. 'So *this* is what goes in their minds!' Did I really want to know this? Was I a better person for knowing this? Would any woman be?

One often hears women say that they dread becoming like their mothers. But as a single mother with full-time responsibility for three young children, I have had occasion to experience the arguably even creepier dread of metamorphosing into my *dad*—or if not my dad, exactly, then The Dad. The Breadwinner from Hell, full of sanctimony and self-importance, yammering on about the lack of 'support' I get at home (what? from a nine-year-old?) or the way my hard-earned dollars are 'squandered' by layabouts (would that be the dog, or the cat?). The day I heard myself thundering at my teenaged daughter that I was more than a 'walking wallet' was beyond Kafka-esque. What would I be doing next, I wondered? Holing up in the shed and playing with my reticulation hoses?

Whatever else they may tell us about ourselves, such experiences reinforce what the research on happiness and gender seems to be suggesting: that the more alike men and women behave, the more alike men and women will feel. No surprises there. Yet, if women are increasingly reporting lower levels of wellbeing, we can conclude that becoming more 'manlike' is not good for us...or we can conclude that becoming more 'manlike' is not good for men either. After all, the point is not to increase the happiness *gap*. It's to increase happiness.

The picture is complicated by the fact that happiness is declining in exactly those places where (one would have thought) the livin' was easy. According to a 2003 survey conducted by the UK's *New Scientist* magazine, the top five happiest countries in the world were among the poorest: Nigeria, Mexico, Venezuela, El Salvador and Puerto Rico. The US ranked sixteenth, Australia thirteenth and Britain twenty-fourth. A study by the Australia Institute found that average incomes had more than trebled since the 1950s, but self-reported happiness remained constant. In the US, where real income has risen 16 percent over the last thirty years, the number of people who describe themselves as 'very happy' has fallen significantly—from 36 percent to 29 percent. Some observers, including Dartmouth economist David Blanchflower, believe that drop is almost entirely gender driven. He points out that men today are 'about as happy' as they were in the early '70s—which means women account for nearly all the decline since that time.

Yet a wider view suggests that the Progress Paradox, as author and critic Gregg Easterbrook calls it, afflicts *all* of us, regardless of gender. Better living conditions, more freedom of choice, greater access to information and more leisure time are the glittering prizes of our unprecedented affluence. But the assumption (until recently wholly unquestioned) that these advantages will make any of us feel better about life generally, or about ourselves specifically, appears not simply doubtful but downright delusional.

It may be true that women are never satisfied. I know I'm not. But Easterbrook remind us—his book *The Progress Paradox* is subtitled 'How Life Gets Better While People Feel Worse'—it's probably more fair to admit that *people* are never satisfied. Studies show, for example, that regardless of how much money Americans earn, they estimate they would need twice that amount to 'live well'. Easterbrook argues that the more material comfort human beings enjoy, the less they…well, enjoy. Part of the problem is 'abundance denial', an elaborate mental rationale affluent people use to convince themselves they are deprived.

Happiness, as my mother would say, is relative. Among other things, that means there is no objective standard by which individuals assess their own wellbeing (no matter how strenuously we may feel that there 'ought' to be). Assessments of our own wellbeing are all tied up with our assessments of the wellbeing of our nearest metaphorical neighbours. If we think we are doing about the same as the other members of our chosen reference group—other new mums, say, or people who graduated from law school in our year—then we will feel satisfied. If we think we are doing slightly better, we will feel happy. If we think we are doing slightly worse, or heaven forbid slightly worse than slightly worse, we will feel unhappy and dissatisfied. Not because we are necessarily 'in denial' about the good things in our life. But because experience shows us—or seems to—that even the best things can be bettered.

If happiness is relative, then who we choose to compare ourselves to is vital. My twelve-year-old son believes he would be perfectly happy if only he had the latest-release handheld game, as do others in his class at school. He's not looking to acquire a Porsche. Then again, he wouldn't be satisfied with a fold-up scooter either, which was his heart's desire a couple of years ago. No surprises there, I suppose.

But that same psychological mechanism gets rather more intriguing when we apply it to the items on our social and political wishlists. I remember reading a study a few years ago that showed that women who compared their marriages to those of their parents at a similar stage of life felt happy and satisfied with their lot. Those who compared their experience of marriage to that of their husbands, on the other hand, did not. Arguably, the world would be a happier place if we could all find a reference group that made us feel fortunate by comparison. ('You don't like Brussels sprouts? Think of the starving Biafrans! They would kill for those Brussels sprouts!') Inevitably, it would also be a place more riddled with injustice, stagnation and conservatism. The injunction to Be Grateful for What You've Got is the refrain of those who've got even more. You don't see Bill Gates being grateful for what he's got—and you don't see anyone expecting him to be either.

Social progress can also, paradoxically, erode our sense of security. And this is a point with particular salience for women making their way through a postfeminist thicket of broken certainties and tangled expectations. Growing up—which is what women have in a sense been doing these past forty years—may increase wisdom. But it also diminishes, or at least alloys, our happiness. 'Ignorance is bliss,' we say. Probably 'innocence' would be a better way of putting it.

Autonomy is a more evolved state of being than dependence. But it is also a scarier one. It means, 'Nobody's taking care of you anymore,' notes Harvard professor of government Christopher Jencks, 'so it feels like everything is getting more worrisome, even if objectively everything is getting better.' For women today, the sense that 'nobody is taking care of us anymore' is particularly acute.

In trying to understand why greater equality for women has not necessarily translated into greater happiness for women, it is necessary to take a closer look at what we mean by that innocent bystander of a word, 'happiness'. We all agree that 'happiness is what it's all about'. In this we are following an ancient intellectual tradition, reaching back at least as far as Aristotle, who regarded the exploration of the nature and requirements of happiness as the central task of all philosophy. Aristippus taught that the goal of life is to experience the maximum amount of pleasure. Herodotus, rather more pessimistically, believed happiness to be so slippery a conceptual commodity that no person should be judged happy until after her death! That seems to me to be delaying gratification a step too far. Yet there is no denying the difficulties that arise when we try to nail the jellyfish to the wall.

Today, happily, there are more and more thinkers who seem willing to have a shot at it anyway. After centuries of scholarly indifference, the pursuit of happiness has become a growth industry, with the burgeoning field of 'happiness studies' and 'positive psychology' attracting increasing attention from psychologists, sociologists, economists and others. Their findings—while still tentative and piecemeal—make for fascinating reading, in part because they explode so much of the modern mythology of happiness.

Part of that mythology has been the conviction that human happiness is either a naïve construct—which is what Freud believed—or a dangerous one, which is what Plato argued. Freud's observation that the aim of therapy was 'the transformation of hysteric misery into common unhappiness' is well known and widely cited even today. (Mark Twain anticipated this sentiment, observing that 'Sanity and happiness are an impossible combination.') Rather more grandiosely, Freud was emphatic in his belief that 'the intention that man should be "happy" is not included in the plan of Creation.' Wittgenstein evidently agreed. 'I don't know why we are here,' he wrote, 'but I'm pretty sure that it is not in order to enjoy ourselves.' (If I was a nicer person I would resist pointing out that both of these great thinkers led distinctly unjoyful lives.)

At the simplest level, researchers today define 'subjective

wellbeing' as a function of three factors: life satisfaction (as self-rated by an individual), positive mood and absence of negative mood. Whatever else happiness may or may not mean, therefore, it cannot be limited to mere pleasurable sensation. Of course, to speak of happiness *without* 'mere pleasurable sensation' doesn't make a lot of sense either.

Most contemporary research approaches happiness from one of two perspectives: hedonics, which comes from the same root as 'hedonist' (lover of pleasure); and eudaemonics, which comes closer to what most of us mean by 'fulfilment'. Hedonics is about feeling good, full stop—whatever 'good' may mean to you. Eudaemonics, from the root word 'daimon' meaning 'true self', is primarily concerned with life's meaning, and those experiences that deepen our apprehension of who we are, and how we connect to the wider world.

Common sense would suggest that the good life would have to include ticks in both of these boxes. It's a hunch that's been consistently verified by the evidence. People yearn not only to feel good, in the short-term sense, but to feel good about themselves—to act with integrity and in accordance with a set of higher goals that help us define a purpose in life. As positive psychology founder Martin Seligman puts it in his book *Authentic Happiness*, 'It is not just positive feelings we want, we want to be entitled to our positive feelings.'

The literature also tells us—as if we needed reminding!—that feeling good and behaving well are not necessarily linked. Short-term pain is often necessary to bring about long-term gain, as anyone who's ever tried to get fit or stay married can attest. Parenting provides another classic illustration. It has been well established that the birth of a first child erodes the hedonic wellbeing of most women, often substantially and over a long period of time. Yet, from a eudaemonic perspective, parenting is so rewarding most of us don't *care* how bad it makes us feel.

My own first child has just entered her third year of high school, and I am still waiting to get my groove back. Maybe that's not exactly typical, but there is no doubt that women who are new mothers enjoy less sleep, less leisure, less sex and less unstructured time off, including time for personal grooming or even toileting. Put it this way. When indulging in 'me time' means going grocery shopping or mopping the floors without interruption or—as in my own case a few years ago—looking forward to having a root canal done, for the peace and quiet, you can be pretty sure your hedonic happiness is at low ebb. Having a baby—let alone two or three—can be enormously depleting. At the same time, the Hallmark cards and your mother-in-law are right. It will also infuse your life with meaning and purpose. Eventually.

Hedonically, then, the transition to motherhood can be a disaster, at least as our society orchestrates it. Eudaemonically, it is frequently, and *at the same time*, a godsend. (This is not to say that individual women cannot or do not have a very different experience of motherhood. These are general observations only.)

Researchers in the hedonic tradition don't really care about deeper meanings. They are not interested in arguing about what happiness 'really' is. A bit like my mother, with her 'happiness is where you find it' philosophy, they favour a bottom-up approach to human happiness, and focus exclusively on people's own assessments of what makes them feel good, moment to moment.

They also have to live with the limitations of this framework, which can include large-scale fluctuations in response to relatively trivial life circumstances. Like the finding that people inevitably report a higher degree of wellbeing in face-to-face interviews than they do in mail surveys—especially when interviewed by someone of the opposite sex! Or the research that found specialist doctors to be more efficient diagnosticians after they'd been given a packet of candy. Or the experiments that confirm that most of us not only report being in better moods on sunny days, but actually being more satisfied with life as a whole. To a degree, then, the observation that our wellbeing, and therefore our 'well functioning', is a perception that may blow with the prevailing wind is completely accurate.

As Nobel Prize-winning economist Daniel Kahneman writes, it makes sense to call a person objectively happy 'if she spent most of her time in March engaged in activities that she would rather have continued than stopped, little time in situations she wished to escape, and—very important because life is short—not too much time in a neutral state in which she would not care either way'. From such a perspective, stalking the bluebird becomes a much more straightforward exercise. A happy life may be tricky to choreograph, but it's not really all that difficult to define. Simply put, it is a life in which the sum of our moments of pleasure is greater than the sum of our moments of pain.

Politically, this simple idea goes by the name of 'utilitarianism', from the nineteenth-century movement dedicated to achieving 'the greatest happiness for the greatest number'. John Stuart Mill, one of its principal proponents, who also happened to be a passionate feminist, pointed out that happiness was not necessarily 'a life of rapture' but rather 'an existence made up of few and transitory pains' and 'many and various pleasures'.

Mill added two further conditions to this elegantly simple prescription. The first was that we should aim for 'a decided predominance of the active over the passive'—a reminder that pleasures you 'take in' (like a doughnut, say, or television) are rarely as satisfying as those that get you to 'put out' (having good sex, say, or creating a good meal).

It's an intuition that the research supports on many levels. Anyone who has ever spent any time around children, or husbands for that matter, will not be surprised by the finding that television-watching is a happiness *depressant*, while participating in sports—even a ten-minute walk around the block—is one of nature's magical mood enhancers.

Getting the active/passive thing right was vital to achieving happiness, Mill believed. But even more important—in fact, the foundation of the whole transaction—was getting the expectations/reality thing right. 'Not to expect more from life than it is capable of bestowing', is how Mill put it in *Utilitarianism*. If there is a single secret to lasting happiness, this may be it: to find the cruising altitude that lies somewhere between goals that are sufficiently challenging and expectations that are sufficiently achievable.

Modern happiness research has tended to confirm this conclusion (although it would have been quicker to check with your mother). It has certainly demonstrated that evaluative comparisons not only influence how we feel about our lives, but can actually cause pain or pleasure. 'Emotional amplification', for example, refers to the process by which abnormal or unexpected events will provoke a much more intense effect, whether positive or negative, than the same events when they are framed as normal and expected.

Childbirth is a fascinating case in point. When a woman learns, or has experienced first-hand, that the outrageous pain of labour is in fact 'normal', the impact on her ability to deal with that pain is akin to a blast of nitrous oxide for the soul. This does not make labour fun, exactly. As one researcher has noted, there is no context in which cutting oneself shaving can be regarded as a pleasant experience. But a person who routinely inflicts three cuts on himself may legitimately feel pleased on mornings when he's gotten away with only one.

In the same way, comparing one's actual experience to 'what might have been' leads almost inevitably to feelings of regret, frustration and guilt, no matter what the arena. A 1995 study of Olympic athletes, for example, found bronze-medal winners to be happier with their achievements than silver medallists for exactly this reason. The former were often surprised and delighted to have won anything at all, while the latter were much more likely to ruminate on what they'd missed out on. To use the technical language for this, bronze winners tended to engage in 'downward counterfactuals'—basically, imagining a worse- (not worst-) case scenario—while silver medallists indulged in 'upward counterfactuals'.

Again, the childbirth parallels seem obvious. A hundred years ago, women who *survived* childbirth considered themselves fortunate. Today, we are likely to be disappointed if the experience has not attained the level of performance art. Among those who expect a natural childbirth, having a successful caesarean section (or other form of assisted birth) feels like 'failure'. And this despite the fact that in many hospital settings, the actual percentage of naturally delivered babies is no higher than 10 to 20 percent.

A. C. Michalos's 'Michigan Model' of wellbeing, also known as the Goal–Achievement Gap Model, more or less defines happiness as a function of the gap between aspirations on the one hand and actual accomplishments on the other. As a working mother who has always strived to keep her standards low, I can relate to that.

My own idea of a perfectly happy Monday, I am somewhat abashed to admit, is one in which I both finish my column *and* go grocery shopping. On an acceptable Monday I will have finished my column by the time the children arrive home from school. And on a miserable Monday I'll still be tinkering with it at bedtime. On a perfectly happy Tuesday, on the other hand, I may aim no higher than to answer emails and do some extreme ironing.

When my children were toddlers, my standards were even lower. I was pretty much satisfied with any day where no one drew blood, threw up or wandered into the bush to be eaten by native animals (and we live in a capital city). Now that they are fourteen, ten and twelve, life is a little more complicated. Naturally, I expect more. It is predictable that I am more easily disappointed as well.

There is a mediating factor in the goal–achievement gap, however, which is that our personal scorekeeping is deeply influenced by social factors. In other words, we do not simply compare the fit between what we hoped to achieve and what we have achieved. As we have already observed, people tend to calculate the gap between their own perform-ance and that of a chosen reference group (the one they imagine to be 'average'), whether consciously or not. When it comes to parenting, for example, my own happiness self-ratings can see-saw wildly depending on whether I compare myself to other mothers generally (especially those who work part time or not at all), to other mothers who work full time for pay, or to other working single mothers.

The old saw about a sorrow shared being a sorrow halved expresses another side of this dynamic. I was surprised at the number of married readers who wrote to tell me that my book *Wifework*, despite painting a grim picture of contemporary marriage, actually made them feel better. I'm not sure why this surprised me, because that was exactly the effect the book had on *me*. Writing it forced me to confront the negatives head on, not just about my own marriages but about marriage generally. In the process, I realised I was not alone in what I had experienced—far from it. In a sense, doing the research into equality and marriage allowed me to join a more realistic reference group. My marriages had not been like my parents' marriage, and it had not been like my best friend's marriage (both of which, for very different reasons, I now recognise as exceptional). But there were plenty of marriages with which I could compare them—and feel less of a failure.

The notion is widely held that happiness is bestowed, not earned, or that it alights on us like a butterfly or a bluebird—or not, as the case may be. Nor is that entirely fanciful. We would all very much like to believe that happiness is a choice, perhaps those of us who write books on the topic more than anyone. And in important respects it is, or at least can be.

To take a prosaic example (my forte, after all): half an hour ago, I returned from dropping my children off at school to a house that felt drafty and cheerless. On a winter day like today, with a southwesterly squall blowing off the Indian Ocean a few blocks distant, the lounge-room curtains flutter madly in the wind. And the windows are *shut*. It's a sight that always depresses me.

'If only there was a huge, roaring fire in here,' I sighed to no one in particular—our pug looked concerned, but what pug doesn't?—as I nuked my breakfast coffee one last time, and trudged to my desk. I had a clear choice. I could either wait for something in the loungeroom to spontaneously combust, or I could go out to the wood shed, drag out some kindling and start my own damn fire.

I suspect you will not be surprised to learn that I pursued Option B. After all, happiness is a choice, right? Well, yes and no. Because it also transpired that the only kindling I could find was wet. The fire I attempted to build with it resolutely refused to 'roar', though it did sort of hiss for a while. Eventually, I gave up and turned on the gas. Which turned out to be OK anyway, because half an hour later the sun came out. ('It is better to light one candle than to curse the darkness,' but sometimes your best option is just to roll over and go back to sleep.)

Obviously, happiness is partly a choice—maybe even substantially a choice. Yet it would be naïve to the point of solipsism to pretend that it is exclusively so. For one thing, there is increasing evidence that hedonic capacity, or our ability to experience happiness, is an inherited trait. A landmark 1998 study of 300 twin pairs by University of Minnesota psychologist David Lykken showed that overall happiness is at least 50 percent, and possibly as much as 90 percent, determined by our genes.

Each of us appears to have a particular 'set point' for happiness—a kind of wellbeing thermostat programmed to keep us on course no matter what circumstances life may dish out. And it is our genes that have done the programming. Some research suggests that up to 52 percent of the variance in adult happiness can be accounted for by genetic inheritance, and direct family and social factors perhaps no more than 3 percent. People who appear to be chronically 'a couple of drinks behind', this research suggests, may have been hard-wired that way. Similarly, the notion that 'some people are just born happy' is not as far fetched as it may seem.

Set-point theory also explains why winning the lottery rarely brings lasting happiness. It explains too why becoming a paraplegic, say, rarely brings lasting *un*happiness. Extremely positive or extremely negative events can create sharp short-term spikes or dips. But sooner or later—and often it's much sooner than common sense would suggest—happiness levels have a tendency to revert to psychological sea level. It's an effect researchers call, somewhat oxymoronically, the hedonic treadmill.

One study of 22 lottery winners found that, after a period of initial euphoria, all eventually returned to the same happiness set point they had started out with. In the end, they were no happier than 22 matched controls who hadn't won a dime. Not only will money not bring lasting happiness, such research suggests. Perhaps *nothing* will—or nothing external to the self, at any rate. I think of this as the Dorothy Gale Theorem of Human Happiness, after the heroine of *The Wizard of Oz* who discovers the homely truth that, 'If I ever go searching for my heart's desire again, I won't look any further than my own backyard. Because if it isn't there, I never really lost it to begin with.' Whether you see this as impossibly defeatist or intriguingly Zen is, I suspect, partly a function of gender.

The concept of the hedonic treadmill helps explain why improvements in our standard of living do not necessarily result in improvements to our perceived wellbeing. We quickly get used to living well. And the result is not increased satisfaction but increased drive to live 'better than well', to borrow a phrase from bioethicist Carl Elliot.

Daniel Kahneman points out that our almost spooky ability to adapt is a factor we seldom take into account in making life decisions. We overestimate the difference that almost *any* change in circumstance will make to our own wellbeing, from changing husbands to changing hairstyle. To an inspiring and sometimes dismaying degree, the human ability to roll with punches—which psychologists call adaptation—is an extraordinarily efficient form of emotional insulation. Kahneman tells the story of his wife's choice of bedroom curtains. At first, he found them 'perfectly dreadful'. A bit later, he was relieved to find, they'd become all but 'invisible'. Eight years on, when the family moved house, he was 'really sorry to leave those curtains behind'.

Familiarity does not necessarily breed contempt; indeed, more often it spawns indifference. And the path of least resistance is the one that returns us, like Dorothy or Odysseus, to the place we started out from.

love in a vinegar jug

Vast improvements in our life circumstances will not necessarily make us happier, although on the plus side—sort of—deteriorations in life circumstance will not necessarily make us unhappier either. But enough of my relationship history! In fact, the oddly comforting trend toward homeostasis that we discovered in the last chapter is evident in many areas of life, from our physical health to our financial wellbeing.

Let's take a seemingly extreme case. People who become paraplegics following an accident, studies show, experience a sharp decline in wellbeing. Well, what else could possibly be expected? But the extraordinary thing is that a mere eight weeks later, most will already be reporting more positive emotion than negative. Within a few more years, people with paraplegia are on average only slightly less contented than the average non-disabled person. One recent study of quadriplegics, for example, found that 84 percent rated their lives as 'average' or 'above average'.

Similar patterns emerge with respect to other kinds of disadvantage—for example, in repressive institutions like work camps, orphanages and prisons, or in wartime. Life has a wonderfully stubborn way of forging ahead, no matter what. And our happiness 'set point', like a true north of the spirit, has a way of steering us through even the densest terrain.

The psychological processes of adaptation help us understand why even attaining our heart's desire—or what certainly seemed like our heart's desire last Tuesday—may fail to lastingly enhance our day-to-day experience. Martin Seligman cites the example of eating a dish of vanilla ice cream. The first, long-anticipated taste is heaven. You savour it, swooning. The second spoonful is marvellous, too. Ummmm! The third is good, the fourth not bad and the fifth…well, frankly, it doesn't really taste like much at all. You might almost say that the *idea* of vanilla ice cream is more delicious than the reality.

Essentially the same story as Seligman's parable of the vanilla ice cream is told in the classic fairytale 'The Fisherman and His Wife'. Although generally regarded as a morality tale about greed or, for the more politically minded, the evils of social mobility, it is a story that speaks eloquently of how our longings for 'more'—whether for vanilla ice cream or anything else—may undermine our own best chances for happiness.

The story is a simple one. A humble couple who live in a vinegar jug (as you do) make the acquaintance of a magical fish, who can make wishes come true. Naturally enough, the wife's first wish—which is communicated to the fish through her tool of a husband—is for a bigger kitchen and a second bathroom. Well, OK, a cottage. The fish grants the wish, and the wife is delighted. So is the husband, of course, but what does he know? He thought the vinegar jug was prime real estate.

A few weeks of bliss ensue. The wife has everything she ever wanted and swears she will never wish for another thing as long as she lives. Well, the remainder of the story is predictable, I suppose. She does keep wishing, and she does keep getting. First a mansion, then a palace, then a series of palaces. Eventually, she asks the fish to make her Pope. He obliges, somewhat sourly to be sure, but she is still not entirely satisfied. What she really wants, she tells her husband, is to be God— whereupon the fish pulls the pin on the whole scam and dumps them both, unceremoniously, back in the vinegar jug. 'And there they live to this day,' concludes our version of the story. ('At least they got immortal life, then,' noted my son philosophically the last time we read it.)

The iconic Insatiable Female, the fisherman's wife is at one level just another gender stereotyped storybook villainess—a downmarket evil stepmother (tellingly, perhaps, the couple are childless) whose immense appetite for More is the source of her own destruction. Like Eve, the fisherman's wife is the sharp cookie of the family, the one who 'gets it'. But her ambition and vision—qualities normally associated with success in life—prove ultimately corrupting. 'Give a woman an inch,' the story seems to be saying, 'and she'll take a mile.'

More damning still, that mile she 'takes' will get her nowhere she really wants to go. Her heart's desire will continue to elude her no matter *how* far she travels. In the end, the fisherman's wife Has it All, if you'll forgive the expression. But the place she's ended up brings her no more joy—and arguably less—than the one she started out from.

From the perspective of feminist theory, it would be hard to find a less politically correct fable than 'The Fisherman and His Wife'. Yet I am convinced that there is more here than a sermon about uppity women who need to be stoppered. Maybe it's just wishful thinking on my part, but for me, the story contains much insight about the dynamics of human happiness that transcend gender entirely. (Sometimes a cigar is just a cigar, as Freud once remarked—and sometimes a wife is just a plot device.)

At the very least, the tale provides a magnificent illustration of adaptation in overdrive. Gratification, it turns out, does not follow additive rules but some other kind of logic altogether. In other words, just because one spoonful of vanilla ice cream tastes good does not mean that a hundred spoonfuls will taste a hundred times as good. Just because having two bathrooms has improved your quality of life does not mean that having three bathrooms or—like a suburban mansion I visited recently, five—will do the same. The fisherman's wife is exactly like one of those lottery winners. Winning the lottery made them happy, unquestionably. But *living* with the winnings turned out to be another story.

Our tendency to focus on what I think of as happiness flash-points—events that mark a turning point in our fortunes, like buying a house or landing a new job or getting married—is part of the reason we can miscalculate our life sums so disastrously. Researchers call this 'impact bias': the gap between what we predict we will feel in response to a set of changes, and what we actually do feel.

This kind of 'miswanting', as Harvard psychology professor Daniel Gilbert calls it, is responsible for the discontents (especially the vague ones) that continue to afflict people who otherwise would seem to have everything. Just like you and me.

Daniel Kahneman, who happens to live in New Jersey, likes to cite the example of people who live in New Jersey but dream of moving to California—where, despite the sunshine and fresh air, people are in fact no more and no less contented with their lives than they are in any other state. While moving interstate may prove exhilarating in the early weeks, after a while life returns more or less to normal. Sooner or later, the same things that made you miserable in New Jersey will make you miserable in California (because most of them probably lie between your ears...).

My own experience of moving from high-stress New York to laid-back Western Australia was something out of a wellbeing textbook in this regard. In New York, where my daily commute took two and a half hours one way, I was constantly bemoaning my lack of time. In Perth, where my daily commute took fifteen minutes, I was still constantly bemoaning my lack of time. My intolerance of traffic, far from dissipating, simply adjusted itself to my new conditions. Now, I found myself getting frustrated at a *one-minute* delay. I still do.

My adaptation to Perth's decadent Mediterranean-style climate followed along much the same lines. In time, I came to *expect* perfect weather. Nineteen years of cloudless skies later (the occasional winter storm notwithstanding), I have lost the ability to tolerate even the smallest deviations from the norm—an air temperature just slightly chilly or a little bit too warm. Like most other West Australians, I have become a princess chafing against a meteorological pea.

Marriage provides another classic case of impact bias, in which the flashpoint called 'getting married'—very much dominated by a wedding and all the big, fat hoopla that goes with it—may distract couples from thinking deeply about 'being married'. On a more mundane level, impact bias is also what's going on when we convince ourselves that an upgraded computer or a car with electric windows is going to substantially alter our lives for the better. This is an easy point to grasp in the abstract. It is much, much more difficult when you're standing in the showroom or the whitegoods department. (And I speak as a person who wrestles with her conscience every six months at least about the life-enhancing potential of an ice-cube dispenser.)

The question whether 'stuff' makes us happy is similar to the question of whether money does. The answer is an unequivocal 'yes and no'. As the fisherman's wife learned the hard way, enough really *is* as good as a feast—and the research supports that insight absolutely. People who live in poverty, which is to say, below the subsistence level, enjoy life less than people who don't. Having enough money, and enough of the comforts that money can buy, is vital to human happiness. The hard part of course is figuring out what 'enough' *means*.

In part it will be defined by our reference group, as we have already observed. One woman I know took legal action against her ex-husband for failing to provide enough child support for an annual European holiday. But 'enough' is also partly a function of culture. In Australia, a clothes dryer is still regarded as something of a luxury item. In America, it is a staple. In my parents' neighbourhood, local statutes actually forbid the hanging out of laundry. It is believed to mar the landscape.

Perceptions of sufficiency are also subject to personal beliefs and values. There are individual families in every community who don't own television sets, for example, and profess to feel not the slightest bit disadvantaged. But they are anomalous, both socially and statistically. For the great mass of humanity, the only commodity that will reliably buy happiness is *belonging*. Even the television-free families illustrate this principle: they hang out with other television-free families!

The fisherman's wife provides a perfect case study of the hedonic treadmill on turbo-boost. With each objective improvement in living conditions, she feels a short-term rush of satisfaction. Adaptation ensures that the hedonic high is short lived, however. In order to maintain the same level of satisfaction, she is driven to continually increase the dosage. Her demands for more intense and more frequent pleasures may appear ill-mannered and outrageous, and ungrateful in the extreme—yet, in a socially mobile and competitive society, the same dynamic writ large is what drives most of the rest of us most of the time. Objective life circumstances, so long as they are not horrendously deprived, account for less than 5 percent of our subjective wellbeing. That is both a sobering thought and, potentially, an extraordinarily liberating one.

In crude terms, the link between income and happiness is almost laughably weak, according to massive reviews of the literature. This is especially true in affluent countries like America and Australia, where most people earn well above subsistence levels. In such countries, where it is rare for people to die of exposure or starvation, expanding the social welfare net also fails to increase happiness, notes Dutch sociologist Ruut Veenhoven, editor of the *International Journal of Happiness Studies*. A study conducted during the 1990s among tens of thousands of individuals in 64 countries found that beyond about US$13,000 of gross domestic product per capita—roughly half the American level—additional income does not enhance wellbeing at all.

Research conducted in 2001 by Professor Bob Cummins and colleagues at Australia's Deakin University showed that people in the lowest income group (those earning less than $15,000 a year) had an average satisfaction level only six percentage points lower than those in the highest group (earning more than $90,000 a year). On the other hand, the romantic notion of poor but happy peasants is as delusional as the myth of the barefoot and pregnant wife. 'Learned helplessness' is not the same as wellbeing, though it may share some of the same outward features (such as a disinclination to complain or to alter the status quo).

People who don't whinge about living in vinegar jugs may absolutely love vinegar jugs. Or they may simply lack a wider frame of reference. Gender role research has shown that women not only earn less than men; they are also in many instances *satisfied* with less. Childcare workers compare their salaries to those of other childcare workers. They do not compare them to those of auto mechanics or fitters and turners, let alone to dentists or family lawyers.

By the same token, people who compare their own circumstances with a less fortunate reference group will revise their satisfaction levels upward. When I had three kids under four, I was convinced my friends visited me solely to feel better about their own lives. ('Not *solely*,' they protested lamely.)

Howard Cutler, co-author of the Dalai Lama's *The Art of Human Happiness*, cites a University of Wisconsin study in which women were either shown harsh living conditions in their city at the turn of the last century or asked to visualise and write about being burned or disfigured. Afterwards, they were asked to rate the quality of their own lives—with entirely predictable results.

An even simpler trial at the State University of New York (Buffalo) asked subjects to complete the sentence, 'I'm glad I'm not a…'. After five repetitions, life satisfaction underwent a distinct elevation. Those who had been asked to complete five sentences beginning 'I wish I were a…', on the other hand, felt measurably worse.

At the same time, those who score high on materialism scales are less happy than others. One survey looked at 800 alumni of New York's Hobart and William Smith Colleges to determine whether those with 'yuppie' lifestyles were more satisfied with their lives. You will not be shocked, I'm certain, to discover that they weren't. In fact, those people who rated high income, occupational success and prestige over having close friends and a good marriage were twice as likely to describe themselves as unhappy. Those Who Die with the Most Toys, it seems, Lose.

Yet before we get too sanctimonious, other research has shown that the effect on happiness of social class—a category comprising job status, income, education, area of residence and 'lifestyle'—can be quite large. Interestingly, it is not income per se that is the salient factor here, but occupational status. Professional people consistently describe themselves as being more happy than those in less highly regarded jobs. This is a finding which may help explain why housewives, for example, who often enjoy a relatively high standard of living, nevertheless report lower wellbeing and more depression than many other occupational groups. In fact, housewifery is a highly skilled job—at least as much so as many other well-paying blue collar trades. But in terms of status and prestige, it is traditionally among the lowest rated jobs in the world.

It is interesting to speculate how the current revival of interest in housewifery may affect the wellbeing of women today. The opt-out generation—young, highly skilled and educated women who make a 'lifestyle choice' to turn their back on the paid workforce—are obviously very differently placed from their grandmothers in the '50s and '60s, who stayed home because that's what women did, or because marriage rendered them ineligible for employment in their own fields.

Among my mother's generation, full-time housewives professed to feel sorry for women who 'had' to work. Their daughters, in turn, felt sorry for women who 'had' to stay home. That is appropriate: status and choice are in fact closely related.

Today, those who can afford to opt out are in the privileged position of not 'having' to take either of those paths. The eagerness of these young women to re-imagine what used to be called home duties as a vocation or calling, complete with professional associations, technical and inspirational texts and attendance at virtual meetings, will change not only the way housewifery is performed but more importantly how it is perceived. If people like Martin Seligman are right, and 'our economy is rapidly changing from a money economy to a satisfaction economy', then the decision to cocoon—which is nevertheless wholly dependent on money (albeit somebody else's)—may be seen as an increasingly high status choice.

It is sobering to be reminded that people who see themselves as ranking high on the social ladder are also among the most contented —and this is truer still in contexts where the social ladder is a highly visible structure. In India, for example, 58 percent of self-described upper-class people rate themselves as 'very happy', compared with 18 percent of middle-class folk and a mere 1 percent of those who see themselves as 'lowest class'. In America fifty years ago, 46 percent of professional workers versus 28 percent of unskilled workers rated themselves as 'happy'. Yet by the late '70s, the difference was almost nil.

The 'social ladder' is just another way of referring to status, of course. The wellbeing of those who suffer from what Alain de Botton calls 'status anxiety' is impaired almost by definition. De Botton observes that the 'most evident feature of the struggle to achieve status is uncertainty'. If so, it is hardly to be wondered that women today are experiencing diminished wellbeing. A radical increase in the level of uncertainty in our lives is the dark side of the open options policy that feminism has fought so hard and so well to implement.

Our grandmothers had their life courses laid out for them like suburban street maps, with every crossroads clearly marked. For women today, it's more a case of being handed a pair of hiking boots and a backpack. The sense of adventure can be exhilarating—but it can also be terrifying. Having so many choices—which was the solution forty years ago—has now become part of the problem. The responsibility for making the *right* choices used to belong elsewhere. Our fathers, our husbands, our churches. No more. Now it is all up to us. We wanted the freedom, but we never reckoned on the anxiety, let alone the guilt, that goes along with it. For all but the most intrepid among us, it is certainty—closure, even—that allows us to sleep peacefully. And sleep, you will not be surprised to learn, is correlated directly with wellbeing.

Yet the society we live in is positively fetishistic about freedom of choice, notes Nobel Prize-winning economist Amartya Sen in *Development as Freedom*. He joins a growing number of social critics who are worried about the costs to human health and happiness when options are too abundant. Instead of mindlessly seeking to multiply options, Sen believes we need to ask whether unlimited freedom of choice 'nourishes us or deprives us, whether it makes us mobile or hems us in, whether it enhances self-respect or diminishes it, and whether it enables us to participate in our communities or prevents us from doing so'.

I found myself thinking about this quote yesterday, as I stood in front of the dairy case in my local supermarket, searching fruitlessly for the brand of yoghurt my children prefer out of the two hundred or so varieties on display. 'Just how important is it to have the option of sucking yoghurt from a squeezable tube?' I found myself wondering. (I know what my ten-year-old's answer would be: 'Very.')

Social theorist Barry Schwartz, author of *The Paradox of Choice:*

Why Less Is More, asks the same question. He cites the example of a study titled 'When Choice is Demotivating' that showed gourmet-shop patrons bought more jam when there were six varieties to choose from than when there were twenty-four. Too little choice may be perceived as repressive. Too much choice can be perceived as oppressive. This appears to be as true in the world outside the supermarket as it is within. Even when it comes to religion, we may stagger under the weight of options overload.

Like it or not, religious observance—particularly when it involves membership in a community of believers—is highly correlated with wellbeing. In times past, people inherited the religion of their parents the way they inherited their eye colour or bone structure—and with about as much choice in the matter. Today an increasing number of adults believe children should be allowed to choose to 'be' religious (as we now say) or not. The fact that these same children struggle to choose a brand of running shoes does not deter us. Arguably, many in the west have simply replaced a naïve faith in Christianity with a naïve faith in the religion we call Freedom of Choice. Perhaps this helps explain the paradox that, as Schwartz observes, 'most Americans seem to lead thoroughly secular lives' while 'the nation as a whole professes to be deeply religious'.

Indeed, Schwartz goes so far as to propose that the problem of options overload may be the real reason for the epidemic of clinical depression afflicting much of the western world—especially the female half. The fact that women suffer depression at twice the rate men do is certainly suggestive in this regard.

The Brothers Grimm provide no data on the subjective wellbeing of the fisherman's wife after she is returned, presumably in perpetuity, to the vinegar jug. But other research suggests she may have been secretly relieved to 'opt out'. Maybe she decided to put her energy into her marriage—or into finally biting the bullet and finding a life partner more suited to her in temperament and ambition. The research suggests that either choice would have been a sound investment in her own wellbeing.

In fact, having a satisfying, committed relationship is one of the most important pieces of the wellbeing puzzle, albeit one of the trickiest ones to fit into place. Perhaps she and the fisherman, or the new man—a real estate agent?—decided to have a child or to adopt one. This would not necessarily have made life more fun, especially in the short term. But the experience of motherhood, while it might decimate her earnings potential (calculated over a lifetime), would almost inevitably have increased her sense of purpose and meaning in life. So too would having a challenging job outside the vinegar jug, into which to pour her considerable energies.

The research shows conclusively that one-off intense positive experiences—like winning your dream home, or being made Pope, for example—don't really have that much effect on happiness. Happiness, like evil, is a disconcertingly mundane matter. The main positive life events that contribute to a sense of genuine wellbeing are almost ridiculously achievable on any budget: the basic pleasures of food, drink, sleep and sex; and relationships with friends.

I can't think of a single fairytale that ends with a group of friends living happily ever after. Yet most women say their happiest moments are not the ones they spend on the job, or with their partners or even with their children. They are the ones they spend with their girlfriends. Possibly the chronic dissatisfaction felt by the fisherman's wife has more to do with her social isolation than it does with her status anxiety. The evidence is clear that no human being, no matter how exalted their job title or how hip their kitchen appliances, will be happy without a sense of *belonging*. And this, incidentally, helps explain why church membership is a more salient predictor of wellbeing than, say, intelligence. It also helps explain why, on the whole, those who conform to society's expectations report higher wellbeing than those who challenge or defy them. There's a reason most of us are so resistant to stepping outside our vinegar jugs. Because we're on our own out there.

In some ways, the fisherman's wife is the ultimate control freak. Her final wish, after all, is to control even the rising and the setting of the sun! Ironically, it is the out-of-control nature of her ambitions to control that finally seal her fate. Yet it's important to acknowledge that the drive towards mastery—which sounds so much nicer than the rage to control—is not in itself evil or even maladaptive. On the contrary, quality of life research has shown that 'autonomy', to use another positive word for the same basic impulse, is essential to adult wellbeing. Autonomy—which is often, in the real world at least, the result of a degree of social or economic power—is the yin to the yang of relatedness or belonging.

Being dependent on others for the fulfilment of one's basic needs and desires, as for example wives have traditionally been within the confines of wedlock (so named for a reason), is a recipe for discontent, this research assures us. And this is especially true in 'developed' cultures like our own, which prize individuality over broader, more collectivist goals. Too much autonomy, on the other hand—and this, it could be argued, has been the experience of husbands in the traditional confines of wedlock—is obviously equally hazardous to happiness. When Having it All means Controlling it All, Taking Responsibility for it All, Worrying Constantly about the Possibility of Losing it All, no one lives happily ever after.

After autonomy and relatedness, the third essential element of authentic or eudaemonic happiness is—not surprisingly—competence. Freud's famous dictum that 'love and work are the corners of our humanness' probably says exactly the same thing with a bit more style. For most of us, whether male or female, autonomy and competence are related directly to the work that we do, though the picture can be a bit fuzzier for those who are full-time parents, or others whose vocations are outside the mainstream of the paid workforce.

Competence is a quality that cannot be cultivated in the abstract. We can't think our way towards it, or imagine it into being. Nor can it be bestowed by another. Competence derives from action—from doing stuff, and doing it well, and being seen to do it well. (The 'being seen' part helps explain why housework rarely bestows the same psychic rewards as other kinds of skilled labour. It's not because it's demoralising, or hard, or 'never done'—though it is all that. The real bitch about housework is that it is functionally invisible.)

A sense of competence is what assures us that the good things in life that we enjoy are the things that we deserve, that we have earned. And earned rewards pack a punch that no unearned prize, no matter how lavish, really can. This is one reason that work is so essential to wellbeing. Nor is it necessarily even about money, though to be honest it usually is. Think of the taste of a tomato one has grown from seed, or an orange picked from a tree carefully pruned and fertilised throughout the year.

We hear so much about the importance of 'self esteem' to our health and happiness. Yet the research is clear that self esteem is nothing more than a by-product of competence. What makes us feel good inside our own skins is achieving something good outside of our own skins. Hearing from others—whether courtiers, bishops or any other subordinates—how wonderful we are does not, in and of itself, produce wonderful feelings. On the contrary, it may produce only cynicism, emptiness and self-loathing. Surely part of the discontent suffered by the fisherman's wife in the first place was the result of a competence deficit. The fisherman, tool though he was, was clearly happy in his work. He may not have known much, but he knew how to fish, and he was good at it. And that was enough. Like so many men before and since, he was puzzled by his wife's obscure discontents and unreasonable demands. But I suspect if he'd been a fisherwoman's husband—without a clear sense of his own competence in the world outside the vinegar jug—the clog would have been on the other foot.

Possibly, the fisherman's wife was simply relieved to be 'put in her place' at the end of the story. Any woman who has ever secretly fantasised about turning the clocks back to a simpler place and time—and isn't that all of us?—can relate to that. Yet there is where the fairytale parallels end. For those of us who live in a world where enchanted fish are regrettably rare, there is no going back again—and no amount of neoconservative wish-fulfilment will change that.

It's funny though. When you've gained everything you knew for certain you'd always wanted, you'd think living happily ever after would be the easy part. Obviously, it's time to think again.

women who feel too much

'There's nothing mysterious about what women want…They want everything. Just like us. What's interesting is what they'll settle for…'
Richard Russo *Straight Man*

In the psycho-sexual stone-age in which I grew up—America in the suburban '60s—kids learned early on that happiness was a magical mask that could make you invisible to grown-ups. Especially if you were a girl. Maybe little boys were not supposed to cry, but little girls were not even allowed to look *solemn*. Happiness was something grown-ups expected of you if you were a girl. It was a duty, like setting the table.

In my own case, I felt happy enough. I just didn't look happy enough. I didn't exhibit enough happiness. The problem, I think, was in my mouth. I have one of those mouths that, at rest, looks…well, not exactly tragic but let's say pensive (it sounds so much nicer than sulky). There were few adults who could let this pass without comment. 'Why the long face?' they'd ask. Or 'Come on. It can't be all that bad.' Even total strangers used to exhort me to 'Smile!' ('There's a good girl!')

I hated being unable to sit invisibly, and the fact that my normal expression failed to meet adult expectations. I resented the implication that, unless I was grinning like an idiot, I must be feeling sad. And that feeling sad was something a little girl must learn to cover up with a smile, like wearing an undershirt in summer, or crossing your legs at the ankle—things no boy was ever expected to do.

We don't normally think of happiness as having a gender. Then again, we don't normally think of emotion as having a gender either. People feel what they feel, we are inclined to believe, by virtue of being people—not because they happen to be male people, or female people. This is entirely reasonable. It is laudably PC. And it is defiantly untrue. In short, the belief that emotion is entirely gender neutral is a classic case of 'wonderful theory, wrong species', as E. O. Wilson is said to have remarked about Marxism.

Ideologically unsound or not, the evidence is clear that women and men do 'feel' differently, distinctively. To be sure, most of those differences are the result of nurture, not nature. Although we are born female (or not), it is at least equally true to say that we become female (or not). We learn how to be girls, and later how to be women. And part of that learning process is what Flaubert calls our 'sentimental educa-tion': learning how to feel what we're supposed to feel—in this case, what we are supposed to feel as daughters and sisters, wives and mothers, workers and girlfriends.

We have already observed that, overall, women report more happi-ness than men do (although the happiness gap also appears to be shrinking). A meta-analysis of 93 recent studies of gender differences in wellbeing, for example, showed that women were 'significantly' happier than men—that is, the difference was large enough to be more than chance. Another large-scale study, this one based on data from the (US) General Social Surveys of more than 12 000 individuals, confirmed that finding: in every subgroup, in every stratum of society, women were more satisfied with life than men were.

Which is all very interesting...but what does it really mean? Because another, equally emphatic finding is that women in every subgroup and every stratum of society are also more *depressed* about life than men are. Not just a little bit more depressed. A lot more depressed. In fact, women's rates of depression are double those of men. What's more, female depression has an earlier onset, higher rate of recurrence, longer duration and lower rate of spontaneous remission. Women also invariably score higher than men in measures of both guilt and shame, say experts. And the gender difference is no more subtle than it is in the case of depression. (Not surprisingly, guilt-proneness and depression are linked.)

Women experience more joy in life than men do. But then, women experience more of *every* emotion than men do—including, against all the stereotypes, anger. According to the accumulated evidence of decades of research, women don't necessary feel 'better' than men do. But as a gender, we do tend to feel *more* than men do.

The technical term for this emotional virtuosity—or vulnerability, depending on your point of view—is 'affect intensity': the predisposition to experience emotions strongly, both positive and negative. Over large populations, and across the lifespan, men consistently report lower levels of affect intensity than women do. Other researchers prefer to speak of 'expressiveness' (as opposed to 'instrumentality') to describe an emotional style in which, shall we say, the volume is turned up just a little louder. (Research that attempts to avoid gender-stereotyping may use 'expressive individuals' and 'instrumental individuals' as a way to avoid talking about females versus males.) In fact, the question whether women *feel* emotion more keenly, or are simply more open about—or more skilled at—expressing it, remains a topic of lively debate.

One thing that is clear, however: happiness, no matter how joyous or profound, does not cancel out unhappiness. The relationship between positive emotions and negative ones, in other words, is 'non-reciprocal'. The research shows that this is both the good news and the bad news about affect intensity. On the one hand, it's true that experiencing lots of peaks provides only moderate insurance against life's inevitable potholes. But on the upside—in a way—feeling totally and utterly miserable from time to time in no way destroys your chances of feeling totally and utterly euphoric—let alone your capacity to do so. In fact, one reading of the available evidence is that the happiest people in the world are also the most dissatisfied. That's what affect intensity is all about: intensity across the entire range of emotions.

Personally, I find that idea a little strange, and deeply reassuring. It is certainly an accurate description of my own emotional blueprint. Growing up, I was convinced that the nursery rhyme about the little girl who was either 'very very good' or 'horrid' had been written for me personally, while that silly one about 'sugar and spice and everything nice' was clearly intended to mess with a girl's head.

My daughters are the same. They may have inherited their eye colour from their father. But their emotional colouring is—alas!—a direct inheritance from the distaff side. My son's emotive style—for the sins of his feminist mother, no doubt—so closely parallels the male stereotype of low expressivity/low intensity/high avoidance it's as if he sprang fully formed—or should I say in glorious two-dimensions?— out of John Gray's head.

Psychologists who study emotion are careful not to make the same mistake all those grown-ups did when I was a solemn-faced child. They try to be scrupulous in distinguishing
- how we express emotion,
- how we 'do' emotion, by transmuting feeling into behaviour, and
- how emotion registers physiologically, as measured by heart rate, skin conductivity, and so on.

People who say they are happy do not necessarily feel happy, a fact which wreaks no end of methodological havoc for happiness researchers, let alone the rest of us. People who feel happy do not necessarily act happy—whether they are pensive five-year-olds or false, schadenfreudian friends. And of course people who act happy do not necessarily feel happy (think: professional clowns, professional politicians…).

Smiling is a good case in point. As the 'outward and visible sign' of happiness, the smile is a highly charged form of symbolic behaviour. Cross-cultural research confirms that women smile more than men do, both in public and in private. In fact, studies show that people *associate* smiling with femininity. They associate non-smiling, interestingly, with power and dominance. On a fairly basic level, this explains why Barbie smiles more than Alan Greenspan does.

The so-called 'oppression hypothesis'—I prefer to think of it as the Happy Darky Phenomenon—holds that more-frequent smiling is a strategy by which a less-powerful group attempts to ingratiate itself with a more-powerful group. People in positions of dominance smile less, this theory goes, because they don't need to be liked in order to get their needs met. In job interviews, it is the applicants who do most of the smiling, not the employers, and studies confirm that. A beauty pageant judge who attempted to dazzle contestants with his smile would be as out of place as one who paraded around in a swimsuit and heels.

Like the rest of us, psychologists distinguish between real smiling and fake smiling, between spontaneous expressions and managed *impressions* of wellbeing. They call the real thing a Duchenne smile, after the nineteenth-century French physician, Guillaume Duchenne, who first identified the telltale physiological patterns that distinguish wanna-be grins from the real thing. Any alert six-year-old could probably tell you the same thing: a real smile involves the musculature around the eyes as much as it does the mouth and lips. It's an effect that is almost impossible to fake (unlike getting the corners of your mouth to turn up, which any chimpanzee can do).

'Empty' smiles, by contrast—sometimes called Pan American smiles, after the air hostesses who helped raise them to a fine art—are smiles which represent the form of happiness but none of its content. Although the practice is hardly limited by gender—think used car salesmen and fundamentalist preachers—I'd wager most of us associate this type of smile with women much more than we do with men. The Stepford Wives, or Victoria Beckham ('David and I are more in love than ever!'), or perhaps even our own mother smiling frigidly at our in-laws-to-be.

(Bizarrely, though, research by psychologist Paul Ekman has shown that fake smiling, while it may not reflect happiness, may in fact induce it. Evidently, forcing your mouth into a smiley shape—even if it means clenching a pencil between your teeth—stimulates increased activity in the left prefrontal cortex, the seat of positive emotions in the brain. Your fake smile may not fool anybody else, but the last laugh could be on you.)

We have already observed that the happiness gap between men and women appears to be shrinking throughout the developed world—a finding that some observers have blamed on feminism's failure to bring genuine fulfilment to women's lives. An alternative explanation might be that women are not really less happy today, but simply more honest. Maybe we feel less pressure to do the zippity-doo-dah thing and pretend everything is satisfactual because we are more empowered now. Maybe we have reached the point where we feel entitled to complain.

And while we're on the subject of complaining, women do more of that as well, especially within the context of a relationship. For all of our supposed superiority in enjoying the good things life has to offer, we are also the first to sweat the small stuff. (Although it needs to be said that one man's 'small stuff' may be another woman's grounds for divorce.)

Recent research has shown that married women are significantly less likely than married men to report being 'very happy' with their relationships, citing as key issues the division of housework, childcare and leisure. One recent study by Australian sociologist Ken Dempsey found that 70 percent of men were satisfied with their marriages just the way they were, compared to 42 percent of women. Whether this is owing to women's greater affect intensity, or simply because they have more, objectively speaking, to whinge about, remains an open question.

Anyone who accepts the gender stereotype that women express more happiness but men express more anger has obviously never been married (or read the research). In fact, the evidence is clear that overall men express far *less* anger than women do, indeed far less of any negative emotion, including sadness, remorse and shame. Possibly, the stereotype reflects the fact that when men do express their anger, they do so in tangible and dramatic ways, whether facially, through grimacing and frowning, or in physical acts of aggression.

'I feel so angry almost all of the time,' my friend Marion admits. We are at a book club meeting. Or what started out as a book club meeting—it is now two a.m., and the book in question has long since been discarded for the pretext it always was. The unsettling thing is not Marion's confession per se. It's the smile she proffers along with it, like a cocktail napkin or a thoughtfully chosen hostess gift. I'm not saying I don't believe that she feels angry. She's my friend. Why should she lie? What I don't believe is that she feels entitled to that anger. The smile is like an apology, a way of softening or containing the anger, making it more acceptable. But it is also—and I know Marion well enough to say this—a reflex.

Marion is nobody's doormat. Aged fifty, she is a senior architect in a successful practice, with two wonderful daughters and a husband she not only still loves but still likes. Marion is a feminist. So is her husband. So are her friends and most of her associates. She takes it as a given that women and men are entitled to the same opportunities, the same treatment under the law. Her behaviour makes that absolutely clear. Marion also takes it as a given that women and men are entitled to the same *emotional* bill of rights. But in this case, the mismatch between her belief and her behaviour is almost comical.

If somebody asked Marion to participate in a gender and emotion study, she would clearly be amongst the majority of women who report feeling anger that is frequent and intense. Equally clearly, Marion is a person who has 'issues' with anger—issues that her feminist convictions have not entirely succeeded in resolving. Of course, things could be worse. Marion's mother, whose prefeminist upbringing included the overt message that angry feelings were 'unfeminine', is unable to admit to feeling anger at all, let alone to expressing it.

'Mother doesn't get angry,' Marion explains. 'She gets "palpitations".'

Feeling authentically happy, we have observed, isn't just about having good feelings. It's about feeling entitled to those feelings. The experience of feeling 'authentically angry' appears to be similar. The conviction that one's anger is, for want of a better word, deserved—earned even—remains problematic for many women.

'Feeling your feelings' may not be difficult. Assigning meaning to those feelings may well be. Psychologists believe it is how we evaluate or *appraise* what we feel, what sort of frame we put around it, that determines our wellbeing. How we think about cause and effect is particularly critical. Consider a car accident, for example, in which you are convinced that the other party was at fault. You will still feel shaken by the experience, and you will still wish that it had never happened. But your predominant emotion is likely to be anger. If, on the other hand, you appraise the accident as self-inflicted—the result of your own poor judgment—you will not feel angry at all, but rather guilty or regretful. In the first case, you have 'externalised' the event. In the second case, you have 'internalised' it. And the consequences of the choice for your emotional wellbeing will be enormous.

I suspect you know where all this is leading. And yes, I hate to be so predictable, but it does seem to be the case that women, even card-carrying postfeminist women, are more likely to internalise negative feelings while men, regardless of their sexual politics, are more likely to externalise them. This is one reason, say researchers, why women are so overrepresented among the ranks of the clinically depressed—and why men's rates of alcoholism, domestic violence and other forms of aggression are equally skewed. Antisocial personality disorder, for example, is four to five times more prevalent among men, and substance abuse is twice as common. Women may accentuate the positive, but we internalise the negative.

Our capacity to internalise *success*, on the other hand, is nowhere near as proficient. A study published in 2003 in the *Journal of Personality and Social Psychology* found that men are far more likely than women to 'self-handicap'—that is, to make lame but self-protective excuses for poor performance.

'The goals of self-handicapping are to disregard ability as the causal factor for a poor performance and to embrace ability as the causal factor for success,' explains Edward Hirt, a University of Indiana (Bloomington) psychologist who has spent a decade researching the phenomenon. Hirt has found that, on the whole, females are not only less likely to engage in self-handicapping, but also less likely to tolerate it in others. They are unlikely to believe that negative events 'just happen', and tend to judge self-handicappers as 'lazy, unmotivated or lacking in self-control'.

The old stereotype that women are flighty and irresponsible—what I think of as the I Love Lucy Fallacy—is almost cruelly untrue. By and large, we suffer from exactly the opposite tendency. We take too much responsibility, especially when things go wrong. This is one reason why, compared to our men (who, we like to assure one another, are 'just big kids'), we so often feel like the real grown-ups in the house. The truth is, we are often not simply more mature. We are hyper-mature. Pathologically mature.

The result, of course, is guilt—one of the so-called moral emotions that women excel at, along with shame, embarrassment, gratitude and empathy. Looking at the relationship between guilt and responsibility can help us to see guilt as a *control* issue as well, perhaps even a control freak issue.

'When I bring friends to a restaurant where the food doesn't measure up,' one female writer confesses, 'my reflex response is to tell them I'm sorry. I have apologised for the lack of snow at a ski resort, the lack of sun on a picnic, and for the mistakes of others—even to the extent of saying "excuse me" when somebody bumps into me on the street.'

Obviously, guilt means always having to say you're sorry, but there's more going on here. Such rampaging guilt suggests a certain grandiosity, even hubris. There's a thin line between being a responsible adult and sitting at God's right hand pulling the snow lever, and this lady's definitely crossed it.

We'll look at guilt in more detail later on, but for now—and I feel absolutely awful about this—I'd just like to say a word about masochism. For our extraordinary capacity to torment ourselves is, I'm afraid, another of woman's special gifts.

Early-twentieth-century psychoanalytic theory held that females were by nature masochistic—and to look at the lives and relationships of many women, even today, it is not hard to see why. Freud saw masochism as an inevitable feature of female sexuality, as did many other influential psychoanalysts.

Helene Deutsch, for example, theorised that, because women suffer physically in menstruation, childbirth and (initially) sex, pain and pleasure become inextricably enmeshed. Feminine sexual development, Deutsch concluded, constituted a 'series of self-denials'— a sequence that was particularly adaptive and healthy because it was so well suited to the mothering role! Deutsch clinched her argument by pointing out that any woman who *failed* to develop the requisite degree of masochism would have too much ego left to be a good mother. (Deutsch's own mother, who is said to have beaten her regularly because, in the words of one biographer, 'she was not a boy', was an obvious inspiration.)

Today, we are inclined to shake our heads at such nonsense. Yet, perhaps more often than we care to admit, masochism remains a feature in the lives of many otherwise liberated women. In a twisted sort of way, our masochistic feelings may even make us feel powerful. Self-denial is not fun, exactly. But it can be a surprisingly useful tool for manipulating others.

Remember the old lightbulb joke about the Jewish mother? How many Jewish mothers does it take to screw in a lightbulb? 'Don't worry. I'll sit here in the dark.' I love that joke. To me, it's a joke about power: the power that comes from *not having needs*. Jungian Sylvia Brinton Perera observes that guilt can provide a source of positive identity for the scapegoat, 'an enormously grandiose strength compensating the fragility and masochism of the victim-ego'. No wonder so many wives and mothers develop what one observer has called a 'proud and passive stoicism—often with a sense of righteous martyrdom'.

Are you happy now?

the girlfriend's guide to guilt and depression

When I first came to Australia nearly twenty years ago, I was struck by the apologetic nature of so much of women's discourse. Women were always saying they were sorry. Even when they wanted the salt they were sorry. 'Sorry, but would you mind passing the salt?' I'd never heard that before. Why should a person be sorry for wanting salt? Weren't women supposed to like salt? I asked my then-husband. He thought I was being a smart ass. Which I was, of course. But it was also a serious question. A question about needs, and who was entitled to have them.

We have already observed that guilt-proneness is associated with depression, and that being female is a risk factor for both. Generally speaking, women suffer from depression at twice the rate that men do. On this basic statistic all observers agree. The question that remains is why? Are women more depressed because that's the way women *are*, or because that's what women *learn*? Or is it simply the case that women have more to be depressed *about*? The answer, depressingly enough, seems to be a combination of all three.

Like guilt, depression is a deeply personal experience whose political implications for women have been disastrously underexamined. If greater happiness for a greater number is what women *really* want next, understanding depression needs to be made an urgent priority—not just from the perspective of public health, but from the point of view of women's status, rights and opportunities.

Depression afflicts males too, of course. Over the past forty years, rates of depression throughout the developed world have increased by a factor of ten for both males and females. Depression hits earlier today, too. In 1960, the average age of onset was 29.5. Today, it's 14.5. Statistics like these tend to confirm—for me, anyway—the hunch that depression is not primarily a matter of biology (whether sex-linked or not) but of sociology.

Researchers who argue that depression *is* biologically determined point out that the two-to-one ratio of female to male depression has been reported in numerous cultural settings around the world. Those who suspect it is simply gender-linked—the result of how we construct sexual identity—point to exceptions to this 'rule'. For example, that women who live in Amish communities in rural Pennsylvania have a rate of depression one-tenth that of their sisters who live down the road in Philadelphia. Or that recently widowed men are more depressed than recently widowed women. Or that depression rates on US college campuses and in developing nations—on the face of it, a rather curious coupling—are much more evenly distributed between males and females.

In girls, rates of anxiety and depression skyrocket in early adolescence, a finding often cited in support of a biological explanation. Yet recent research has shown that this spike does not appear to be tied to endocrinological changes at all. Some researchers have suggested that teenage girls may be more prone to depression because they find the physical changes of puberty more upsetting. Boys tend to welcome unequivocally the changes to their adolescent bodies; girls, for a variety of *social* reasons, are more ambivalent.

'In particular,' notes Yale psychologist Susan Nolen-Hoeksema, 'girls dislike the weight they gain in fat, and their loss of the long, lithe look that is idealised in modern fashions. Boys, in contrast, value the increase in muscle mass.' Before adolescence, there is little difference in the depression rates for boys and girls. But by age fifteen, according to figures from the National Institute of Mental Health, depressed girls outnumber depressed boys by that familiar two-to-one ratio.

The view that 'her hormones made her do it' has been further eroded by research into the link between depression and menopause. Contrary to popular belief, it seems there isn't one. Although depressive illness at menopause was once considered a standard disorder, research has now shown that women are no more prone to depression at this time of life than at any other. Nor, despite widespread publicity, does there appear to be any clinical evidence for a gender-specific empty nest syndrome—feelings of loss of identity and purpose that supposedly follow when children grow up and leave home. On the contrary, studies now show the immediate empty-nest years to be a time of renewed vigour for women.

Data on the neurobiology of depression are inconclusive at present; however, some researchers have proposed that women's higher susceptibility may stem from specific (but as yet undetermined) ways in which the female body metabolises the neurotransmitters involved in depressive illness. In other words: because our brains are different.

Far less speculative are the data showing a direct link between depressive disorders and child sexual abuse, findings that are particularly relevant to understanding the gender skew in depression rates. It's hardly necessary to drag in neurotransmitters, kicking and screaming, when you consider that females are four times more likely to be sexually abused as children than males are—or that half of all rape victims are under eighteen. One large-scale study published in 1998 in the

British Medical Journal found that among adult women who had suffered severe sexual abuse as children (penetration or attempted penetration), *all of them* were depressed as adults. Other research has shown that fully a quarter of all depressed women report a history of sexual abuse, compared with only 6 percent of the non-depressed population.

Other gender-related stressors that may be relevant include domestic violence and sexual harassment on the job. Recent US figures show that a quarter of all Caucasian women and half of all African-American women who have attempted suicide have been the victims of domestic violence (operationally defined as 'the use or threat of use of physical, emotional, verbal or sexual abuse with the intent of instilling fear, intimidating, and controlling behaviour'). Sixty percent of women who live with domestic violence are depressed, according to the National Center for Post Traumatic Stress Disorder.

Depression is also associated with the experience of sexual harassment on the job. Experts estimate that women are the victims of 85 percent of all incidents of sexual harassment, with young women particular targets for this form of abuse. In Australia, the federal Human Rights and Equal Opportunities Commission reports that 75 percent of sexual harassment claims that proceed to public trial involve women under twenty. US research published in 2002 that looked at a sample of 712 high school students holding part-time jobs found that almost two-thirds of the girls (compared to just over a third of the boys) reported experiencing sexual harassment.

According to a review of the literature conducted by the National Women's Law Center, more severe forms of sexual harassment can have devastating consequences for women's physical and emotional health, including anxiety, depression and sleep disturbance. US psychologist Louise Fitzgerald, author of the widely used Sexual Experiences Questionnaire for measuring harassment behaviourally, echoes the view that depression is a common response to frequent and severe sexual harassment.

Women's coping styles appear to be another contributor to the gender gap in depression rates—though the question whether such strategies are themselves innate or acquired remains to be answered. We have seen, for example, that females are less likely than males to 'self-handicap'. Women are also more likely to report low self esteem, to rely on the opinion of others, and to blame themselves for failure. The Woman Who Has No Needs—who, in the words of Susan Nolen-Hoeksema, has succeeded in 'silencing the self' in relationships in favour of maintaining a 'positive emotional tone'—is particularly vulnerable to depressive illness.

'Feeling too responsible' is linked in early adolescence with depression for both boys and girls, but girls are far more prone to such worries. This is especially true within the context of family or couple relationships, where women overwhelmingly assume responsibility for the emotionwork.

Whether women's well-documented virtuosity in caregiving turns out to be a) entirely learned behaviour or b) some genetically endowed gift of emotional intelligence—and the answer, almost certainly, will be c) all of the above—one thing is certain: our interpersonal assets are at best a mixed blessing. The ability to 'de-self' may be adaptive for the group, especially the family group, but it can wreak havoc on women's personal wellbeing.

Too little empathy can make Jack seem heartless and hardboiled. Too much empathy can turn Jill's ego boundaries to scrambled eggs. Think about it. When you empathise so expertly you are not always certain where you end and the next person begins, how stable can your wellbeing really be?

Not surprisingly, what psychologists call 'dispositional empathy'—a temperamental orientation towards responding vicariously to the emotional states of others—is higher among women. Equally unsurprising is the link between dispositional empathy and susceptibility to depressed mood.

'You poor little stone!' my youngest daughter cried when she accidentally kicked a pebble. At around the same age, my son's favourite game was exterminating garden snails with a brick. 'Works!' he'd cry when he came across a live one. 'Doesn't work!' he'd announce gleefully after mashing it to a fine paste. (The Curse of the Feminist Mother strikes again. Do our toddlers sit up nights studying textbooks on gender stereotypes, or what?)

It's a huge generalisation—but if you look at large enough populations, it does hold true. Females *do* tend to do more of life's empathising. On the other hand, they also tend to do more of life's toilet scrubbing, and we'd hardly describe that as 'innate'. Equally, and rather less appealingly, we tend to do more of life's ruminating—a psychological habit—or vice, really—that turns out to be related to depression even more strongly than dispositional empathy.

Over the last decade or so, rumination has emerged as a key predictor of susceptibility to depression. Defined as the tendency to 'passively focus attention on one's symptoms of distress and on all the possible causes and consequences of those symptoms', rumination can take many forms, from continually reminding yourself of your own fatigue levels to 're-running' negative incidents and events. In layman's terms, rumination is self-focused worry that serves no productive purpose. Ruminators are people who feel compelled to keep taking their own emotional temperature, but never seem to get up and take a Panadol. They are also overwhelmingly female.

The link between rumination and depression is so strong that some psychologists have argued that it is this gender-linked habit—and not gender per se—that accounts for the difference between male and female depression rates. Even if this is true, however, it doesn't explain *why* women ruminate. Some observers have argued that rumination, like smiling, is a psychological adaptation that arises from women's lower status. As subordinates, we really are more vulnerable to experiencing negative events, so our need to be more vigilant about potential dangers isn't paranoid; it's adaptive. And in a sense, rumination is simply vigilance on steroids. Women learn to 'go looking for trouble' because if they don't, trouble will almost certainly go looking for them.

At the same time, part of our sentimental education involves 'sadness lessons' learned at Mother's knee. For example, research has shown that mothers engage their daughters in significantly more discussion of both sadness and fear than they do sons. By age two, girls have a broader emotional vocabulary than boys do—which is not surprising because both mothers and fathers use a greater variety of emotion words when talking to their daughters.

Of course, as my snail story suggests, it is possible that in doing so mothers are exploiting a pre-existing disposition. After all, most self-fulfilling prophecies abhor a vacuum.

A recent study of depressed teenagers found that parents tended to provide positive reinforcement for girls' moods—the tea and sympathy route—while boys were basically given a kick up the butt and told to stop feeling sorry for themselves. Mothers—even in the 'postfeminist' noughties—still tend to punish boys for being emotionally expressive, being far more likely, for example, to send a son to his room for being sad. The assumption that men ought to be able to control their sadness appears to be shared by men and women alike. A study conducted in 1993, hardly the dark ages of gender stereotyping, found that depressed men caused those around them to feel angry and resentful. We punish men for daring to reveal their sadness—and then we wonder why they seem so 'out of touch with their feelings'!

There are multiple ironies in all this—not least, the increasing weight of evidence that being out of touch with your feelings may have distinct mental health *benefits*. The suggestion that denial can be therapeutic seems counterintuitive in today's 'ventilationist' climate (to use Martin Seligman's term for it) in which we take it as an article of faith that the only good emotion is a fully expressed emotion. Many people, particularly Americans, are convinced that anger is like a volatile gas that must find an outlet in order to be safely discharged. The view that unexpressed rage will eventually leak out to create potential hazards (heart disease, tumours, neurosis, even cancer) is widespread; indeed, the injunction to 'feel your anger' is one of the most fundamental assumptions of modern psychotherapy.

Yet there is surprisingly little clinical evidence for such beliefs. On the contrary, studies show that when subjects suppress their anger, blood pressure actually goes down. Often, anger simply breeds more bad feeling, not less, and people who habitually express their rage may simply be perfecting their negativity—rehearsing it, really—rather than discharging it. The research on rumination suggests that feelings of sadness, pain and hurt may operate in exactly the same way—at least some of the time. Encouraging girls and young women, however implicitly, to get in touch with their inner depressive may be one of the *least* empowering strategies we can adopt.

Yet as long as women continue to be assigned (and to assign themselves) the role of emotional caseworker in couples and families—taking responsibility for servicing and maintaining relationships—our hypervigilance to sad and painful feelings will make sense.

Whether it makes us happy is of course another question. Susan Nolen-Hoeksema, like many other experts in the field, is convinced that what underlies these differences in our emotional destiny is not anatomy—or hormones or chromosomes or neurotransmitters—but beliefs and values and behaviours. Her research has shown that ruminators, for example, are people who:

- perceive themselves to have low mastery or competence,
- believe negative emotions to be fundamentally uncontrollable, and
- have accepted responsibility for emotionwork.

The majority of such people—in fact, the vast majority—are women. But there is nothing essentially, let alone biologically, female in any of these conditions. Emotional style is not a sex-linked characteristic, in other words. It does not inevitably 'go with the terri-tory'. On the other hand, the way we respond to the world emotionally is clearly and emphatically gender-linked. To feel, in Dylan's words, 'just like a woman' is to acquire a skill-set of habits and routines. It is something we *learn*.

The finding that women are harder on themselves, and harder on others, is hardly a surprise. We have already observed—hell, most of us have spent a lifetime observing—that guilt is very much a girl thing. Women feel guilty about almost every potential pleasure that life can offer, from full-time work to full-fat milk. We are told that our fore-mothers felt guilty when they had sexual feelings they couldn't control. Women today feel guilty when we *don't* have sexual feelings we can't control. We feel guilty about our leisure time—or we would if we had any. We feel guilty about what we buy, and what we eat, about the mould in the shower recess, the fungus on the roses and the dog's vaccination status. And perhaps most of all we feel guilty about our children. Unless we don't have any—in which case we feel guilty about that instead.

In addition to all this primary guilt, many women suffer a secondary guilt about feeling guilty in the first place. The 'I feel guilty when I feel guilty' set—and anecdotal evidence suggests they are a growing demographic—are, like my friend Marion, educated, middle-class and often card-carrying feminists. Politically evolved enough to know better, yet socialised from an early age to accept other life lessons, this sandwich generation is especially susceptible to feelings of futility and self-blame.

'Guilt is a pointless form of anxiety that never got anybody anywhere,' is how I heard one psychiatrist describe it a few years ago. A specialist in postnatal depression with a thriving practice in a large city, she was addressing a large regional gathering of young working mothers. 'The first thing I tell my clients,' she went on briskly, 'is "Get rid of the guilt." It's not doing you any good, and it's not doing your family any good either.' I don't really remember what she said after that. To be honest, I couldn't concentrate anymore. 'Get rid of guilt'? Just 'Get rid of it'! To me, it was like telling an audience of heroin addicts to just take up knitting.

Of course, the expert—who incidentally was childless—was right about guilt getting you nowhere. In this it is different from remorse, which is a response to wrongdoing for which one experiences regret and takes appropriate responsibility. You feel remorse for having run over the cat or voted Republican, or for marrying a man who collects airsick bags. Whether accidental or not, the unwanted outcome is unambivalent. You did the wrong thing. You are sorry. You are clear why. You alter, or attempt to alter, your behaviour next time. You move on.

Guilt is what happens when we internalise unwanted outcomes, and it becomes neurotic or maladaptive when the focus of our emotional energy is not reparative—directed towards righting the wrong—but self-punitive. In *Civilisation and Its Discontents*, Freud argued that the 'loss of happiness' people experience as a result of guilt is 'the price we pay for our advance in civilisation'. (At the same time, neurotic or obsessional guilt makes achievement impossible. It does not motivate. It paralyses.)

Freud was something of a cheerleader for guilt. More recent research confirms his view that guilt, like greed, can be good. It has demonstrated for example that guilt-prone individuals are unusually understanding and forgiving. We also know that guilt can be a tremendous motivator. It's getting this chapter written, for example. And of course guilt helps keep complacency at bay. As Rabbi Harold Kushner has observed, 'Guilt makes you strive to be the best person you can be.' My mother would agree with that. So would most parents, I suspect. A world full of self-handicappers would be a world in which mediocrity was not only tolerated, but probably celebrated. A bit like the public service, perhaps.

At the risk of being reductive, we might say that guilt is like stress, or strychnine. The key is calibrating the dose. How much guilt is enough guilt—for an individual or indeed for a civilisation? And what about the distribution of guilt? Clearly, there are groups in society that 'carry' more guilt than others—that do the guiltwork for all of us. As a woman, and as a mother, I belong to two of those groups. Of the many emotions that women feel too much, I would argue, guilt is among the most self-sabotaging.

At the same time, women's guilt today seems to be less about good old-fashioned masochism than it is about fear—especially the fear that we are cutting too many important corners, that the price of Having it All is not only Doing it All, but Doing Most of it Badly.

More than 25 years ago, psychologists Pauline Clance and Suzanne Imes noticed that high-achieving women were vulnerable to a phenomenon they called the Impostor Syndrome, defined as a persistent belief in one's own lack of competence, skill or intelligence in the face of consistent objective data to the contrary. Today, a better term might be Impostor Epidemic. As our equality of opportunity has expanded, so too, it sometimes seems, have our insecurities— particularly surrounding that elusive quality psychologists call 'authenticity'. The number of competent women out there who secretly believe that they are 'faking it'—whether as mother, employer, partner or simply 'real woman'—is nothing short of unreal.

I was on a panel recently which turned out to be an all-female group. The participants were an especially formidable bunch. They included a respected philosopher, a high-profile broadcaster, a best-selling novelist, a kick-ass critic and a gentle, kind-hearted columnist. The youngest of our group was in her early thirties, the oldest perhaps 55. Well, the moderator asked us each how we'd like to be introduced. Within moments, she'd reduced this group of hard-nosed heavy-hitters into a circle of snivelling simps, present company included.

'Oh, I always feel like such a fraud when I'm introduced as a "philosopher",' the philosopher said. 'It sounds so…pretentious. Can't you just say I'm an academic?' The best-selling novelist, who'd just won a major national prize, demurred that, with only one book under her belt, she didn't really think of herself as a 'writer' yet. And on and on it went. It was as if we all thought we were getting away with something, that we'd somehow succeeded in hoodwinking our employers—or publishers or readers or whatever—all these years but in our heart of hearts we knew, and they knew, and we knew that they knew, that we were frauds.

'Lord, I am not worthy to receive you,' say Anglicans and Catholics before receiving communion. The words have an eerie resonance for women who do too much yet still expect too little. It's almost as if we're being punished for something—or punishing ourselves. But for what? Our success? Our competence? Our failure to 'know our place'? Our decision—however consciously applauded—to break ranks with the kinds of lives our mothers and grandmothers had? One thing is clear: women's guilt, our anxiety about 'doing the right thing'—by our families, by our employers, by ourselves—is rising faster than our ability either to conceal or manage it.

Women who are feeling guilty, dis-entitled and inauthentic are unlikely to be the life of anybody's party. Yet negative emotions like these, despite the intensely personal ways in which we experience them, have an often-overlooked political significance as well. On a broader canvas, it is possible to see women's guilt as a collective repository of bad feeling and inaction—a glass ceiling of the soul, as it were. In fact, I would go so far as to propose that women's guilt, and the ambivalence about gender roles and boundaries that almost certainly underlies it, is significantly responsible for the failure of feminism to completely fulfil even its most moderate agenda, including equal pay for equal work in the marketplace, and an equitable distribution of domestic labour.

Psychoanalyst Carl Jung argued that guilt is all tied up with the experience of being an outcast, set apart, fractured from the dominant group. Guilt, in this view, is the emotional fall-out from alienation: a panicky free-fall triggered by the fear we no longer fit in or 'belong'. Feeling guilty is synonymous with feeling exiled—whether from God, or parents, or peer or gender group. Psychologists observe that our primal experience of guilt arises out of rebellion against our primary caregivers, usually our mothers. Breaking away from parental authority is developmentally appropriate (whether we are learning to crawl or learning to drive), but that doesn't mean it's easy. Teething is developmentally appropriate too, and it still hurts like hell.

If all this is true, it may help explain what social researcher Barbara Pocock has called 'the epidemic of guilt' afflicting so many women today—especially those of us who came of age during the Gender Revolution. Psychologically, we have made ourselves permanent exiles from our mothers' experience. The brave new world we have entered as women—a world that permits and even expects our participation in the public sphere—has moved us into an entirely different orbit from the one our own mothers probably occupied. No wonder Planet Mum seems to belong to a distant galaxy. And then we have children of our own, and worlds *really* start to collide.

It is easy to forget how entirely unprecedented it is to grow up, as so many baby boomers have grown up, determined to dissociate from our mothers. We haven't simply broken the apron strings to Mother. We have chewed them into little pieces and made confetti out of them. In fact, we have taken a sharp pair of shears to the whole maternal outfit—from the housecoat to the hostess gown.

Oscar Wilde famously observed that 'women always become like their mothers—that's their tragedy,' adding judiciously that 'men never do—that's theirs'. A hundred years ago, it was a funny line. Now—in a culture in which the fear of turning into one's mother ('matriphobia' in shrinkspeak) has become the chief psychological terror in the lives of countless adult women—we are not quite sure whether to laugh or cry or enrol for a re-birthing weekend.

Theory reminds us that guilt is all about boundaries which have been transgressed. Women who have transgressed the boundaries of traditional gender roles may find themselves, or rather feel themselves, painfully outcast—scapegoated, even. Such feelings are perfectly understandable, given the powerful backlash insisting that feminism is to blame for everything that ails our society today, from divorce rates to the poor test performance of senior high school boys.

The political becomes the personal in the lives of families— classically, in cases where a mother's paid job becomes the 'usual suspect' for any and all forms of family dysfunction. Are the kids being bullied at school? Is Dad clinically depressed? Does the guinea pig have ear mites? If only Mum could quit her job and look after everyone *properly*…

All family members may harbour such wishes. But it is a woman's own complicity—or refusal to be complicit—with the role of scapegoat that is more decisive by far.

Quite clearly, the boundaries that feminism succeeded so spectacularly in breaking through have yet to be fully re-drawn. Even women who *know* they are entitled to exactly the same deal as the partners and fathers they live beside—including many of us who are fully supported by our men—may continue to feel guilty and furtive about the freedoms they enjoy (and I use that term advisedly).

It has become commonplace to associate guilt with motherhood, as if the two were somehow hormonally linked. One academic article about maternal guilt I read recently was titled 'It Goes with the Territory', as if guilt, like stretchmarks or perineal tearing, were some regrettable but unavoidable side effect of childbirth. Maybe it makes us feel better to believe that, less 'guilty about feeling guilty.' But the cross-cultural and historical evidence is pretty damning on this one. In fact, guilt is no more intrinsic to motherhood than tantruming is to toddlerhood.

Two-year-olds in Japan rarely throw hissy fits in the supermarket, you may be interested (or dismayed) to learn. In many Asian and African communities, postnatal depression is practically unheard of. In Japan, for instance, where new mothers are lavished with attention, the rate of PND is half what it is in Great Britain. Similarly, your great-great-grandmother may or may not have felt hemmed in by her children, but she certainly didn't feel guilty about them. Nor do contemporary mothers in traditional societies or developing nations. The Tibetan language doesn't even have a word for 'guilt'.

Any attempt to mess with motherhood—which, at the most primitive and fearful level, feminism represents—is the ultimate social transgression, the boundary beyond which social and possibly even biological chaos beckons. It is, if you will, the last frontier. The boundary line that stretches from here to maternity is one we are very far from re-drawing, even today. It is not even accurate to say we have stepped over it—or that we are sure we want to.

having our families and eating them too

'**B**ut Mummy, you promised!'
         Is there a mother alive whose blood does not run cold at those words? Is there a child alive who does not know this?

It is 8.25 on the morning of my ten-year-old's Arts Day, which starts at 8.30, and as a matter of fact I did *not* promise. I mean, yes, sure, OK, I said I'd attend. That is grown-up-speak for 'show up', as every sensible ten-year-old really ought to know by now. It means watching *your* child do her thing in the chorus of Disco Cinderella, snapping some photos of her in *her* Arts Day Headdress, admiring the teddy bear clothes *she* sewed all by herself (with a little help from you and a lot of help from the glue gun), and getting the hell out of there by ten. That's what 'attend' means. What it does not mean is hanging out admiring other people's kids' recorder solos till lunch time—let alone sacrificing an entire work day to it.

'But all the Other Mothers are staying!'

Bingo. I knew something was missing. Well, the gang's all here now. No confrontation would be complete without an appearance by the Other Mothers, whose Godzilla-like presence shadows me like a feral ex-partner or a low-grade menstrual cramp. 'There is no such thing as the Other Mothers!' I long to shout. 'They are a snare and a delusion that exists only in the minds of overly-empowered, exploitative children and their chronically insecure primary caregivers!' Which seems to cover all of us, really.

That's what I long to shout, but I don't of course. Partly because I know she'd say, 'Why are you always shouting? The Other Mothers never shout!' Partly because I'm afraid she might be right.

I start calmly explaining all that Mummy has to do today. This is always a losing strategy, but the forlorn hope that logic will triumph over love, and the infuriatingly irrational needs that attend it, springs eternal in my working mother's breast.

Mummy has to go grocery shopping. Mummy has to pick up brother and take him to saxophone. Mummy has to intimidate her accountant, placate her editor, pay her cleaners and negotiate next weekend's access with Daddy. (This morning, I heard her telling her father all about Arts Day. 'Can you come, Daddy?' There was a pause, pregnant with predictability. 'Oh, that's OK!' I heard her chirp. 'I figured you'd be working. Love you, Dad! Talk to you Saturday, Dad!')

We are both sobbing quietly now. I hand us each a tissue, and we pause to blow our noses, in stereo. I glance furtively out the window to see if anybody is watching us. A woman who looks terrifyingly like an Other Mother—if such a thing existed, I remind myself sternly—is carrying a cake shaped and decorated like a poodle dog, with mini-marshmallows for fur and long licorice eyelashes. She smiles serenely ahead. I start hiccupping. Somehow, this doesn't seem like the most auspicious moment to confide to my daughter that Mummy's real priority right now is to start her chapter on motherhood and…um, happiness.

In the end, we negotiate. Isn't that what families do these days?

I call the photographer and cancel our morning meeting; my make-up could pass as fingerpainting by now anyway. My daughter agrees that there's really not that much going on after eleven on Arts Day. Eventually, the colour drains from our eyes and noses, and we feel safe enough to get out of the car and pretend we were just hanging out there (for twenty minutes) as we run like hell for the Hat and Headdress Parade.

There are days when I feel like motherhood is the hardest thing I've ever had to do, and then there are days when I *know* it is. Forty years of feminism has arguably revolutionised women's lives. Yet the mute, mammalian tasks of motherhood remain majestically unaltered. Pregnancy, childbirth, lactation, Arts Day. The routines of waking and sleeping, dressing and bathing, eating and eliminating. We can talk all we like about how our lives have changed. But there is so much about motherhood, as both a set of routines and a set of mind, that seems to lie so far beyond the talk. Or perhaps so far beneath it.

Feminism, like a fortysomething MBA, has come late to motherhood—and not altogether gracefully. Or perhaps I should say feminism has been late in getting back to motherhood. For it was critiques of nuclear-family life—a life in which motherhood featured as a kind of radioactive core—that decisively detonated feminism's first wave. What Marx and Engels had done for capitalism, books like Betty Friedan's *The Feminine Mystique*, Germaine Greer's *The Female Eunuch*, and Shulamith Firestone's *The Dialectic of Sex* did for the politics of reproduction. Motherhood, these writers agreed, lay squarely at the foundations of women's oppression, providing the pivot around which the entire, lumbering machinery of the patriarchy revolved.

For both Friedan (whom American feminists would later dub the Mother of Us All) and Greer, women's reproductive power was a centre of intellectual gravity that proved impossible to resist. Both began by attacking motherhood as The Problem. Both ended up convinced it was The Answer. Then again, motherhood is like that. Like a Zen paradox, or a teething two-year-old, it is almost impossible to pin down.

By and large, however, early-wave feminists spent less time thinking about how to do motherhood than they did how to undo it. The wishlist seemed to centre on ways to elude motherhood, whether via exit strategies like free and universal childcare or abortion rights, or through access to preventative measures like the pill, IUDs or even the outright rejection of heterosexual sex.

We no longer regard motherhood as women's inevitable social and biological destiny—and that deceptively simple re-fit in our framing of the female experience constitutes a cataclysmic shift in human evolution. It is true to say, and vital to acknowledge, that motherhood remains at the centre of most adult women's lives. Yet motherhood is no longer what women *do*. It is no longer the default setting for our lives but rather a single option among many competing options—and the difference that this difference makes is impossible to overstate. Every second day, it seems, a journalist—usually one in her twenties— reminds us that up to a quarter of young women will remain child-free, many of them by choice. Becoming a mother is no longer something that just happens to a woman, like adolescence, say, or a car crash. It is now—at least some of the time—a decision, like whether to build on a second bathroom or take out life insurance.

Of course, it is possible to overstate the extent of our control over all this. It's exceedingly difficult to 'choose' motherhood in the absence of a suitable and/or willing male partner, or when you are faced with fertility problems, or when you miscarry, to name but three obvious examples. 'Choosing' to remain child-free can obviously also be prob- lematic. One of the most delightful children I know was conceived while his mother was on the mini-pill *and* using a condom—'just in case'—which, as his father remarked, is enough to make you believe in the existence of a Conception Fairy.

The social pressure for women to conceive, bear and raise

children is nowhere near as strong as it was a generation or two ago. But it remains formidable. Ask any childless woman over the age of thirty if she feels it is entirely her 'choice' to remain that way. If you wait around long enough for her to stop laughing, she'll explain it to you.

Our control over our reproductive destiny remains imperfect. Yet even imperfect control—hell, even the *illusion* of control—is revolutionary stuff. At the very least, it has meant that motherhood can now be held at arm's length, an object of conjecture, of analysis, of reflection. Forty years ago, the only books on mothering that existed were babycare manuals written by men. It kind of gives you colic just thinking about it. Even ten years ago, whatever public discourse existed—and there was precious little—still tended to frame motherhood as either a set of skills to be mastered, or a workplace disability to be overcome. The proposal for my book *The Mask of Motherhood* was rejected by one publisher in 1995 on the grounds that 'mothers have no interest in books about themselves—they want to read about their children'!

Today, of course, there is an entire literary subgenre devoted to women's reflections on the experience of motherhood. Some of these works are serious and academic. Others are autobiographical and sidesplittingly funny. Yet the really striking thing about this important new body of work—apart from how overdue it is—is how *negative* it is. Titles like *Misconceptions, The Bitch in the House, The Mommy Myth, Dispatches from an Imperfect Life* make it clear that motherhood isn't for girls anymore. The gloves are off now. Or is it the nipple shields? Whatever else it may or may not be, motherhood ain't no motherhood issue for today's women. Not by a long shot.

To borrow Ann Oakley's phrase, we are learning at last to take motherhood like a woman. Which, we are realising, does *not* mean 'keeping mum' about the messy bits or the unfair bits, or the downright terrifying bits. Taking it like a woman does not mean suffering in silence—it means suffering NOISILY. Volubly. People credit Freud with having invented the talking cure. What nonsense. *Women* invented the talking cure.

I wrote *The Mask of Motherhood* during the year my children were two, four and six—in other words, a lifetime ago. I always envisioned it as the book I wish I'd read before I had kids: the book that would tell you what all the other parenting books left out. Which is to say, the truth. It's not that I believed anybody had lied to me, exactly, though I still maintain Penelope Leach has a lot to answer for. It was more the stuff they didn't say. The stuff that wasn't on the syllabus but turned up on the test anyway. I was sick of reading Hallmark cards about motherhood. I wanted the Cliff Notes.

Obviously, I wasn't alone in the desire to drag motherhood out of the closet. My book did well, and so have a host of others traversing similar territory. At this stage in our maternal development, it is clear that many women are hungry for reassurance that they are not alone in their confusion, or their frustration. The obscure but insistent sense that someone, somehow has sold us a bill of goods—that the price we pay for the privilege of mothering is an unexpectedly exorbitant one— has emerged as one of the key themes of *fin-de-siècle* feminism.

The fact is, for the women we have become, and given the lives we find ourselves living, motherhood really *has* become an outrageously difficult undertaking. Yet the books that lament 'what mama never told us' or that address themselves to the mothers that 'feminism forgot' have missed the point. In fact, Mama didn't tell us what it was like for a very compelling reason: because it wasn't like that for Mama. The struggles faced by women today in resolving the identity crisis we call, with clinical politeness, 'the transition to motherhood' are entirely novel ones. They are not the fault of feminism. But they are the *sequelae* of feminism—the unanticipated aftershocks.

For women of my mother's generation, for whom the question of whether to have babies was as controversial as the question of whether to eat breakfast, motherhood precipitated few identity crises. On the contrary. It prevented them. A woman's identity was *supposed* to revolve around the caregiving role. The selflessness (or de-selfing, as we have been taught to say today) such caregiving entailed was not resisted as a form of psychologically damaging sublimation, but embraced as a means for fulfilment. Indeed, as *the* means for fulfilment. The demands of infantcare were much the same then as they are now—which is to say, arduous. Yet the experience of providing that care could not have been more different.

A woman who has never for a moment entertained the prospect of 'having a life' has nothing to resent when children (and a man) come along to claim her time and attention and vitality. And make no mistake: that has been the experience of the vast majority of women for the vast majority of human history. It is the sheerest arrogance to suggest that this great chain of maternal being failed to qualify as 'living'.

We can look down our noses all we like at the kind of woman who finds fulfilment through subservience to the needs of others. We can call her a doormat or a dingbat or deeply unevolved. We can even accuse her of false consciousness if it makes us feel better. But the plain fact of the matter is that people who only *think* they are happy really *are* happy. Thinking is allowed. In fact, when it comes to human happiness, thinking—in the sense of appraising or evaluating or (as the sociologists say) 'assigning value'—is pretty much all we've got.

One thing women ought to have learned from forty years of feminism is that Tolstoy's oft-quoted remark that all happy families are happy in the same way is simply wrong. (What would a father of thirteen children know about happy families anyway?) The franchise on 'having a life' is not exclusive to employed mothers, or non-mothers, or stay-at-home mothers, or single mothers or empty-nest mothers or any other slice of the maternal demographic. Having said that, the feminist evolution has changed irrevocably our expectations of what 'a life'—aka 'the Good Life'—entails for adult women. Indeed, it has changed irrevocably our very sense of who we are. Of *why* we are. At the present moment, the gap between these vastly altered expectations and the largely unaltered imperatives (both biological and 'constructed') of bearing and rearing children remains enormous.

It is so hard to be who we would like to be as women, and to do what we feel we need to do as mothers, at one and the same time. It's a dilemma no previous generation has ever faced, and if there is a single thing women want next from motherhood it is to resolve it. If 'having a life' is something women can only aspire to do *in spite of* their role as mothers, the implications for our wellbeing are ominous—not only for the 40 percent or so of the population who will mother, but for the 100 percent of us who are of woman born.

In *The Mask of Motherhood*, I tried to provide a few glimpses of the reality behind the rhetoric in family life today. Pregnancy was supposed to make you bloom—then why did I seem to develop root rot? Maternal love was supposed to be unconditional and unambivalent— then why was I having dreams about tossing babies gaily out of a second storey window? Having kids was supposed to bring you closer together as a couple—then why did sex feel as intoxicating as a stainless steel speculum?

I was interested in the differences between what we say about mothering, and how we experience it. But I was at least equally interested in why this gap might exist in the first place. What was the mask made of, really? More to the point, what was holding it in place? Clearly, the concept of mask implied deception. But who was deceiving whom? And whose interests were the deceptions serving?

It's a question I'm still chewing over all these years later. I suspect it will remain with me forever, like an intellectual stretchmark. Now our masks are indeed cracking through, and we are daring to show the real faces of the mothering experience—not just the serene, beatific ones you see in Christian iconography and *Good Housekeeping*, but the gasping-for-breath one, the convulsed-with-laughter one, the angry one, the one that looks like Peter Rabbit's mother in the face of oncoming headlights. Unmasking motherhood is a liberating experience. But it is also a profoundly unsettling one—both personally and politically.

In German, there is a word, *Maskenfreiheit*, that freely translated means 'the freedom we have when we wear masks'. It's a fascinating concept. There's a price to be paid for revelation, that's for sure. The mask of motherhood was inauthentic, but it was safe. What lies beneath, we are discovering, is anything but. With our masks in place, at least we knew who were supposed to be, even if we didn't know exactly who we were. Unmasked…well, frankly, you could be anybody. Maybe that's why to date we've only had glimpses.

The forces 'out there' that once held the mask in place have weakened enormously in the past forty or so years. But there are 'pull factors' that seem stronger than ever—and by that I mean the lines of force emanating from our own hearts, our own minds, our own unfathomable reserves of guilt and self-doubt. Getting real about motherhood—not just reading about it in book club—means holding the mirror up to *ourselves*…and doing it unflinchingly, and in the broad light of day. No wonder we'd rather lobby for changes 'out there'—for better childcare or more family-friendly workplaces or greater participation by our partners. Now don't get me wrong. All those things are consummations devoutly to be wished, and scandalously overdue. But, in a putatively postfeminist world, *they* are no longer the major obstacles to change. *We* are.

What Sharon Hay calls 'the cultural contradictions of motherhood' have conspired to suck the fun not only out of being a mother but out of family life generally. The transformation of parenthood from biological inevitability to artform—which is pretty much what we've done in the last half a century—means today's mothers are infinitely more conscious of parenting as performance, and infinitely more anxious to receive rave reviews. The housewife revivalist movement epitomised by the 'opt-out generation' is an understandable, though ultimately doomed, response to all this.

If educated, affluent adult women really *could* find perfect content-ment in a life devoted to domestic labour, wifework and childcare, we wouldn't need to yearn nostalgically for the '50s. We would still be there. Feminism would never have found a foothold. People don't embrace social change out of boredom, still less because they are 'duped'. After all, there is no stronger force in the world than the force of inertia in human affairs. Resisting that force takes enormous energy, and we are only likely to expend it to gain immediate and compelling advantages.

On the other hand—and this is the part of the equation feminists are likely to fudge—the feminist solution to the riddle of women's well-being has proved partial at best. And that's putting it kindly. True, our hugely increased participation in public life has solved many of the problems plaguing our middle-class mothers and grandmothers in the '50s and '60s. Most of us will never know what it's like to live in a state of chronic financial dependence on a man, for example—or to experi-ence the soul-destroying anomie Betty Friedan called 'the problem with no name'—or to accept discrimination and exploitation as an inevitable feature of Real Life. When I tell my daughters that, aged twelve, I was barred from having a paper route because I wasn't a boy, they are beyond outraged. They are incredulous. I love that.

Compared with previous generations of women, the quality of life we experience today is nothing short of extraordinary. Fortunately or unfortunately, though, it's how we perceive that quality that matters. By any objective measure, we should be beside ourselves with bliss. But bliss *isn't* objective, as the happiness research abundantly demonstrates. Feminism has made our lives freer and more fair. It has expanded our options exponentially—but it is up to us to make the choices that will lead us toward fulfilment *on our own terms*. Feminism taught us to politicise the personal. Now it's time to personalise the political. High time.

At present, we live in a world in which women's depression levels, stress-related disorders and free-floating guilt and anxiety have reached epidemic proportions, among mothers especially. We have the dubious honour of creating the first society in the history of *Homo sapiens* in which becoming a mother is actually corrosive to a woman's wellbeing (and in which, incidentally, having children poses a risk to marital satisfaction). If this is the golden age of female fulfilment envisaged by early feminist leaders, heaven only knows what distress would look like.

Senior political correspondent Elizabeth Kolbert, writing in the *New Yorker*, recalls that motherhood had as much social cachet for young feminist women of her generation as a case of headlice. Serious women simply weren't interested in having babies. On the contrary. They wanted to *do* something. 'Almost without exception, my female classmates either went off to graduate school or found themselves jobs,' she writes. 'If any of us harboured a desire to stay home in order to raise babies, we certainly didn't admit it. (Such a confession would have been received far less warmly than the announcement of, say, an intention to go into pornography.)'

That may be overstating the case just slightly. Inevitably, after all, the Ivy League-educated woman for whom 'getting a job' means writing for the *New Yorker* has one experience of social change, and the woman she hires to clean her house or mind her kids or sell her coffee, quite another. Yet there is no denying that over the past forty or so years, middle-class women have come full circle on the motherhood thing, from enshrining it (fatuously) as the alpha source of women's wellbeing to relegating it (fatuously) to the status of side dish on the dinner menu of life. So now what?

The experience of bearing and raising children is no longer sufficient cause to ensure a woman's long-term fulfilment, if indeed it ever was; for many it is not even necessary. But for most women—perhaps 80 percent, at a guess—motherhood remains a central piece, even *the* central piece, in the larger jigsaw of adult life. Screamingly obvious though this may be to most lay observers, it feels faintly heretical for a feminist to say so in print—a potent reminder of how charged the 'motherhood issue' has become in our time.

When it comes to women's happiness, motherhood matters—not just a little bit, but a great deal. Even among the child-free, women for whom motherhood is a minor issue are few—despite what the fertility crisis seems to be telling us to the contrary. Australian social researcher Leslie Cannold, whose book *What, No Baby?* challenges the 'childless by choice' myth, observes that the average woman in the developed world today wants about 2.5 children. (The reality will end up closer to 1.8.) Even in fertility-challenged Australia, a recent longitudinal study of 39,000 women aged 18 to 22 found that 91 percent wanted to be in a stable relationship, employed and a mother by age 35. Interestingly, the more education a young woman has, the greater the number of children she will report desiring. Yet highly educated women end up producing the *least* offspring.

Childlessness is now seen as a viable life option for most people, the figures suggest—as long as the people in question are *other* people. Little more than a decade ago, only 2 percent of Australians believed having no children or one child was ideal; today almost half (48 percent) do. Demographer Peter McDonald of the Australian National University has estimated that, of the 25 percent of young women presently forecast to remain childless, a mere 7 percent will exercise a conscious choice to do so. According to one American poll, almost two-thirds of non-mothers told researchers they regretted not having children. (The cynic in me cannot help wondering about the proportion of mothers who regretted that they did.)

The challenge of having our families and eating them too is at the very top of the wishlist for women today. We admit to finding the mothering role more problematic. At the same time, we want to have children very badly indeed. The dilemma, alas, is that you can't have kids without becoming a mother. The result is a classic double-bind, with women who have kids worrying constantly that they don't have a Life and are therefore not real people, and women who do have a Life worrying constantly that they don't have kids and are therefore not real women.

Maybe the paradox is not as dumb as it sounds. After all, the 'rewards' of family life are notoriously tricky to tabulate at the best of times. ('Happiness,' observed comedian George Burns, 'is having a large, loving, caring close-knit family…in another city.') A study by University of Michigan sociologist Lois Hoffman suggested that, for most parents, the value of having children isn't fully actualised until old age—at which point fully three-quarters of elderly parents nominate their children as a primary source of love, companionship and joy. And you thought getting them into full-time school would do it.

From the point of view of hedonics—the kind of wellbeing we associate with pleasurable sensations—motherhood can be a total bitch, as we've seen. Yet examined eudaemonically—from the perspective of gaining deeper fulfilment through meaning and purpose—the mothering role is like a pitcher of margaritas for the soul. Go figure.

'Minor adverse events occur as often as once every three minutes when mothers interact with normal preschoolers,' writes researcher Susan Nolen-Hoeksema. Reading that made me feel better about myself— or the self I was a few short years ago, as a single parent with three kids under five in as many rooms. When the baby's nappy was like something out of *The Exorcist*, or the toddlers played dental assistant with the ducted vacuuming, or the dog chewed thoughtfully through another set of Barbie toes, I would cheer myself up by imagining Even-Worse Case Scenarios. 'What if there was a blizzard right now and we were trapped inside for a week,' I'd think. Or, 'I know. Someone could throw up right now.' (Every once in a while someone would, of course, in which case I'd change it to: 'What if someone fell out of bed and concussed. No, wait a minute. What if they *all* did!') Occasionally, when things really got grim, I'd think, dully, about families fleeing from war. About being in a detention centre. About (I am ashamed to admit) Auschwitz.

Mothers of young children, the research tells us, are particularly prone to 'dysphoria'—an awfully pretty word for feelings of stress, depression, anxiety, isolation and helplessness. Did motherhood affect women this way a generation ago? Researchers weren't asking them— the field of 'motherhood studies' is barely toddling even today—but anecdotal evidence suggests that it probably did, but to a much milder degree. Today, according to leading experts Carolyn Pape Cowan and Philip A. Cowan, authors of *When Partners Become Parents*, women who have children under five and lack a supportive partner are at greater risk of clinical depression than any other group of adults. Yet when I mention this to my own mother, she looks genuinely stunned. 'Those were the happiest years of my life,' she tells me. It's an opinion echoed by many older women I've noticed—and in their day, 'supportive partners' hadn't even been invented yet. The babies are the fun part, they say. Just wait till you have teenagers!

There was a time when that struck fear in my heart. But now that I do have a teenager—and a girl to boot—I am getting braver. For me, and maybe for lots of women in my generation, doing the complicated headwork of parenting older children is so far proving infinitely more satisfying and much less destabilising than the physical treadmill of the baby years. Mostly, I think women today struggle in the transition to motherhood not because it is so physically demanding (though it is) or so mentally taxing (though it is that too), but because of the way it eclipses our egos, the way it pushes us out of centrestage. 'There's not much "me" left to think about right now,' one informant told the Cowans six months after the birth of her daughter. Many days, I still feel like that. The difference is, I no longer struggle against it.

Accepting that you don't come first anymore—not even in your own life—is probably the hardest lesson a new mother learns, the gospel according to Whitney Houston ('learning to love yourself is the greatest love of all') notwithstanding. This makes of motherhood an act of deep cultural subversion. Paradoxically, it may also help explain why the enterprise of bearing and rearing children ultimately *enhances* women's wellbeing. It may even explain the persistence of the 'happiness gap' between men and women.

We have already observed that females report higher life satisfaction than males do—despite occupying lower status, enjoying fewer financial resources and exercising less control over their life circumstances generally. In terms of objective wellbeing, and relative to men, women still constitute an underclass. Yet we stubbornly persist in enjoying life more. Why?

I suspect it is the very de-selfing that the mothering role demands that stacks the deck, however narrowly, in our favour. The thing that drives us craziest about life with kids, in other words, is exactly what keeps us sane and grounded and…dare I say it? Fulfilled. This may be a paradox. But it is also the lived reality of family life.

One of my favourite studies ever illustrates the point beautifully. In it, a representative sample of British adults was asked what, if anything, had emotionally strained them the day before. The most common answer they gave was 'Family'. When researchers asked what had given them the most pleasure the day before, the answer was exactly the same.

For women, gratifications in life are even more likely to stem from interpersonal relationships, especially those involving family. For men, research shows, subjective wellbeing will hinge more on career success and material rewards. Well, of course. That is exactly how we have divided up the pie, right? That's what our culture *teaches* men and women to value. As postfeminist women, we know that. What we may not realise is how much women have actually benefited from this arrangement—or what a raw deal it can be for males.

It is a mistake to put all of one's ova in any single basket. Yet the research shows that investing one's emotional energy in relationships really does yield the highest rate of happy returns. For women, for men, for anybody. Freud was right when he observed that, 'Love and work are the cornerstones of our humanness,' but St Paul was right too when he observed, 'and the greatest of these is Love'. Gender role theory aside for the moment, people who need people—and, more importantly, who are needed in return—really *are* the happiest people in the world. No wonder the mother–child bond, the most interdependent relationship imaginable, is so potent a drug.

'Unhappiness,' says the Dalai Lama, 'is always to feel oneself imprisoned in one's own skin, in one's own brain.' The parenting relationship may wear a woman down. It may even wear her out. But it will also, and inevitably, force her out of the private prisons of her own consciousness. Mothering, I have often reflected, is a case of survival of the most empathic.

The happiness research is spangled with findings that support the link between wellbeing and the absence of self-focus. There is even evidence that being other-directed can enhance our physical health. One recent study into the risk factors for heart disease, for example, found that people who were the most self-focused—measured by use of the pronouns 'I', 'me' and 'my' in interviews—were the most vulnerable.

Yet there is a thin line, one suspects, between what you might call 'adaptive selflessness' on the one hand and total self-annihilation on the other—and what women want next from motherhood is to stay on the right side of it. The psychological risks associated with too much self-sacrifice, too much willingness to lose oneself in the needs and desires of others, are well known. Becoming an absence in search of a presence—the stomach-churningly selfless Angel in the House, brandishing her burnt chop before her like a flaming sword—is exactly the fate our feminist foremothers fought to save us from. And thank God for their bravery.

But the danger of…well, throwing the baby out with the bath-water remains a clear and present one. The Woman Who Had No Needs was an emotional vampire who nourished only her own delusions of control. And yet the Woman Who Needs it All, Right Now isn't much of an improvement, I sometimes think (and I speak from personal experience, trust me).

As a feminist, it distresses me to observe that the discourse on maternal happiness is dominated by voices from the neoconservative right, by the Dr Lauras and the Family Firsters and the Danielle Crittendens of this world, by women with what my friend Pat calls Republican hair.

'The guilt we feel for neglecting our children,' writes Crittenden, 'is a by-product of our love for them…Their cry *should* be more compelling than the call from the office.' Yet 'their cry' has rarely kept Crittenden herself from the office. While bringing up three children, she has found time to edit a journal, direct a think-tank, write two books and make countless media appearances.

It seems to me that calls by fully employed women (with fully employed personal assistants and fully employed nannies) for a return to the joys of full-time maternity should be judged in the same way as we judge elderly presidents who urge us to celebrate the glory of death on the battlefield.

At the same time, reflecting on the joys that motherhood can and should bring deserves a place on every thinking woman's agenda, whether child-free or child-tethered. Heaven knows it need not be debased by association with backward-looking social policy or the guilt-mongers who seek to dish it up to us.

For young women who place themselves politically somewhere to the left of Betty Crocker, by contrast, reflections on motherhood can be as inspiring as a bad case of three-month colic. 'If you asked any of the mothers in my set how motherhood has changed us,' writes Caitlin Flanagan in the *Atlantic Monthly*, 'we would tell you—in one way or another—that it has introduced into our lives an almost unbearably powerful form of love and also a ceaseless, grinding anxiety.' In her memoir *A Life's Work: On Becoming a Mother*, British novelist Rachel Cusk confesses her loathing for breastfeeding and documents the degeneration of her marriage into 'feudal relations' after the birth of her child. Calling a woman a 'bad mother' is emotional kryptonite, maintains Peggy Orenstein, author of *Flux: Women on Sex, Work, Love, Kids and Life in a Half-Changed World*. Yet her research found many women who 'seemed relieved to confess that they disliked motherhood and wished they might walk away'. Then there's the recent documentary *Bringing Up Baby*, which follows six professional women through late pregnancy up until their kids are aged two. 'Why aren't we allowed to talk about hating the park?' asks co-producer Donna Wick. 'We want women to be able to say it's OK to dislike parts of being a mother,' she told the *New York Times* recently. 'It's boring, lonely, not valued and not paid. It's mindless and repetitive.'

Is motherhood really this hard on today's women? Or is it only this hard on the kind of woman who writes books or produces documentaries? Maybe it has always been this hard, but women are only now brave enough to broadcast it. Donna Wick is right of course. It *is* OK to dislike parts of being a mother. And it's OK to say so, and to say so loudly and repeatedly. In fact, it's more than OK. It's essential, if we are ever to pay more than lipservice to the goal of combining motherhood and personhood.

At the same time, what women want next, I suspect, is to get beyond the kvetching. If the mothering life is worth living—and with few exceptions, women resoundingly affirm that it is—let's remind ourselves why.

Women take joy in nurturing in part because we are so good at it. Studies of gender and emotion confirm that women's greater emotional range, expressive and otherwise, is adaptive for childcare. We are more skilled as communicators—we listen more, for example—and are more tuned-in and empathic. Compared to males, females start out as parents with a slight emotional edge by nature. But it is by nurture that we consolidate our advantage. Traditionally, this has happened both in the way girls have been encouraged to develop caregiving qualities and in the way boys have been encouraged to suppress them. It is no coincidence that a lesser emotional range tends to be more adaptive for the provider role, with its emphasis on competition and maintaining status within a hierarchy.

Today, as we attempt to raise our girls to take their place as both mothers *and* providers, this traditional division of emotional labour is breaking down. For those of us who were ourselves raised in this way—encouraged to be ambitious, competitive and assertive—it is little wonder that caring for a helpless infant can make us feel panicky and out of our depth. Quite literally, we have had no training for this. The qualities we have been drilled to develop and taught to prize have little place in the booming, buzzing confusion of mother–infant bonding. We long to 'get organised', to 'take charge', to be 'in control'—to be 'on time' even. Perhaps even more doomed is our intense need to *achieve*, to see ourselves as accomplishing something. Motherhood, alas, is antithetical to all such desires. In a sense, we are all Daddies now.

I say 'alas', but I could with equal conviction shout 'hallelujah!' For one of the most valuable lessons motherhood teaches is that there are other ways to live than by productivity alone, that the Achievement Thing is not the royal road to happiness after all. 'We live in a culture that enshrines acquisition but profanes care,' writes feminist psychotherapist Daphne de Morneffe. In her groundbreaking book *Maternal Desire,* de Morneffe urges women to reassess and rediscover the full range of maternal pleasure that is our birthright (quite literally) as women. The desire to mother, she argues—not just the short, sharp urge to 'have' children but the sustained, politically incorrect yearning to 'hold' them, too—has become every bit as sublimated and taboo in our own time as female sexual desire was for a previous generation. If feminism is about celebrating what it means to be fully female, leaving motherhood off the guest list would seem to be a fairly serious omission.

It is also an entirely understandable one, in its own time and place. Today, however, the times have changed, and we are in a different place. It is safe to go back into the water of maternal pleasure now: to revisit the primordial environment of adaptedness in which all females, mothers and non-mothers alike, once swam.

if mama ain't happy, ain't nobody happy

Being a mother is a journey of becoming—a quest, if you will. Yet becoming a mother is not something one achieves, like a promotion or a diploma or a sales quota. It is something one *is*. As a result, the gratifications of the mothering life are often diffuse. (And if that sounds like code for 'frequently non-existent', it is!)

It's not necessarily the things you do with your children, or for your children, that are so dramatically fulfilling—although they may be. It's who you become. It's who *they* become. It's working out that what endures is not the fun, or the misery for that matter, but being caught in a bond of flesh and feeling that is profoundly indifferent to both. Maybe this is why we get so much joy from *watching* our kids (as opposed to directly interacting with them).

When my son was a toddler, one of my favourite outings was to take him into town for a haircut. Bill's normal clinginess—it was at this stage of life that he acquired the richly deserved sobriquet Barnacle Bill—seemed to disappear in the barbershop. I was never sure why.

Maybe he could sense the testosterone in the atmosphere, hanging like a mist over the fading girly calendars and the studded vinyl upholstery. Maybe it was the accents of the older barbers (Scandinavian, Italian, Greek), or the careless strength of their tattooed arms as they airlifted him onto a wooden box and draped him in a cloth, like a pudding. Whatever. The point is Bill would stay put there, on that box, for as long as the haircut took. And I made sure it took as long as possible, even if it meant issuing ridiculously elaborate instructions.

Everyone thought I had a thing about boys and buzzcuts. But the truth was, I just liked to watch him. To behold what God (and I) had wrought: the purity of a cheekline, the slope of those chubby shoulders, the skin so white and blameless at the nape of his neck. Taking Bill to the barbershop was perhaps my first experience of my child as a person, a being wholly separate yet miraculously continuous with my own self.

'Maybe this is what going to church is supposed to be like,' I found myself wondering every time I left that barbershop. I suppose the Lord works in mysterious ways. Why not through styling wax?

Five minutes later, we'd be in a café somewhere and Bill would be squirting tomato sauce into my handbag, and the moment would be gone—taking my temper along with it. Dealing with toddlers was not my strong suit as a mother. At the time, I felt rather ashamed of that. I wanted to be getting more fun out of what everybody kept insisting were 'the best years of my life'. I remember grimly hauling two of my babies through a department store one afternoon and hearing a cosmetics lady call out: 'Enjoy it while it lasts, love! They grow up so quickly!' I felt like hitting her. Surely, the problem was they weren't growing up quickly enough?

Now I would be kinder to both of us in my judgment. Now it seems obvious that we had each, in our own way, fallen prey to what Daniel Kahneman calls a 'focusing illusion'. I was simply too close in to see my offspring for the miracles they most assuredly were. And she was way, way too far off to remember the millstones they could also be.

I needed more of those barbershop moments. And she needed more ketchup in her wallet.

From a distance, we recall of the mothering life only the peak experiences; and for most of us, if we are lucky, the highest highs outweigh in intensity the lowest lows. Like childbirth itself, whose outrageous agony would doom the species to extinction if its joys were not keener still. What fades over time are not the peaks or the valleys, but the vast tracts of the middle distance—the ordinary loneliness, the predictable tedium, the low-pitched quotidian hum of bone-weariness.

Then again, maybe we should simply accept that motherhood has much in common with other acts of creation. No matter how much genius you bring to it, if it does *not* wear you to a nub…well, maybe you're doing it wrong. I think of Dorothy Parker's observation about being a writer: 'I hate writing,' she is said to have remarked. 'But I love having written.' That was me gazing at Bill in the barber's chair. I was as much a work in progress as he was. But for the first time, I felt I had written.

According to a recent Relationships Australia study, 'the most enjoyable thing about being a parent' for most people is…wait for it…watching their children grow up. I laughed when I read that. It reminded me of that Woody Allen joke about the two old ladies complaining about a Catskills resort. 'The food is terrible!' says one. 'Yes!' agrees the other. 'And the portions are so small!'

As a full-time mother at home, I felt deprived of the luxury of distance from my children. They so entirely dominated my field of vision that I had trouble 'seeing' them at all, let alone discerning patterns of growth and change. (Is this why parents universally love to watch their children asleep? I mean, apart from the sheer relief that they *are* asleep.)

All this changed when I started back to work part time, something I probably wouldn't have done at that point if I'd had the option. Suddenly, the focal distance was exactly right. I remember bursting through the back door at the end of one of my first days back at the office, and having the kids crowd around to give me hugs while the babysitter folded my socks and underwear. 'Maybe I should have been a dad all along,' I mused. For parents who work full time, irrespective of gender, there are equal and opposite obstacles to joy. Yet it's important to remember that there are many possible ways to miss out. Quantity time is all very well and good, but my own experience taught me that 'being there' doesn't necessarily mean being, in fact, there.

We take it for granted these days that achieving the life/work balance thing—and it's a phrase I particularly loathe—is a matter of individual taste, like deciding how much chilli to put in the stir-fry. I'm not so sure that's true. My reading of the literature on motherhood and wellbeing confirms that hunch. Family life, like a game of Aussie rules football, only looks like guerrilla warfare. Impossible though it may seem at times, there *are* some rules to the game of Happy Families. I should know. I've broken most of them.

First off, and at the risk of being totally simplistic, motherhood gets off to a far happier and less traumatic start for women who give birth...well, I won't say 'naturally'—for what does that mean these days?—but 'naturally enough', through their vaginas. That's rule number one.

And please, girls, this is not a value judgment on any sister who has had a caesar by choice or circumstance. What would be a value judgment would be to deny or suppress what the research is practically screaming at us: that giving birth is what vaginas *do*, for heaven's sake (OK, and a couple of other things as well) and if we could just let them get on with their business we'd have a whole lot more happy mamas on our hands.

Who says so? Mothers say so. According to the *Listening to Mothers Survey: The First National US Survey of Women's Childbearing Experiences* (2002), women who give birth vaginally are significantly more likely to 'room in' with their babies in hospital and to be breast-feeding at one week, and significantly less likely to experience abdominal pain, bladder and bowel difficulties, headaches and backaches during the postpartum period.

Are caesars sometimes necessary? You bet they are. Are they necessary between 25 and 35 percent of the time? Don't make me laugh (it'll pull my stitches). What women want next from childbirth is *less* distress and discomfort, and all the palaver that's been served up to us about a woman's 'right to choose' her manner of childbirth is just another in a long series of dubious medical interventions.

Probably the smartest thing a woman can do to ensure a smooth postpartum transition, the research suggests, is to be a mother already. That's a tough one if it's your first baby.

Experienced mothers are less likely to use pain medications or other labour interventions, to report negative feelings during labour or to give birth via caesarean. As a group they will report every bit as much fatigue and disorganisation as first-timers. Their only real advantage, the research suggests, is *confidence*. OK, OK. I know what you're thinking. So what's a first-time mother to do? Like an inexperienced waitress who can't get experience because—you guessed it—she has no experience, new mothers cannot acquire a genuinely confident outlook until they are no longer new mothers.

In the days when the average woman could expect to have three or four or more children, usually in quick succession, it may have made some sense to chalk that first kid up to experience. These days, when the average woman will have only one or two children, we cannot afford the luxury of a maternal apprenticeship. We are expected, and expect ourselves, to hit the ground running. No wonder our anxieties about mothering run so high and so hot. We know we might never get a second shot.

From a broader perspective, the fertility patterns in which we are presently mired could not possibly be less amenable to women's well-being. The fact that we are having fewer babies overall is in many ways a huge gain for women. But the distribution of those fewer babies—the fact that we are sowing them thinly, like radishes, across the broader population—has meant fewer economies of scale, financial and otherwise, and steeper opportunity costs for all of us. Large numbers of us 'dabble' in producing children, you might say; but very few are specialising. That sounds odd, I know. Yet the absence of (for want of a better word) intensive farming means the majority of families are living a kind of subsistence existence. More on this in a moment.

Worldwide trends point not simply in the direction of lowered fertility, but toward delayed fertility. Women are having babies later—in many countries in the world, much later—and the implications of this for our own health and wellbeing (let alone those of our children) are alarming. Our reproductive anatomy is no longer our destiny, but it remains a stubbornly salient variable for our health and happiness. No social movement—not even feminism—can repeal biology. That sucks. But the facts remain: women's fertility declines precipitously with age, and for women for whom becoming a mother is a central life goal—and remember, that's most women—the impact of what Leslie Cannold calls 'circumstantial childlessness' will be enormous.

Will most women in their forties who find they've 'left it too late' to have a child survive and find lasting gratifications elsewhere? Yes, they will. Is that the point? No, it's not.

People who miss out on an education, or are denied employment opportunities, generally also survive, and that is worth remembering. But it's hardly an argument for endorsing the status quo.

The fertility issue more than any other reminds us that the iconic '70s bumper sticker was wrong. Girls *cannot* do anything. No one can. It's a drag to be one to have to say this (but then I'm a mother, I'm used to that) but the fact is our options are *not* limitless. Even worse, some of the most important ones have a shelf life.

What women want next is to be able to exercise real choice, and realistic choice, about becoming mothers—and by 'realistic choice' I mean understanding the limits of our own free will and the constraints on our own agency. We cannot change the political and economic waters in which we navigate—not single-handedly anyway, and certainly not overnight. We cannot change vessels either, alas. We can tinker around with the engine a bit, but our bodies are our bodies, and we are pretty much stuck with them.

What we can control—frankly, *all* we can control—are the choices we make in response to those constraints. One choice is not to make a choice, to be blown by the prevailing winds (and whinge every step of the way that we are not getting any closer to our destination). Another choice is to put in the energy to tack *against* that wind. A third choice—dare I say it?—is to steer a middle course.

The Next Big Thing for women who become mothers, as well as for women who don't, is to stop blaming somebody else—whether men, doctors, the patriarchy, our mothers, the nuclear family, globalisation, the church, the media, 'feminists', or our own hormones—for the way our lives are turning out. That's the price of freedom. Not perfect freedom, which is something none of us will ever know. But near-enough, more-or-less freedom. The kind that gives you just enough rope to hang yourself—or to hoist your own sail.

I think here of women like Australian journalist Virginia Hausegger who, childless and peri-menopausal, flung herself on the op-ed pages of the Melbourne *Age* to express her rage toward those 'purple-clad' feminists who brainwashed her into believing that 'female fulfilment came with a leather briefcase'. And I suppose the feminists could blame those pinstripe-clad males for brainwashing them in turn, too. (Those nasty men! How dare they trick us into believing that paid work is where the action is!)

Puh-*lease*. Surely one thing women want next is to put such embarrassing displays of petulance and passivity behind us. 'Female fulfilment', assuming there is such a thing, is nobody's gift to bestow anymore. That is our own privilege now. Equally important, it is our own responsibility.

Motherhood does not 'bring' happiness any more than (heaven forfend) marriage or a mortgage does. Unhappy women are as likely to have children as they are not to have them. Research by US social scientists Grace Baruch and Rosalind Barnett suggests that happiness is determined by the way women frame their maternal status— especially their capacity to accept it and to move on. This can be a particular challenge for younger childless women, especially when the siren song of technological solutions for social infertility (donor sperm, IVF, surrogacy) continues to seduce.

On the other hand, anyone who thinks it is only non-mothers who struggle to accept the hand that fate has dealt them probably needs to spend more time glue-gunning teddy bear clothes. Several studies have found that childless people (both male and female) enjoy *greater* wellbeing—possibly because they also enjoying greater marital satis- faction—than parents do. Where childlessness has been genuinely chosen, research shows, women at midlife express a high level of contentment with their lives.

'Thwarted mothers', as Leslie Cannold calls them, are one group whose wellbeing is compromised by the way we 'do' motherhood today. Another potentially at-risk group are women who have delayed chil- drearing to the eleventh biological hour. The trend towards older motherhood, like the trend toward smaller family sizes, is a by-product of larger socio-economic shifts. The comic-strip character who smacks her forehead and wails 'Omigosh! I forgot to have a baby!' is exactly that: a comic-strip character. Maternity is not the sort of thing that slips a woman's mind. In most cases, it normally takes quite a bit of energy to prevent it.

One often-overlooked reason for the fertility delay is a wider trend towards what you might call adulthood delay. We live in a world where the age of the average video-game player is now exactly the same as the age at which the average Australian woman will have her first baby: 29. Am I the only one who finds that ominous? The rise of 'kidult' and 'adultescent' literature suggests we're not even ready for grown-up *fiction*, let alone parenthood, until we're practically postmenopausal. American market researchers—who, like the Greeks, appear to have a word for everything—call the phenomenon Peterpandemonium. Others would say it's just another sub-strain of the social disease known as 'affluenza'. But whatever you want to call it, it means middle-class men and women are still metaphorically in their nappies till around the age of thirty.

In solidly middle-class countries like Australia, Switzerland and the Netherlands the average woman will have her first child just shy of her third decade. In more socio-economically diverse America, the mean age at first birth is considerably lower at 25; thirty years ago, however, it was 21. In that same time, the number of US women with a university degree has nearly doubled, and female labour force participation has risen by 40 percent.

And the high end just keeps getting higher. Over the last decade, the number of US women giving birth aged forty or older has increased by 95.3 percent, while the percentage of fortysomethings having their first babies has more than doubled. According to figures released by the Australian Institute of Health and Welfare in May 2003, one in ten Australian mothers is 35 or older at first birth. That's twice the rate of a decade ago. The number of Australian women having babies in their forties and fifties has increased four-fold in the past twenty years. In the state of Victoria, there are now more fortysomething mums than there are teenaged mums. In the UK, where National Statistics figures show the number of women having babies past forty has also doubled in the last ten years and most babies are born to women in their early thirties, the figures are much the same. No matter where she happens to live, the more education a woman has, the older she will be when her career as a mother begins; hence, wherever women's education rates are rising (i.e. everywhere) the tendency to delay childbearing will increase also.

Another factor in all this is advances in medical technology—although maybe 'regressions' would be a better word—which today promise to extend the female reproductive lifespan almost indefinitely. 'Reproductive technology is advancing so rapidly,' reported the *Australian* breathlessly in October 2004, 'that within ten years it will be common for women in their fifties to have babies, fertility experts said yesterday.'

The question whether women will actually *want* to have babies in their fifties is evidently less newsworthy. Medical technology, and the institutions that create and sustain it, are notoriously indifferent to women's wellbeing. They are also indifferent to annoying little details like menopause, described recently by fertility expert Alan Trounson as a 'barrier'. Trounson is among a host of cutting-edge researchers who predicts drug therapies will soon have the capacity to prolong women's fertility almost indefinitely. Just as men can continue to father children into their seventies and beyond, elderly women will also be able to...Now, what would you call it? 'Mother' them?

Treatment options within the next few years are expected to expand quicker than a second-trimester waistline, and will include procedures for rejuvenating 'off' eggs (by injecting cytoplasm with new mitochondria); freezing eggs successfully (at the present writing, there has yet to be a baby born in Australia from a frozen ovum); slowing the loss of eggs through drug therapy; and so-called 'therapeutic cloning', a currently non-legal process by which new eggs or sperm are creating outright (using, say, the nucleus of a rabbit ovum as a 'starter'). Women who no longer menstruate need not miss out on any of the fun. 'As long as they've got a womb, that's all they need,' enthuses Professor Robert Norman, head of the Reproductive Medicine Unit at Adelaide University.

At the present stage of our biomedical evolution, however, a woman's age continues to act as...what was that word again? Oh, yes. A barrier. Simply put, the longer a woman delays childrearing, the greater her chances of failing to conceive. (And remember, IVF works best on those women who don't need it: the ones in their prime reproductive years of eighteen to thirty.) We seem to be in collective denial at the moment on this brute fact of our biology. A recent study by FPA Health, reported Australian Associated Press in November 2003, showed that women believed they had a 32 percent chance of pregnancy over the age of fifty. In reality the odds are less than one in one hundred. Fertility rates start to drop significantly at age thirty for women. At thirty-five, they nosedive. By forty—though we may in every other way be as fresh as the proverbial morn—reproductively we are pretty much toast. The fertility of the average forty-year-old is not simply 'impaired'. It is 95 percent *gone*.

OK, but what about women who are successful in conceiving, and who do become mums after thirty-five?

It is beyond politically incorrect for a feminist to admit this, but I have to breathe through the pain and say it anyway: for older women, the experience of motherhood is harder, both physically *and* emotionally. This is not to say that so-called mature-age motherhood is not worth pursuing anyway, or that maturity does not yield some substantial advantages to a parent. It's just that the benefits of youth are greater—pretty obviously and substantially better, in fact.

Women who delay childrearing till their forties are at greater risk to experience complications during labour and delivery, to have an infant with health problems (especially respiratory disease and congenital anomalies) and/or intellectual handicap (a woman in her twenties has a one in a thousand risk of conceiving a child with Down syndrome, for example; for a woman in her forties the risk is one in twenty) and to stagger under the sheer physical demands of infant- and childcare.

After the first year of motherhood, older women also report being less positive about their marital relationships and their sex lives—if any. New research reported in the *Wall Street Journal* in February 2004 raises yet another worrying concern: that children born at intervals of less than three to five years apart may be at increased risk for a host of physical, cognitive and social problems. More to the present point, so may their mothers. The stress of compressed fertility—what my sister calls spittin' 'em out—on women's wellbeing has not been widely studied. But the evidence to date hardly gives cause for premature optimism. (As a proud but somewhat battered veteran of the 'three under four' club, the last of whom was born when I was 36, I speak both scientifically and anecdotally.)

In the US, infant mortality rates climbed for the first time in more than four decades in 2004. Health officials say the trend toward delayed motherhood is the most likely reason why—both because of the higher risk of birth defects and other potentially fatal complications, and because of the higher incidence among older mothers of multiple births, which carry a higher risk of death. In the US in the last twenty years, for example, the number of twins has jumped 74 percent, while the number of higher-order multiples (triplets on up) has increased by a factor of five, according to the National Center for Health Statistics. Most of this increase is the direct result of fertility drugs.

A study released in October 2004 at a national fertility conference in Adelaide found older mums to be more vulnerable during pregnancy, less well served by practical and emotional support networks, and more prone to anxiety about the challenges of parenting. It found too that there were some distinct advantages to later parenthood for women—especially greater maturity and more emotional resilience. In fact, the efforts of the researchers to avoid scare tactics, and to offer a balanced view that supported women's choices, were laudable. Almost too laudable, given the data available.

'I think the constructive thing is to look at how women are managing this, how their partners are managing it and ways in which we can perhaps provide more support if needed,' Macquarie University psychologist and study author Dr Catherine McMahon told ABC radio. That's true, heaven knows—and we hear such warm and practical advice way too rarely in a climate where women tend to get blamed no matter what reproductive choice they make.

Yet I worry too (hey, I'm a mother—that's what I *do*) about the equal and opposite danger of obscuring the risks of delayed motherhood out of a sense of misplaced sisterhood, or a fear of being seen as another in a long, lugubrious line of mother-blamers. The 'constructive thing', ultimately, is to be fearless about confronting the truths we discover, however much they may challenge our sense of right or wrong, fair or foul.

McMahon's carefully worded optimism is echoed by British psychologist Julia C. Berryman, author of *Older Mothers*, who maintains, 'It would be wrong to conclude that there is a right time for motherhood.' Maybe so. But there is an optimal time, and there are less than optimal times. And to attempt to buy into fertility and family life just as your reproductive tract is closing up shop would seem to be among the latter.

Embarking on motherhood at midlife can prove a wonderful and life-affirming adventure, as attested by a raft of recent first-person accounts, from Nancy London's *Hot Flashes Warm Bottles* to Judith Newman's *You Make Me Feel Like an Unnatural Woman*. (Is it only my imagination, or is there a distinct misery-loves-company theme that runs through this literature?) Add that to the list of celebrity mums pushing fifty—or even sixty, in the case of crime writer Lynda La Plante, who recently adopted a baby at 57—and you might begin to believe that midlife motherhood was as natural and normal as…well, midlife fatherhood. Unfortunately, it isn't. And to propose that such an undertaking is unproblematic for women's wellbeing is nothing short of irresponsible.

It is society's attitudes towards motherhood that have to change, not women, argues fertility researcher and author Maggie Kirkman, among many other contemporary feminist observers. If only motherhood were a matter of 'attitude' alone—social or personal—I would agree wholeheartedly. But motherhood is not, alas, something we do exclusively or even primarily with our minds. Nor is it something we do single-handedly or in isolation. Motherhood is not a solo we sing a capella. It is more like a fugue: intricately patterned, multi-voiced, elaborately interwoven. Nor is motherhood something that happens in a single generation. It is rather—as the term 'nuclear family' rather alarmingly suggests—a link in a long chain reaction. It's easy to forget that when we concern ourselves exclusively with our own set of rights and entitlements.

For some women, having a child in middle age is clearly preferable to never having had one at all. As a single mother, I would say the same about single motherhood. Few of us actually 'choose' to go it alone—I know I didn't. But I certainly wouldn't want to live in a world where women didn't have that choice.

On the other hand, maybe what women want next from motherhood is not more choices, but better ones. Putting the best possible face on the trend to delayed motherhood is an understandable response to a perplexing new reality. It is also a humane one. But by emphasising the positives so relentlessly we run the risk of stopping more conversations about women's wellbeing than we are likely to start—and I refer especially to public debate about the factors that incline women to make suboptimal reproductive choices in the first place, and indeed to an even wider critique of the notion of 'choice' itself.

The fact that our present postfeminist world is one which forces women to improvise family life—to throw it together at the last minute, like a potluck dinner from fridge scrapings—is the prior issue. As women who become mothers, or simply as women who are mothers, it's time we stopped cutting corners with our own wellbeing.

So what else makes Mama happy, then? Among the most powerful predictors of maternal wellbeing is a factor researchers call 'social support', and the rest of us call 'help'. It takes a village to raise a child, as we now all acknowledge. Why would a mother's growth and development require anything less? Even having a single, significant other whose support we can rely on can make a huge difference—especially in cases where that single, significant other is related to our child by blood (codename: Daddy).

Recent research published in *Sex Roles: A Journal of Research* found that mothers whose partners most closely approximated a shared-parenting ideal were less stressed than when parenting labour was distributed along more traditional lines. (This research also found that 'approximated' was the operative word, with mothers on the whole doing twice as much of the routine custodial care, whether they were in paid work or not.)

There is a great deal of evidence to suggest that maternal well-being is a product of the fit, or lack thereof, between a woman's expectations of parenthood and the reality she experiences. Women who expect their partners to participate as equal co-parents—and isn't that just about all of us these days?—are especially vulnerable to disappointment and feelings of unfairness during the transition to parenthood.

All of which suggests that a half-evolved New Man—i.e. one who talks the talk but is essentially still slithering through family life—may make life even harder than an unabashedly unevolved Old Man. Research has shown, interestingly, that the unhappiest women of all are mothers in couple families in which both partners share traditional notions about the division of labour by gender but are forced by circumstances to live under non-traditional arrangements with the woman doing the main breadwinning and the man the main caregiving.

On the whole, this research suggests, women today either have higher expectations than men do about father involvement or, to put the same thing in more charitable terms, they don't 'see' the parenting dads do in the same way that men themselves do. Whichever way you want to frame it, the result is the same: when mama feels she's been had, ain't nobody playin' happy families.

Does a zero-sum division of childcare labour—where one person does almost all, the other almost none—make women *less* happy than a more egalitarian shakedown? Not necessarily. What makes the difference for the wellbeing of both partners is not how fair things 'really' are, but how fair they are perceived to be. Full-time breadwinners whose contribution to family life is valued and supported by their stay-at-home partners (whose contribution to family life is in turn equally valued and supported)—no matter what their gender—will be happier on the whole than families in which disputes about paid and unpaid labour, like the proverbial woman's work, are never done.

Having said all that, the fact remains that for most couples today, dividing up the family labour with so blunt an instrument—breadwinners in one corner, caregivers in another—is no longer a viable option. Not so much out of economic necessity, I would argue, as out of its opposite: the imperatives of affluence. Increasingly, dads feel as bored and cheated as mothers do by this arrangement. Men also, we are finally realising, have a yearning to *choose* the manner of parenting to which they would prefer to become accustomed—and their resentment at being denied that choice by what, for want of a better word, we might call 'husbandwork' is more and more deeply felt. Ultimately, that is very good news for women indeed.

Mothers who work for pay, these days, are on the whole happier than those who don't—and that is not just my personal experience but the conclusion of a large and ever-growing body of research. Economist and author Sylvia Ann Hewlett reviews this literature in *Baby Hunger*, noting that researchers have consistently found higher levels of life satisfaction and self esteem—and less depression—among employed mothers compared with their non-employed sisters, in every occupational category. The research shows equally clearly, however, that the majority of mothers are happiest working in part-time or reduced-hours jobs. Not all—but most.

'Not surprisingly,' notes Hewlett, 'working mothers are happier when they have enough leisure time to enjoy their children—to hang out at home, go to movies, play sports, visit museums and parks, travel together, share meals, and just talk.' To make that general observation is neither to blame nor otherwise judge working mothers who choose a different path (or have it chosen for them). Many women and their families positively thrive on a long-hours lifestyle. Every happy family is *not* happy in the same way. For most women, however, long hours of paid employment do *not* predict greater satisfaction with the parenting role. Nor does being a fractional breadwinner necessarily mean a woman is settling for half a loaf.

Child psychologist Donald Winnicott famously observed that 'there is no such thing as a baby'. What he meant was that infants, owing to their utter dependency, achieve definition and identity only in relationship with others. Every child is in this sense a transaction. Babies do not arrive in the world as finished sentences, static and boundaried, but as collections of infinitives awaiting conjugation. Motherhood, I would argue, is much the same. 'There is no such thing as a mother' either—let alone a bad mother or a good mother. We are not born into a maternal identity. We achieve it—or allow it to be thrust upon us.

What women want next is a chance to reintegrate motherhood into the rest of our lives, to find a way to allow it to be central to who we are without swallowing us whole, to lend depth and purpose and joy to lives that are already deep and purposeful and joyful. What we want next from motherhood is, in part, simply to share it more. Not just with our partners—though most of us want that too, and fiercely—but with the wider public world we have been gracious enough to populate.

What we want next from motherhood is permission to take our own wellbeing as seriously as those we care for, and to demand that others follow suit. Motherhood is not an experience we want to 'survive', like an earthquake or a flood. It is not something we need to squeeze into a space small enough for Real Life to accommodate. It *is* Real Life. What women want next, perhaps, is the courage to say so out loud.

balance, schmalance

'No matter what choice we make, we're going to get nailed for it. So
we might as well choose what makes us happy.'

Anna Quindlen *Thinking Out Loud*

I suspect there are two kinds of women in the world: those who seek
balance, and those who say they seek balance but who secretly get
a buzz from those daredevil dismounts off the uneven parallel bars of
life. It only seems fair to declare straight out that I am the second kind.

For me, the concept of the balanced life is rather like the concept
of the balanced meal: laudable but uninspiring. I know this isn't fair,
and it probably isn't even sisterly, but the truth is, I've never really
wanted a meat-and-three-veg kind of a life, consumed dutifully and
at regular intervals. Which is a good thing, because heaven knows
that's not the portion I've been served.

My own experience with life, and with work too for that matter,
has been more a case of splurge and purge. I know this does not make
me typical, exactly. I'm fairly certain it doesn't make me aberrant either.
Yet whenever I start talking about work/life balance, I feel a little like
the workaholic boss exhorting her staff to take up family-friendly leave
entitlements. ('Can't you kids find anywhere else to play?' I bark at my

twelve-year-old through the study door. He and the friends he has brought home after school—a privilege he enjoys thanks to Mummy's flexible, home-based profession—slink guiltily out the back door. 'Mum's obsessed with work/life balance right now,' I hear him whisper apologetically.)

Despite people like me, it has become a truism that Balance is the holy grail that every modern woman seeks. Balance between work and life—as if work were somehow conducted in the spirit world—between care and leisure, between Them and Us. Ten or twenty years ago, we spoke of women 'juggling' their multiple roles, a metaphor whose Barnum and Baileyesque backstory we have rightly rejected now. A woman who juggled succeeded only by never, ever stopping. The balance metaphor, by contrast, emphasises stasis, harmony. That quiet, grounded quality that Bridget Jones calls 'inner poise'…usually just before she falls flat on her face.

Whatever else it may entail, work/life balance requires just enough work to keep a woman 'stimulated', just enough life to keep her grounded…or is it tethered? The woman in balance is like the fulcrum in the see-saw of family life. Men and children experience the ups and downs. She stays so centred she can hardly be said to move at all.

Yet we are also clear these days that work/life balance is good for guys too. It's not a *women's* issue, we say now, defensively—as if any issue that did primarily affect females were by definition less urgent, or less worth remarking. Today, the experts remind us, work/life balance is a goal for *all of us*. And men agree. In theory. (Don't forget that men also agree on the equal sharing of parenting, housework and the remote control.)

Yet most of the successful men we see around us, whether politicians, artists, businesspeople, athletes or academics, do not really exemplify balance as an ideal at all. Harmony is not really their thing. Winning is.

A generation ago, at the dawning of the equal opportunity era, the question of what women wanted next from work was easier to answer. We wanted more work and more challenging work; we wanted better pay and greater opportunities for promotion; we wanted to create a level playing field by way of maternity leave, childcare and flexibility. What we wanted from paid work was the privilege of doing it as men did—preferably full time and at full throttle—and for the same guaranteed reward package: salary, benefits, prestige. We also assumed that taking up cudgels in the paid workplace would involve putting down cudgels—what the hell *is* a cudgel anyway?—in the unpaid workplace we call the family home. In any rational or just world, this expectation, which sociologists call the 'revolving door theory' of social change, would have made perfect sense. But in *this* world, it didn't have a prayer.

As the decades clocked in and out, the women who had poured into the paid workforce waited hopefully for the trade-off to descend. Like tired children staying up late for Santa, their belief in the Equity Elf was touching, and tragically misplaced. What we learned to call the second shift meant that, for partnered women, and especially for partnered women with children, paid work did not replace unpaid work, the way it did for men. It just deferred it till the weekend. Employed women today, whether they work full time or part time, still perform roughly two-thirds of all household labour. And this despite the fact that men now contribute about twice the amount of housework they did forty years ago.

We don't do as much housework as our mothers did—in fact, we've managed to lop off about ten hours a week on average. (Remember ironed tea towels? Cooked puddings? Spring cleaning? No, I don't either.) But we do more of it than we 'ought' to at this stage in our social history, and much, much more than anybody would ever have predicted. If the entry of women into the paid workforce has been feminism's greatest achievement, the persistence of the second shift is perhaps its most keenly felt failure.

In part, it helps us explain why, forty years on, what many women want most from paid work seems to be less of it. A generation ago, women fought for the privilege to work as men did, and for the same rewards. Today we're not so sure. Playing hardball looked so thrilling when we watched it from the sidelines. Up close and personal, it's a game we're not even sure we want to play, let alone to win. And as far as taking men as our role models, let's just be polite and say that most of us want less of that as well.

In fact, many observers now insist that gender is no longer even the issue. In a way they are right. It is certainly the case that the great workplace divide today is the one between the 'child-free' (operationally defined as people with no kids, or people without primary responsibility for kids, no matter what their gender or relationship status) and the 'childbound' (operationally defined as those people who function as the main caregivers of children and take front-line responsibility for performing, or delegating, most other unpaid labour). Gender is hardly irrelevant to this divide—so much so that economists like Harvard's Claudia Goldin refer to 'men and childless women' as a single economic category. Quite obviously, women are over-represented among the childbound by a ratio of perhaps nine to one—and that's a generous estimate. The hard question is what that disproportion represents, and whether—or how—we should continue to worry about it.

Gender still stacks the odds, but it no longer determines which side of the divide we end up on. That the overwhelming majority of the childbound are female need not obscure the basic fact that we are talking about roles, not sex per se. It is not who we *are* that makes the biggest difference in what people say they want from paid work. It's what we *do*—whether by choice or economic necessity, whether by virtue of our temperaments or talents, or simply because that's the way we've been socialised. Biological theories that oppose men's 'drive to compete' with women's 'drive to affiliate' are fascinating, but beside the point—a bit like analysing an efficient factory production line by positing an 'assembly instinct' versus a 'packaging instinct'. A specialist division of labour that happens to work efficiently needs no Grand Unifying Theory to justify its existence.

The division of human labour by gender into the material and the affiliative, the public and the private, the productive and the reproductive, obviously does have a biological base. But the reason for its persistence into the present has nothing, or almost nothing, to do with biology. It is clear that females can and do function just as efficiently as males in the provider role, under the conditions of a level playing field; and it is equally clear that males can be as effective at nurture and nest-building. Can we agree once and for all that that's a case we don't need to make anymore?

I think of the husband of a girlfriend of mine who swiped her copy of *Wifework* and was horrified to discover—as he told everyone for months—'My God. I'm the Wife!' As a single mum who's been the sole breadwinner for more than a decade, I don't feel the need to read any more case histories. Why should I, when I probably qualify as one? It's not as if breadwinning were an ignoble calling or anything. In fact, once you get with the program it can be deeply gratifying. But the fact is, like most boomer women, I wasn't raised to it. Not really—no more than my ex-partners were raised to plan dinner parties or remove those stubborn stains.

My own mother was a stay-at-home housewife whose CV, if she'd had one, would have stopped at 1953, the year, aged 22, she gave up her job as a model in New York City's garment district to marry my father. 'I don't *want* to explore new horizons,' my mother would snap whenever one of us tried to consciousness-raise. 'I don't like having to *be* anywhere.' (Honestly, I'd think to myself. That woman has the consciousness of an anvil.)

The women's movement of the '60s and '70s had no outward impact on our family's traditional infrastructure. It didn't change the way we did things. But its effect on the way we framed things—all of us—was profound. For one thing, we started to realise that we were a certain kind of family: a 'traditional' one. Before, it never would have occurred to us there was any other kind.

My mother taught my sister and me how to dust and vacuum, how to make a bed with crisp hospital corners, and even how to scrub a toilet. I remember that last lesson vividly. I was five. When I tell my ten-year-old daughter all this—a sixth-grader who still struggles to put her school blouse on a coathanger—her eyes grow as wide as CD-ROMs. 'Wow,' she says. 'Just like "Little House on the Prairie"!'

But we girls were also taught that we would need to learn how to earn our living in the world, to 'become' something, as my mother had not—preferably something highly skilled and reasonably paid. She was happy enough with her lot in life: her house, her marriage and her children, quite possibly in that order. But the women's movement hammered home the unromantic point that she'd had little choice in the matter—that her financial dependence made domestic tranquillity not simply desirable but imperative. At the same time, my mother said she hoped that we wouldn't *have* to work—a reference, we knew, to the expectation that we would marry well, or well enough to know the luxury of choice.

This particular mixed message has followed us all of our adult lives. In fact, I would go so far as to say that it has followed our entire generation. In my own case, it turned out that I did 'have to' work. So did my sister, though for different reasons. (In my case, a marriage that self-destructed; in her case, a mortgage that didn't.) Yet for both of us, I think it's fair to say, it was only when we 'had to' that we came to realise how much we actually wanted to. Not having the luxury to opt out, or to opt in for that matter, didn't change the rules of the game. But it certainly changed the intensity with which we played it.

The word 'revolution' is bandied around a lot these days, applied indiscriminately to everything from feminine hygiene protection to ziploc bags. But in our own lifetimes, the entry of women, especially women who are mothers, into the paid workforce qualifies as a genuine revolution. In OECD countries between 1954 and 2000, the employment rate among women has more than doubled. It is now 61 percent. (In Australia the figure is 73 percent.) Among mothers, the market share has grown even more spectacularly. In the US, the percentage of employed mothers *quadrupled* between 1950 and 2000. In the developed world today, almost half of all mothers with children under five—45 percent—are presently in the paid workforce.

A generation ago, it was common for women to retire from paid work upon marriage. With the birth of a first child, it was practically compulsory. It is easy to forget how recently we have amended the handbook. As late as 1976, for example, Australian census figures show that the average mother with two children spent a *decade* at home, as George Megalogenis points out in *Faultlines: Race, Work and the Politics of Changing Australia.* Today, only 23 percent of Australian families with dependent children default to Ozzie and Harriet mode. In the US, the figure is even lower. Here, it has been estimated that families that *choose* to operate in single-breadwinner mode constitute a mere 10 percent of all households.

What the research tells us very plainly is that most women today do work for pay. It also tells us that most women want to work for pay, and are happier when they do. We'll look at some of the evidence for that later. For now, let's be clear that what women want next from work is not, on the whole, a return to full-time domesticity—and never will be.

The other side of the story is that the upward trajectory of women's, let us say, 'enthusiasm' for paid work appears to have reached its upper limit. The evidence is equally clear that once a woman has had children (as, conservatively, three-quarters of us will eventually do), she will work many fewer paid hours than singletons and she will do so, by and large, by choice.

For most adult women, paid work is now an integral part of our identity. Yet the research shows that, as a group, most of us continue to rank family priorities higher than professional ones. Men, in case you were wondering, do also these days. The difference is that women actually alter their behaviour to reflect those priorities. It is women who choose to work shorter weeks, to take advantage of family-friendly entitlements, to forgo promotion and to opt for part-time work, where it exists, in preference to full-time.

The abysmal figures on women's workforce participation at the highest levels, once read as transparent evidence of institutional gender discrimination, are being reassessed today within the context of what US author and executive coach Michele Kremen Bolton calls 'the internal glass ceiling'. The suggestion is that the barriers to success we face today—arguably the highest and most intractable of all—are the ones we have built with our own hands, within our own hearts. If women are not assuming leadership roles because they are paralysed by maternal guilt, for example, or because they fear for the consequences of a long-hours lifestyle on the quality of their marriages, it seems clear that we may need to rethink the whole concept of 'obstacles to women's workforce participation'. Pointing out that men in equivalent situations *don't* suffer from such guilt or worry doesn't really move us forward (unless we take it as a given that being like men is our goal—*eew!*).

Choosing not to compete out of fear or self-doubt is every bit as devastating to our chances for success as any external bar that might be erected. In fact it's more devastating in some ways, because less susceptible to manipulation through legislation or policy change. This does not suggest that having equal opportunity policies in place is irrelevant or unimportant, but what we have to face now is the confronting truth that policy—even at its most inspired—may not be enough.

Here's an even more subversive thought: maybe it is. Maybe women's persistent preference to remain more focused on relationships than on achievements isn't an 'obstacle' at all. Maybe, just maybe, it is our greatest asset. The underrepresentation of women in leadership roles—like the underrepresentation of men in nurturing roles—has been a standard item on the feminist shitlist for so long that it takes an effort of the will even to imagine its persistence as anything other than the most grievous defeat, but imagine it we must.

Maybe *New York Times* journalist Lisa Belkin is right, and the answer to the question Why Don't Women Run the World? is simpler than any of us ever imagined: *Because We Don't Want To.*

Or perhaps, to be more accurate, because 80 percent of us don't want to. Here in Australia, many feminists continue to insist that we have structured our workplaces in a way that virtually guarantees that women will never achieve more than a toehold. Yet there is compelling evidence to suggest that perhaps only 20 percent of women are work-centred enough to mind—quite possibly the same 20 percent who identify most strongly with feminism in the first place. If only a fraction of us *want* to play hardball with the big boys, no wonder we're looking at such dismal batting averages.

'It's not just that the workplace has failed women. It is also that women are rejecting the workplace,' Belkin has observed, and research carried out by London School of Economics sociologist Catherine Hakim provides hard evidence for that somewhat impressionistic thesis. Hakim has enjoyed—or should I say endured?—a similar reception, as vintage feminists who, like the hard-working parents of spoilt children who despise them for their 'materialism', have thrown up their hands in despair.

It is easy to understand why this older generation feels betrayed. But it is, equally, impossible to deny that the solutions to one set of problems—achieving equality, say—almost inevitably give rise to a new and improved set of problems—appreciating diversity, say. Of *course* young women today take so much for granted. That's not a sign of feminism's failure. It's a sign of how far we've come.

What women wanted a generation ago was the opportunity for

more and better work. Now, we tell the enchanted fish, what we want is more and better *time*. Family time, quality time, 'me' time. If time is the new money—and there are plenty of indications that, in an affluent society, that's exactly what it is—then what women want next is a substantial pay rise. And they are willing to forgo many of the privileges their mothers fought for in order to get it.

Ironically, of course, part-time employment rarely translates into a net loss of hours worked. This is especially true for mothers, for whom working fractional hours will spell an almost one-for-one exchange of paid work for unpaid work at home. Yet judging by women's preferences, the conclusion is inescapable that work very definitely ain't work. Doing the weekly grocery shopping, or cleaning the oven, or supervising a major afterschool playdate are not exactly what you'd call leisure time activities. But for many, this sort of work is not only perceived as qualitatively different from the other sort, but evidently ranked as qualitatively higher.

In Australia, where women work part time at twice the rate they do in the US and the UK, the effect is particularly striking. A recent large-scale Australian study of work-hour preferences found that almost all men and women surveyed, regardless of marital or parental status or whether they worked full or part time, wanted to be spending slightly less time at work than they did currently. (The single exception was sole mothers.) Yet for all groups the difference between actual and desired hours was astonishingly small. According to this study, conducted by researchers Robert Drago and Yi-Ping Tseng using data from more than 7500 households, the average male in a dual-earner household worked for pay twenty hours longer than the average female. But the desired gap—and it was shared by both genders—clocked in at a barely distinguishable eighteen.

Specifically, for the average couple with children, men's stated preference was to work 44 hours a week while women wanted only 26 hours of paid work. Even in the subsample of families Drago and

Tseng called 'egalitarian'—in which both adults worked full time and the care of children was shared—the gender gap in preferred work hours was significant, with women desiring on average a 36-hour week to men's preferred 41 hours. Even among singletons, the situation was similar. In this demographic, the average man worked five hours longer per week than the average woman, and was basically happy with those hours. The average single woman, on the other hand, preferred to work an additional half an hour less.

In Australia at least, then, what women seem to want from work in quantitative terms is pretty much what they get, and that is: not too much of it. The strong preference among partnered Australian women for part-time employment is matched by the reality. In fact, the household type that social researchers have started to call 'neotraditional'—He works full time for pay and She works part time—has become the new typical Australian family.

By definition, the neotraditional family consists of two parents who participate in both paid and unpaid labour. But the division of that labour 'is highly unequal, with the man performing a disproportionate amount of paid work and the woman undertaking most unpaid work for the family', in the words of Drago and Tseng.

In Australia, part-time work and women's work are so closely associated that some observers have argued that virtually *all* of women's increased labour force participation over the past four decades can be accounted for by the expansion of part-time jobs. Of all employed women, 44 percent of us work part time. Among employed mothers, more than 56 percent do. (By contrast, only 5 percent of Australian fathers work part time.) That's double the figure for mothers in the US. There, only about a quarter of mums work part time, though the evidence strongly suggests that many more would prefer to do so.

Not surprisingly, the division of unpaid labour reflects these skews. Whereas in the US, recent time-use studies show significant increases in the domestic labour performed by men—particularly with regard to childcare—here in Australia real change has been negligible. Most of us now say we *believe* men and women should share equally as parents and partners. But then most of us still say we're Christians, too—and look at the figures on church attendance.

Many observers have suggested—myself included, if memory serves—that the rhetoric of egalitarian family life is about the only thing we *have* managed to successfully redistribute, and that the ghettoisation of women in part-time work is an obvious reason why. Part-time work, the argument goes, is work on P-plates: Mummy track work that, no matter how conscientiously pursued, exists in relation to full time as Pepsi is to Coke (i.e. not-quite-the-real thing). Here in Australia, permanent part-time employees have been guaranteed pay equity since the '70s, and lose neither superannuation nor health benefits when down-shifting from full time. At the same time, fully two-thirds of all part-time jobs are casual, subject to unregulated fluctuations in rates of pay and benefits and offering minimal job security. Achieving big promotions—or, in many cases, any promotion at all—is an impossible dream for most part-timers.

Most of the time, making the choice to work part time means trading off power for convenience, prestige for flexibility, challenge for security—and, as we have already observed—paid hours for unpaid hours. It means playing softball: a safer, slower game that will never get you into the majors but still keeps you in circulation. Above all, part-time work is a status-quo saver, creating a family structure that allows women's labour to be exploited to the max while enabling men to continue to function as Big Cheese breadwinners with all the rights and privileges attached thereto (because, after all, 'He works so hard!').

Part-time work requires no major structural changes with regard to child-rearing practices either. It means you can get away with finding ad-hoc care for kids while they're little—neighbours, grandparents, babysitters, dads—without making any inconvenient demands for institutional daycare. All of which explains the standard feminist line that sees the feminisation of part-time work as, in author Joan Peters' words, 'more a symptom of an overworked culture, not a cure'.

And yet…and yet. It's easy for people like Joan Peters and (if I'm honest) myself to make this case. As highly educated, highly skilled and—at least in relative terms—highly paid journalists, we are hardly typical members of the working mothers' constituency. For one thing, we don't just have jobs. We have careers—and those careers are extremely important to us. (In my own case, as a single mother and sole breadwinner for a family of three, paying the mortgage is extremely important, too.) Let's face it: most of the women who carry the public debate about women and work—and heaven knows just about every feminist author *ever*—are in more or less the same position. We are career-focused women. Women for whom paid work represents not just a paycheque but an important source of identity and gratification.

Personally, I think I'm fortunate—though I am aware that others would disagree with that assessment, especially if they saw me on a deadline day. But I never delude myself that I am normal. Or even average.

I often think about a stunning young mum—she couldn't have been more than 22—I met at my daughter's preschool more than a decade ago. After weeks of watching me barrel through the school gates at 2.59 (she was always first in line, as composed as a Botticelli Madonna), she shyly asked me what I did for a living. When I told her she nodded sympathetically, as if I'd just confessed that I suffered some congenital mental illness.

'And what about you?' I asked. 'Oh, I'm lucky,' she smiled radiantly. 'I don't have to work.' It made me chuckle at the time. It still does, actually. The fact is, I consider myself lucky too. Not because I 'have to' work, but because I want to despite having to. Because for me, work is not just a means to an end, but *meaningful* in and of itself.

According to controversial, but really rather unremarkable, research conducted by Catherine Hakim, I am in that 20 percent of women who describe themselves as work-centred—that is, who give priority to paid employment or other activities in the public sphere. (Despite this, I might add, I still work part time, and have done so since the birth of my first child. My first act upon learning that I was pregnant was to shriek with joy. My second was to call the childcare centre at Curtin University and put my name on the waiting list for a full-time place. When our number came up, about six weeks after my daughter's birth, I rang to say I wasn't quite ready yet. Fifteen years and two more kids later, and I am still not quite ready. I now accept that I probably never will be.)

An equal minority, Hakim reports in her 2001 book *Work-Lifestyle Choices in the 21st Century: Preference Theory,* are like the Botticelli mum: home-centred and happy to be that way. The remaining 60 percent—in other words most of us—fall somewhere between these stools. Hakim calls this group 'adaptives', but they are exactly the same women that Drago and Tseng would call 'neotraditional': looking for the best of both worlds and finding it, give or take, in the 1.5 bread-winner family.

Hakim's findings have inspired fear and loathing among establishment feminists, who scoff at the notion of 'choice'—especially when it's the wrong choice!—and imply that compromise is a particularly pernicious form of false consciousness. In mainstream political circles, meanwhile—especially here in Australia—Hakim has been hailed as something of a postfeminist messiah. Her research has lit something of a fire under policymakers on both sides of politics as they wrestle to provide a platter of fertility-friendly incentives for all working women. (The fact that Hakim's findings appear to relegate paid maternity leave to the bottom of the political porkbarrel is an added bonus.)

For me, Catherine Hakim's research proves only one thing: that nothing starts an argument faster than a statement of the obvious. Her central finding—that women's work and child-rearing preferences are too diverse to conform to any one-size-fits-all solution—is as contentious as motherhood and apple pie.

What is scary—and I would be lying if I pretended to be entirely comfortable with it myself—is the implication that we are moving towards a post-equality ethos. Whether this turns out to be a fancy way of saying 'moving backwards', or proves a genuine advance on feminism's evolutionary ladder, remains open to conjecture. But my own experience suggests strongly that it is possible to make conventional choices for revolutionary reasons.

Women who choose to privilege relationships over paid work are no less a feminist success story than their career-oriented sisters. And at this point in our history, we need to be clear, many women *are* so choosing. And conspiracy theories to the contrary—like Anne Summers' argument in *The End of Equality* that 'the federal government and other powerful agents' have concocted 'a powerful new [*sic*] ideology that defines women first and foremost as mothers'—ring increasingly hollow.

What women want next from work—not simply what governments or employers or male partners or children want next for us, but what *we* want next—is a level playing field for those who want to play that particular game, and a *different* playing field for those who don't.

Drago and Tseng's study of work preferences provides further support for this slightly unsettling notion. We have already observed that the neotraditional family accounts for the largest proportion of Australian household types. But a closer look at the figures shows that there really isn't a 'typical' family of any kind anymore. In 27 percent of families, Dad works full time for pay and Mum part time. But in an almost equal number, 23 percent, Dad is the sole breadwinner while Mum works full time at home. Another 23 percent is comprised of single-parent households (the vast majority female-headed), in half of which the parent is in paid employment. Genuine dual-career households, in which both adults work full time, constitute another hefty hunk of the pie at 17 percent. In the remaining 6 percent of families, neither adult works. The picture is further complicated by the fact that a third of us don't live in 'families' at all. In the larger context of Australian social trends, the single-person household now represents the largest segment of all: 35 percent of our total population.

In the US, the figures have a slightly different skew, but much the same pattern of elaborate diversity. Here, 16 percent of all households are headed by sole parents, three-quarters of them female. Single-breadwinner couple families account for one in five or 19 percent of total households. 'Dual-earner' married couples constitute another 39 percent, with wives working an average of almost eight fewer hours per week than husbands. Of all married women, just over 60 percent work full time, year round.

The diversity of demographic orbits out there is positively awe-inspiring, especially when compared to the Dick-and-Dora world many of us grew up in as late as the 1960s and '70s. So too is the move-ment between those orbits, the chaotic commuter traffic from one household type to another and back again. Writing the paragraph above, for example, it struck me that in the last twenty years I have at one time or another been a member of every single household type I've just mentioned. (I'm not sure whether that's an achievement, or a sign that I need more therapy.) This may not be exactly typical, but it's hardly unusual either.

No wonder adult life, formerly a tightly woven drama in five acts, so often feels like an improvisation—a pastiche we make up as we go along, aided by a cultural prop closet overflowing with possibilities. 'Flexibility' is no longer an asset in such a world. It's a survival tool.

waiting for the no-fault fairy

It's not just employment patterns that have altered in the last half century. It's not just the rules that govern the way we do family life. Our very definitions of *self* have mutated. The struggle to achieve work/life balance is not just about finding enough hours in the day. It's about finding who we *are*, as women and as people.

The perception that the boundaries between male and female are harder and harder to discern is more than a curmudgeonly complaint. It's quite demonstrably true. It's demonstrably unbalancing, too. We may buy books that insist that men are from Mars and women from Venus—possibly because it makes us nostalgic for the days when the lines between Us and Them were still clearly drawn. But the reality is that men and women today are extraordinarily alike in their expectations and experience. Depending on our point of view, we either praise feminism for this, or we blame it.

At the same time we must beware of exaggerating the extent of these changes. In fact, some of the very boundaries we thought would be easiest to bend have turned out to have rods of steel inside, and none more so than the redistribution of paid and unpaid labour. All the rhetoric, and all the legislation, and all the family-friendly policymaking aside, the fact remains that the long-hours lifestyle—another name for Catherine Hakim's work-centredness—appears to make most men feel good about themselves, and to make most women, especially if they are mothers, feel bad about themselves. And not just bad, but *wrong*.

Sociologists observe that our workplaces are built around an 'ideal worker norm' that rewards people who make paid work the focus of their lives. Critics point out that this is a 'masculine' model of success, and that is true of course. But it is true too that in today's workplaces, gender explains less and less of the variance in occupational attainment between men and women. A woman who chooses to behave as an ideal worker, in other words, is as likely to succeed as a man who does. The difference is, many fewer women do so choose. Catherine Hakim found that the proportion of men who described themselves as work-centred was 55 percent—more than double the rate for women.

For many observers, myself most emphatically included, the argument that the persistence of the ambition gap is the result of discrimination or disadvantage increasingly fails to persuade. 'It's not about talent, dedication, experience, or the ability to take the heat' either, insists entrepreneur Mary Lou Quinlan. 'Women simply say, "I just don't like that kitchen."'

Quinlan ought to know. She resigned her position as CEO of New York advertising agency NW Ayer in 1998 to found Just Ask a Woman, a consulting firm that advises corporate clients on doing business with women.

Of course, the news weeklies are full of stories of corporate drop-outs—sorry, opt-outs. Nothing sells a magazine faster, it seems, than another heartwarming story about a female executive who, like the Grinch Who Stole Christmas, discovers that the true meaning of life lies in service (unpaid) to others. The interesting thing about Mary

Lou Quinlan is that she didn't opt out to spend more time with the family—in fact, she is childless—but *because she wanted to*.

Could the Mary Lou Quinlans of the world represent feminism's next new wave? Lisa Belkin was practically pilloried when she hinted as much (hell hath no fury like a second-wave feminist scorned). Her 2003 *New York Times Magazine* article, 'The Opt-Out Generation', profiled a group of high-achieving, Ivy League-educated Have it Alls who made the decision to pull out or cut back on their careers simply because—to all appearances—they wanted to.

Belkin was well aware that the women in question were atypical: superbly qualified, socially powerful and supported to an enviable degree by loving partners whose ultra-high earnings made the opt-out question a viable one in the first place. The fact that these women were so highly privileged was the whole point. If any group of women could be said to be able to make a free and unconstrained choice, surely this was it.

Belkin began by pointing out some unsettling statistics. That, for instance, women comprise half of all Ivy League law school graduates, but only 16 percent of partners in law firms. That men and women today enter corporate training programs in equal numbers, but that women remain outnumbered in corporate officer positions by a ratio of greater than one to four. That, of the 108 females who have been featured by *Fortune* magazine as the Most Powerful Women in Corporate America, at least twenty have abandoned their jobs (most of them voluntarily) for 'less intense and more fulfilling' lives. That only 67 percent of white women with MBAs currently work full time, compared to 97 percent of their male counterparts. That, according to US Census figures, the number of children being cared for by stay-at-home mothers has increased nearly 13 percent in the last decade.

'As these women look up at the "top",' Belkin wrote, 'they are increasingly deciding they don't want to do what it takes to get there.'

Not 'can't do'. Not 'aren't allowed to do'. But 'don't want to do'.

'Financially, it gets better,' is how one informant nutshelled it, 'but in terms of my actual life, it gets worse.'

Feminist and evolutionary anthropologist Sarah Blaffer Hrdy believes that most women opt out for the sake of their children. At this moment in our social development, she argues, 'Seeking clout in a male world does not correlate with child wellbeing. Today, striving for status usually means leaving your children with an au pair who's just there for a year, or in inadequate day care.' Females are competitive all right, Hrdy insists (and she has spent a good deal of her fascinating career showing exactly how and why). They just 'don't want to compete along the lines that are not compatible with their other goals'. And for mothers, the number-one goal is the wellbeing of offspring.

In the '70s and '80s, radical feminists agitated for free and universal childcare, on the assumption—rational enough—that child welfare, far from being 'women's work' ought to be considered a *community* responsibility. Personally, I still believe that's true. Yet the evidence has persuaded me, as it has many others, that long-hours daycare is not the way to achieve that goal. In fact, the snapshot that has emerged from the last several decades of research into the impact of institutional care is distinctly unflattering. The 'myth' that Mother (Or a Reasonable Facsimile Thereof) Cares Best has turned out to be almost alarmingly substantial.

What began as a 'trickle of disconcerting evidence' about the effects of long-hours daycare, in the words of leading researcher Jay Belsky, has now become a veritable white-water rapid. In an extensive review of the literature in the *Journal of Child Psychology and Psychiatry* in 2001, Belsky presented a round-up of findings on the effect of institutional care on everything from parent–child bonding to socialisation to school achievement—and the news is about as gladsome as an epidemic of pinworms. Without going into the minutiae (because I'm depressed enough right now), the clear message is that daycare for more than about twenty hours a week is *not* 'just as good for kids'; it is demonstrably worse. And that's regardless of the quality of care.

We can go on shooting the bearers of such tidings—Belsky himself, an avowed and committed feminist, is as full of lead as a 2B pencil—but the message itself remains intact, for anyone brave enough to unplug their ears and hear it.

Let's take a step back, lest in our moral panic we deduce from these premises some absurd or hysterical conclusion (like 'mothers shouldn't work', or 'daycare is a dumping ground'). First of all, in many cases the disadvantages to children in long-hours care—while definite—are slight to the point of insignificance, especially when they are tracked over time. More broadly, it is not a matter of daycare 'damaging' kids, let alone 'destroying' them.

On the other hand, from the perspective of a parent who wants only the best for his or her child—and, really, isn't that all of us?—that seems awfully cold comfort. I remember when my marriage broke up how angry I would get when well-meaning friends assured me my children would 'survive'. As parents, 'survival' is not what we aim for. Perhaps most importantly of all, though, we need to remember that the research on daycare effects pits institutional care against home-based care in general, *not* against mothercare specifically.

The take-home message here is not Mother Cares Best, but that Families Care Best. (And in case you're wondering about nannies, I am too. I have searched in vain for research that has compared home-based commercial care with family care.) There is no evidence at all that *mothers*, or any other females for that matter, provide better care for children in the early years of life than, for example, fathers do.

Yet the temptation to throw the problem at women still proves irresistible. 'Working Mums Harm Kids' scream the headlines when such research is reported in the media, and biased or downright inaccurate reporting of findings is more often the rule than the exception. I found it amusing—and instructive—to follow up one recent report in the British press alleging that working mothers' kids suffered educationally. When I read the original research, conducted at the Institute for Social and Economic Research at the University of Essex, I found that that was true. Sort of. It turned out that mothers' full-time employment did have a very small negative effect on children's educational achievement—*but so did fathers'*! Somehow or other, the headline 'Working Dads Harm Kids' never makes it to the front page. Or any page, for that matter.

The gravitational imperative—I'll be politic and avoid that other 'I' word, instinct—for mothers to provide hands-on care for their offspring has been well established, and the implications of that imperative for women's working lives are obvious both logically and empirically. But one of the most fascinating features of Belkin's interviews was how convinced these young women were that, by opting out, they were putting their *own* wellbeing first. If their children or their partners reaped some benefit too—well, so much the better. But that was a secondary concern. One woman Belkin spoke to, a theatre artist and teacher with a masters degree in English, admitted sheepishly that maternity had simply provided her with 'an escape hatch…a graceful and convenient exit'. And of course there are plenty of non-mothers, like Mary Lou Quinlan, who are also making the choice to downshift for reasons of *self*-care.

Men and women alike worry about the impact of the dual-career lifestyle on the quality of their relationships. Yet when there is slack to be cut, it is almost inevitably women's employment that gets the snip. The problem is knowing whether that's a problem, especially where there is no evidence to suggest that the privileging of men's paid work is not a mutual decision.

A Relationships Australia study published in December 2003 found that, in the dramatic words of one journalist, 'Nine out of ten Australians believe work—particularly the drive for both partners to have careers—is threatening to destroy relationships.' When both partners worked for pay, respondents alleged, the three main difficulties were: lack of time (38 percent), lack of understanding (27 percent) and failure to communicate (21 percent). The same study found that 93 percent of both men and women believed that being a good husband or a good wife was the most important aspect of their identity, followed closely by parenthood (91 percent).

Our *values* as men and women converge. But the way we express these values has remained stubbornly divergent. 'Being a good wife' and 'being a good husband' only seem like equivalent goals. In fact, they are achieved in very different ways. Being a good husband *means* working full time—and being a good father only intensifies the provider imperative. Being a good wife or a good mother, on the other hand, calls to mind an entirely different set of responsibilities, to which paid work is neither inimical nor necessarily even relevant.

A look at employment trends for men confirms this. It is true that the breadwinner role is more and more frequently shared between men and women in families. Indeed, in the US, more than a quarter of wives contribute as much or more income than their husbands do. Yet the work/life solution for dual-earner families that in many ways seems the most obvious—for everybody to work part time for pay and part time at home—has inspired as much enthusiasm among guys as a Saturday afternoon of sock-matching.

According to research commissioned by the Australian federal government and carried out by the Social Policy Research Centre in 2004, only 2 percent of Australian men have moved to part-time work to care for children. The study also found that, while 81 percent of workplace agreements contained at least one family-friendly provision, only 18 percent of male workers took advantage of any. The authors concluded that 'despite the enthusiastic adoption of a child-centred view of family life and a commitment to the idea of shared parenting, most male employees…tended to give work priority over family.'

Other research has shown that so-called family-friendly

entitlements have little impact on the way either gender copes with work/life pressures. US researcher Ellin Galinsky found that working parents with access to such benefits 'experienced no less conflict between their work and personal/family lives and only slightly less stress'. The factors that really did make a difference for parents, Galinsky found, were things like having more autonomy at work and greater job security. Those who simply had less hectic and demanding jobs also, if you can believe it, reported less *sturm und drang*.

Galinsky also found that employed mothers were much more likely than employed fathers to stay at their current level of responsibility, and much more likely to say they would trade job advancement for part-time work, home-based work or flextime. US research firm Catalyst points out that women managers more often gravitate to lower-paying, lower-stress staff jobs, like marketing and human resources, rather than line jobs, where managers have direct bottom-line responsibility. Such findings suggest strongly that, rhetorical window-dressing aside, the only real competitive edge guys enjoy is their determination to 'win'—and what *that* boils down to is often a willingness to put career before family.

Research by Stanford Business School's Charles A. O'Reilly III has shown precisely this. Success is no longer a matter of whether you're male or female, O'Reilly found. It's how you play the game. Opt-out homecoming queen Brenda Barnes, the Pepsico CEO who dropped out in 1997 at the height of her corporate powers, told the *Australian Financial Review* in 2002, 'When you talk about those big jobs, those CEO jobs, you just have to give them your life. You can't alter them to make them accommodate women any better than men. It's just the way it is.'

Alice O'Keeffe, writing in the *Observer* in January 2004, cites UK research showing that male and female graduates with the same degree will often enter entirely different fields—forget about levelling them—with the women choosing careers with lower status and higher flexibility. Just three years after they leave university, females' earnings are 76 percent of males'. The reason why isn't rocket science. Hell, it's hardly even sociology. In the field of engineering and technology, for example, most female graduates become—wait for it—*teachers*. Most male graduates become scientists and managers.

O'Keeffe quotes one recent Oxford graduate whose acquaintances were 'genuinely shocked' when she chose nursing over medicine. (How much more shocked they would have been if she'd been a man!) Single and childless at the time she made her decision, this young woman explained she was determined to think *ahead* about the challenges of combining family life with a career—including that pesky little detail about having enough energy to spare to enjoy them. Call her decision cripplingly cautious, or impressively mature. But at this stage of our social evolution, can we at least agree it's a judgment call every woman has a right to make for herself?

As far as job *satisfaction* goes, the evidence shows that women experience at least as much of it as men do, despite having lesser outward success. In one intriguing study cited by psychologist Leslie Brody, male and female participants recorded their emotions whenever they were randomly beeped by pagers. Women reported more positive moods—describing themselves as 'happy', 'cheerful' or 'friendly' as opposed to 'unhappy', 'irritable' or 'angry'—when they were at work, and more negative moods when they were at home. Exactly the reverse was true for men. The reason, Brody speculates, may be that women have more choices at work, and men have more choices at home.

We have already looked at some of the evidence that people with lower incomes report less life satisfaction than those who earn more, and observed that the difference between the two groups is surprisingly, shall we say, stingy. The 2001 Australian Personal Wellbeing Index, to take just one recent example, found that those in the lowest annual income stratum—$15,000 per household—had an average life satisfaction level of 72 percent compared to 78 percent for people in the highest income group, who earned six times that amount (\$90,000+). Other research has suggested there may be a tipping point for earnings, below which wellbeing may be impaired but above which fluctuations in self-reported happiness are small.

My favourite such study, which was conducted in 1996 at the University of Michigan, found that women who earn \$40,000 or more feel a greater sense of belonging and function better psychologically than women who earn less, perceiving less conflict and reporting more social support from others.

Adjusting that figure for inflation, one could answer the question 'what do women want next from work?' very succinctly: about a grand a week.

Equally fascinating was the finding that it wasn't salary per se that made the difference but the extent to which earnings influenced a woman's sense of *belonging*—a factor which, in its turn, had a profound impact on her levels of depression, anxiety, loneliness and vulnerability to suicidal thoughts.

When a sample of female Harvard Business School graduates was asked recently what term best described how they felt about their working lives, the word 'exhaustion' came top of the list. Not surprisingly, perhaps, a quarter of these women had left the workplace entirely. And yet, as *The Third Shift* author Michele Kremen Bolton wryly notes, 'Like Air Force pilots bragging about how many missions they've flown without being shot down, women today take great pride in their ability to manage multiple roles.' Quite right too. The idea that you can be exhausted and at the same time deeply gratified certainly makes perfect sense to this single mother.

The masculine ideal worker norm is all about devoting oneself body, soul and briefcase to a single role in life: the worker role. (Time spent out of the office, if any, is devoted to the slacker role.) The 'overtime junkies' among us, as leading Australian sociologist Barbara

Pocock calls them, think nothing of working ten, twenty or even thirty extra unpaid hours a week. In fact, two-thirds of all overtime in Australia is unpaid. Recent studies show that Australia has the second-longest working day in the world, second only to Korea—a finding that recently prompted Australia Institute senior fellow Richard Denniss to propose a national Go Home on Time Day. Economists observe that the trend is partly the result of the shift from an 'hours worked' mentality to standards based on 'outcomes achieved'. Maybe so. But there is little evidence that the long-hours lifestyle means anyone is actually working harder, let alone smarter. Just more.

At the same time, workers who pursue better balance—regardless of their gender—find themselves precariously placed when it comes to promotions and pay rises. 'People have told me they have taken two or three mornings off to go to school functions and at their yearly appraisal they are described as abusive of the process,' observes men's health specialist Stephen Carroll. The result for many executives, Carroll notes, is an 'existential crisis' that can lead to a radical reordering of priorities.

Women who opt out make some feminists uneasy, while men who do the same are hailed as cultural champions. I suspect this is another one of those '70s holdovers we need to get beyond—the moral equiv-alent of a Nehru jacket, or a fringed poncho. Carroll cites the example of a male lawyer who downshifted to a more tame career in conveyancing in order to devote more billable minutes to his family. How gorgeous is that? we sigh. Yet the young woman who chooses nursing over medicine, or general practice over a specialty, or teaching over admin makes us nervous. For Him, it's a clear case of 'the road less travelled'. For Her, we worry about the path of least resistance.

There are female overtime junkies, too, of course—and we cut them a whole lot less slack. A friend reports a conversation overheard between two over-accessorised children on a suburban train: 'My mum is so-o sad,' the first girl complains. 'She has like two jobs and dresses up in this suit and tries to do everything. Like she said she had to go to parents' night…And she fell asleep? Right in the middle of everything?' ('When she fell asleep,' asks the friend, 'was it during a boring part?')

The dad who works two jobs and falls asleep at parent teacher night is still more likely to be seen (and to see himself) as a legend, not a buffoon. And the father who baths his children every night, come what may at the office, as selfless and committed. The wives of men who behave like this are still more likely to describe themselves as 'lucky' than 'oppressed'. Their children feel secure and cherished. They don't really *expect* any more than this from Daddy. Neither, if truth be told, do most of the rest of us.

On the whole, Women Who Do Too Much are less likely to be overtime junkies than they are to OD on multitasking: a nice word for doing almost everything, and doing it half-assed. 'Role strain', researchers used to call it. Today we know that managing multiple roles—much as women complain about it—is something a good many of us actually thrive on. And when I say this I do not mean to imply that women should learn to love their exhaustion. Working the second shift is *not* good sport, and being forced to grab your 'me' time by bolting yourself into the bathroom for five minutes isn't either. But having responsibility for multiple roles is something different. And the research shows it is actually *more* protective of women's mental health and physical wellbeing. Rates of depression among women are highest among stay-at-homes.

Paradoxically, feelings of guilt and self-doubt may be too, say experts. Such women may experience little role strain, notes Michele Kremen Bolton, but in many cases the object of the guilt they may have felt while working simply transfers itself 'from self-reproach about the time spent with one's family to a sense of betrayal of one's education or the women's movement'.

Lisa Belkin believes that such guilt may be what sociologists call a 'period effect'—that is, a phenomenon associated with a particular historical moment. Among the stay-at-home mothers Belkin profiled was a woman in her fifties who suffered enormous guilt for having opted out; a woman in her early forties, who was much less conflicted about her choice; and a thirtysomething, who expressed no guilt and no qualms at all. 'Even before I became a mother, I suspected I wouldn't go back to work,' she told Belkin. (I almost wrote, she 'confessed' to Belkin—a verb choice which would as good as carbon-date me.)

'Women Today Lead Messy Lives' accuses a *USA Today* feature. Yet, as *New York Times* columnist Margaret Talbot notes, with notorious good sense, 'how much better "messy", with all its implications of fullness, than "neat"'. Given the choice between a life that was tidy but threadbare, and one just slightly overstuffed—or maybe even splitting at the seams from time to time—I know which one I'd choose. And, really, sometimes the search for the perfect solution to the work/life conundrum can get as tiresome as the search for the perfect anything else—whether handbag, home or husband.

'On a personal level, and as a matter of social policy,' writes Marjorie Williams in the *Washington Post*, 'we often seem to be waiting for the No-Fault Fairy to come and explain at last how our deepest conflicts can be managed away.' Happiness is not, ultimately, a matter of having no more problems to solve. By that definition, my son's goldfish would be more fulfilled than I am.

Accepting that our lives are not problems to be solved, or a set of scales that may one day be righted—that our deepest conflicts exist in part because being fully human requires it, demands it in fact—may be the toughest assignment of all.

the last blow job?

Forty years ago, the sexual revolution seduced us into thinking that the Pill would set us free. Today that notion seems as quaint as a pair of vinyl go-go boots. The sense of anti-climax is unmistakable. Or maybe it's just the discovery that 'freedom' isn't really all it's cracked up to be. The sexual revolution was supposed to simplify sex: to reduce it to essentials, to return it to nature—as if there were anything remotely 'natural' about unmooring sex from reproduction. Yet sex today is more problematic than ever. Certainly our take on it as a society has never been more schizoid. True, we have succeeded in dismantling the old sexual politics. Whatever else it may or may not be, sex is no longer a game men play with women's bodies. Nor is it any longer a transaction brokered by breeding females, a calculated exchange of pleasure for protection. We have stripped sex of its biology with spectacular success. At the same time, we have unwound the tangled overlay of ritual and romance that for earlier generations set human sexuality definitively apart—in theory at least.

Dragging sex out of the top bureau drawer and into the sunshine seemed like such a good idea at the time. But the clear light of day has a way of exposing flaws and fissures that go unnoticed in the dark. ('At night,' I hear my grandmother say, '*all* the cats are grey.') Most unsettling of all, perhaps, the question of what sex *means*—especially given the promise that, if we played our cards right, it wouldn't mean anything at all—has never seemed more urgent.

For women, the sexual revolution promised an end to the double standard. We were now free to have sex without strings, whether of the reproductive, matrimonial or economic kind. The resulting euphoria, like a long-delayed orgasm, was almost disorienting in its intensity. For a brief time, notes Kay S. Hymowitz, a contributor to *Modern Sex: Liberation and Its Discontents*, 'Promiscuity became almost a matter of principle for many women newly liberated from old-fashioned notions of what good girls could and couldn't do.' Sleeping around for the sisterhood was nice work if you could get it—'sexual variety and abundance did not merely promise pleasure; they asserted women's freedom and independence,' notes Hymowitz—but it was hardly standard practice for any but the most politicised feminist. For most women, even I daresay for most feminists, sex remained a defiantly personal act.

Overturning the double standard was the fun part. The tricky bit was figuring out what to replace it with. It still is. The double standard that allowed boys to be boys and girls to be their mothers had been grossly inequitable on its face. Jettisoning it not only felt good. It felt right. The single-standard alternative—which is really just shorthand for the traditional male standard—is self-evidently less unjust to women, but arguably no more conducive to their sexual happiness.

Coming of age during a time of sexual revolution, as we have done, has meant that sex has been foregrounded in our lives, and in our culture, as never before. No wonder our perspective seems a little off at times.

As I drive my daughters to school each morning along an

otherwise bland stretch of suburban highway, we pass a series of bill-boards prurient enough to make a sailor blush, except that blushing seems to have gone out with crinolines and monogrammed hankies. One is an ad for a new kind of SIM card (JUST STICK IT IN!). Another is for a sports car, THE PERFECT BUTT captioning an image of the car's rear end positioned between those of two young women. A third is advertising a softdrink. GO ON, it leers. YOU KNOW YOU WANT IT.

I hate these billboards. I hate them, as the Psalmist says, with a perfect hatred. Yet—like so much else that I despise, from Australian xenophobia to low-rise jeans for eight-year-olds—I try to see them in historical perspective. It's cheaper than Prozac.

'Sexual intercourse began / In nineteen sixty-three,' Philip Larkin deadpanned. He was overstating the case just slightly. But there is no doubt that in that forty-odd-year stretch, our sexual consciousness has been raised to unprecedented heights. So too have our sexual expecta-tions. Ironically, the revolution that was supposed to get us to lighten up about our sexuality—and has to a large degree succeeded—has also forced sex to carry an impossibly heavy cargo of demands and expectations.

Previous generations accepted, indeed welcomed, the waning of sexual desire as a natural part of the lifecycle (although shorter life expectancies meant relatively few were fortunate enough to outlast their libido). For women who went the distance, surviving multiple preg-nancies and childbirths, the menopause must have been welcomed as a gift, and the associated waning of sexual attention a reward for serv-ices rendered. 'To be unwanted,' as Germaine Greer notes in *The Change*, 'is also to be free.'

One certainly can't imagine such women trying to 'fix' menopause, or god forbid forestall it. Today, we expect—in fact we demand—to remain sexual beings till the grave. And we are quite prepared to do what needs doing to achieve that end: whether it's prescription drugs, cosmetic surgery, psychotherapy or some other form of self-sculpture. Just as we expect to keep our teeth, we expect to keep our sexuality.

Yet it is not always entirely clear who 'we' are—or where our anxiety is coming from. The drive to remain sexual at any cost, at least as far as women are concerned, too often seems to be powered by some external engine, our partners, perhaps, or 'society' by way of a sexual script that still casts females as featured players in a boys' own adventure.

'One no longer hears even the disapproving "tsk-tsk" of respectable middle-age matrons,' notes the *Wall Street Journal*'s Meghan Cox Gurdon. 'They're all at Pilates classes trying to stay sexy lest their husbands replace them with younger models.' One can't help but wonder: is this what the sexual revolution has 'freed' us for?

In some ways, sex seems too central to the way we live our lives. Omnipresent, like those billboards. But banal like those billboards too. The sexual revolution helped to expose human sexuality in all its diversity and perversity. But today it is a case of overexposure. Sex is everywhere; hence, it is also nowhere—invisible or at least unremarkable.

'Where's the mystery?' my mother asks in exasperation, as we pass a well-groomed young woman in a midriff top whose brand of thong is as clearly visible as her navel ring. 'Why does there have to be mystery?' I respond testily. But really, it's just a reflex. I know exactly what she means. I not only know, but in a sense I agree (which is much, much scarier). Shining a bright light on our sexuality has made us more knowledgeable, more emotionally intelligent, and more accepting of our bodies and our desires. And all of that is wonderful. But forbidden fruit just doesn't taste as good when it's been cored, peeled and cut into bite-sized pieces.

'Do you believe sex is dirty?' someone once asked Woody Allen. 'Yes,' he replied without hesitation. 'But only if you're doing it right.' I suspect most young people today wouldn't even understand that joke, and maybe that's progress. These days, sex has become such good, clean fun. No wonder we need extraordinary measures to keep us interested.

We spend so much more time now looking at sex and hearing about sex and talking about sex. The irony, of course, is that we have never spent less time actually doing it—with the significant exception of young people, who are doing it more, and earlier, than ever. The rise—though perhaps detumescence would be a better word—of Generation Sexless is the latest unplanned child of the sexual revolution (the eldest sibling being feminism itself).

In part, I suspect, sex has lost some of its sexiness simply because we have so many alternative sources of gratification now, so many competing seductions. In an electronic environment, what you might call our social erogenous zones have multiplied exponentially. Sex (the Activity) used to be what grown-ups did for fun—entertainment, even. Today, we have DVDs for that. Not to mention the internet, computer games, email and wall-to-wall home theatres. Leisure is increasingly an out-of-body experience. And sex is no exception.

Sex surveys from around the world confirm that the trend toward having less sex—like the presumably linked phenomenon of having fewer babies—is as much a part of postmodern life as global terrorism, or reality television. A large-scale Australian study published in 2003 identified 'lack of interest' as the nation's number-one sexual dysfunction, affecting almost a quarter of males and more than half of females. More than *half*. In my day, this would have qualified a social condition as average, not aberrant.

But it's not just Australians who are forfeiting the game for lack of interest. In the US, public concern about Generation Sexless (as *New York* magazine dubbed it in 2003) has heated up rapidly over the last several years. According to the University of Chicago's national Health and Social Life Survey (1999), a comprehensive look at sex in the US, one in seven women reported problems with arousal and one in five, low sexual desire. A study reported recently in *USA Today* claims 'more than 40 million Americans are mired in a low-sex or no-sex marriage'. And it's not just women who are turning off the tap. Thirty percent of American men say they couldn't be fussed either.

According to a lengthy review article in the *Atlantic Monthly*, women in the Frigid Fifties were seeing more action than their counterparts today. It's an opinion seconded by Kinsey Institute director Dr John Bancroft. Women—particularly married women—are reporting less sex than at any other time in recent history. Not that it's an easy stat to ferret out. Informants notoriously over-report the amount of sex they have (men especially). 'When pressed, nearly everyone defaults to a respectable "once or twice a week",' notes a *Newsweek* article titled 'Not in the Mood'.

Asking adults about sex is now a little like asking us about our eating habits, or our exercise routine. Like a high-fibre diet, sex has become something we know we really ought to be having more of. But also like a high-fibre diet, it is something vast numbers of us seem to be honouring in the breach. Sociologist Pepper Schwartz, author of *Everything You Know about Sex and Love Is Wrong*, believes that when people are given 'permission' to be honest, they often admit to having sex less than once a month. 'And these are couples that like each other!' she adds. Some psychologists estimate that up to 20 percent of couples have a 'sexless marriage'—operationally defined as having sex no more than ten times a year. According to therapist Michele Weiner Davis, author of *The Sex Starved Marriage*, the number of such marriages has been 'grossly underreported'. Books like the ominously titled *Resurrecting Sex* and *Rekindling Desire: A Step-by-Step Program to Help Low-Sex and No-Sex Marriages* make the same point. Even Dr Phil calls it an 'epidemic' (but then, what doesn't Dr Phil call an epidemic?).

Anecdotally, the problem is said to be particularly acute in families where both adults work full time for pay. Couples who started life as carefree DINKS (double income no kids) undergo a grim meta-morphosis after the arrival of the first child, emerging by their mid-thirties as DINS (double income no sex). Other observers dismiss DINS as an urban myth. It's 'a cocktail party phenomenon. The data show that it's not true', insists psychologist Janet Hyde of the University of Wisconsin. According to Hyde's research, there is no correlation at all between the hours partners work and the amount (or quality) of sex they enjoy.

British women are among the least sexually active in the world, according to recent research. One study found fully a quarter of all British women have sex once a month or less. In June 2001, website redirect.co.uk found a quarter of more than 3000 women aged 18–45 said they 'can't be bothered' to have sex, another quarter adding they were 'happy with a cuddle'. Yet they are certainly keeping a stiff upper lip about it all, because their 'happiness' scores are through the roof. Whether despite or because of their rock-bottom erotic life, it is impossible to say.

One of the top-selling novels of 2003, Allison Pearson's savagely funny novel of working motherhood, *I Don't Know How She Does It*, features a heroine who approaches sex with her husband the same way she approaches hosting a dinner party for eight: warily, and only after every delaying tactic has been exhausted. She prefers to give her husband oral sex, she admits. It's quicker that way. Neater too.

But women aren't the only violets who are shrinking. One recent BBC report, headlined 'Men Choose Sleep Over Sex' (think 'Man Bites Dog'), reported that, 'given the chance of an extra hour in bed, most working men say they would rather spend it asleep than having sex'. Although a survey 'confirmed the long-held belief that men spend much of their time day-dreaming about sex'—thanks for clearing that up, guys—it also found that 'the pace of modern life leaves them too tired for the real thing'. Not at all coincidentally, it must be admitted, this research was conducted by Berocca, the vitamin company, whose vested interest in putting the b-b-bounce back into all of us is well known.

At least the new sexual apathy—which perhaps only seems apathetic compared with the unrealistically high sexual expectations adults now stagger under—makes for passionate debate. Neoconservative observers argue that it is just another example of postfeminist fall-out. Women's exhaustion and anger, the argument goes, have combined to create a potent appetite suppressant—and it's all our own fault, too, especially if we insist on the folly of pursuing a dual-career lifestyle.

I am as offended as anybody by this rhetoric. On the other hand, it must be admitted that the impact of the 'time drought' on every form of adult leisure—sex most emphatically included—has been documentably devastating. This is particularly true for couples with young children. Any three-year-old could do the math: when there is no time to scratch yourself, heaven knows there's no time to scratch anybody else. Women and men both suffer from sex-defying exhaustion in modern families. Yet the persistence of the double shift means that women suffer more, and the 'lack of interest' statistics bear this out.

More subtle but perhaps equally salient in de-sexing family life are shifts in our notions of parenting itself. The couple-centred family of the mid-twentieth century—with its locked bedrooms, adult-only parties and sex manuals under the mattress—is as passé as a quilted douche bag. So too unfortunately are adult privacy, adult leisure and a sense of adult entitlement to time alone.

Despite the dual-earner phenomenon—or perhaps even because of it—today's families revolve around the needs of children. When I was a child, we had to ask permission to *enter* my parents' bedroom. Today, we are more likely to ask our kids' permission to enter theirs. Adults who want to keep their beds to themselves—even occasionally—are seen as churlish or withholding. Beds belong to *families* now. And sex belongs…well, largely to partners who haven't become parents yet. Typically, it is not until the kids have grown into sexually active teenagers that couples finally feel entitled to that 'parents' retreat'. I have one friend who says the chief advantage of having a parents' retreat is that they can't hear their sons having sex with their girlfriends downstairs. 'We spend more time grappling with the remote control than we do with each other,' she adds drily.

The Lysistrata Effect—angry women going on 'sexual strike', as they do in Aristophanes' famous comedy—has been cited as another factor in the cooling down of modern adult life. In the play, a group of concerned wives club together to harness their sexual power as a political strategy to prevent their men going to war. Today the situation is rather more complex.

Sure, there are instances in which modern women use sex, or withhold it, for specific ends—like the wife who gives her husband a blow job for remembering to take the bin out. In most cases, though, the relationship between sex, reward and punishment is both more diffuse and less conscious. Women who feel anger towards their male partners—typically, over inequities in the distribution of unpaid labour—may express their frustration by withholding sex, and even by suppressing sexual feelings more broadly: 'My husband acts like a four-year-old—and then he wonders why I don't want to sleep with him.'

Women in families may complain, with justice, of being 'too tired' for sex. Yet when you consider how much energy couples put into arguing about *not* having it, you've got to wonder. Is it time drought? Or is it anger avalanche? 'A lot of women out there are mad,' *Newsweek* observed,

> …Working mothers, stay-at-home moms, even women without kids. They're mad that their husband couldn't find the babysitter's home number if his life depended on it. Mad that he would never think to pick up diapers or milk on his way home. Mad that he doesn't have to sing all the verses of 'The Wheels on the Bus' while trying to blow dry his hair.

The deep-seated desire to have what guys had was how a previous generation dealt with the power imbalance. Freud called this penis envy. Today, it may be more a matter of vagina vengeance (usually wielded unconsciously). In a nicer world, maybe women wouldn't use sex as a weapon. But in a nicer world, they wouldn't feel they needed to.

There are plenty of furious men out there as well—guys who feel they've been pulling twice the weight of any previous generation of males for a fraction of the benefit. Men who feel they are not respected for what they contribute to a relationship—in the form of both paid and unpaid labour—are rubbed as raw as their female partners. And their sense of deprivation, though it may take different forms, is no less acute.

It is easy to forget that having regular access to a sexual partner has been, until shockingly recently, the entire point of marriage from a male perspective. In a low- or no-sex marriage, men who find themselves doing around the house at least double what their own fathers did—and perhaps double that again in childcare—feel at best unrewarded and at worst like absolute suckers. As one 35-year-old husband told *Newsweek* journalist Kathleen Deveny, 'The big loser between job, kids and the dogs is me. I need more sex, but that's not the whole story. I want more time alone with my wife, and I want more attention.'

As we have already observed, the idea of the 'wifely duty'—that regular sex is the breadwinner's right and the housewife's obligation—is hard to imagine without the inverted commas these days. At least in theory, nuptial rights are now, like everything else, equal rights. When we are reminded of books like Marabel Morgan's 1973 opus *The Total Woman*—which cheerfully advised wives to initiate 'super sex' in the bedroom if they wanted superior white goods in the kitchen—it's hard to know whether to laugh or cry or let out a deep, guttural moan.

Except that it's easier to laugh. And so we do. On the other hand, we also laugh at the joke about the groom who whispers to his best man, 'I just had the *best* blow job of my entire life!' and his blushing bride who whispers to her bridesmaid, 'I just gave the *last* blow job of my entire life!' Women no longer come to marriage in order to become sexually active—as their mothers and grandmothers may have done—but to take a well-deserved rest from sexual activity. To hang up the Wonderbra and relax, already. There seems no evidence (anecdotal or otherwise) that men share this view, or that they are in any way attracted to marriage as a haven *from* sex.

Blow jobs for the boys notwithstanding, sex is no longer a service women render to men. Yet among the very young at least it is more utilitarian than ever. On college campuses, 'booty calls'—a kind of sexual distress signal—are every bit as common (and seemingly every bit as emotion-charged) as calling up for a pizza. You get hungry, you eat. You want sex, you find someone to screw. Not to sleep with—to screw, for booty call etiquette requires spent participants to return to their respective dorm rooms when it's time to do something really intimate (i.e. fall asleep). Compared to the average booty call, a one-night stand looks like a serious commitment. This kind of hooking up is not 'relational sex', explains University of Chicago sociologist Edward O. Laumann in *The Sexual Organization of the City*. It's 'transactional sex'—an exchange of pleasure, pure and simple. Well, simple anyway.

For this generation, real intimacy is not hinged to sex per se, or even necessarily to sex *at all,* and even the least cutting-edge romantic comedy takes this as axiomatic. *Love, Actually*, for example—a film whose sexual politics is otherwise about as radical as an episode of 'I Love Lucy'—features a sub-plot about a well-brought-up young porn star who fellates on cue for the camera, but gets all tongue-tied when the fellatee shyly asks her for a date. The irony is as light of touch as a vibrator set to turbo-boost. Dating, which is presumably about fantasy and longing and—well, mystery—has become sexy in a way that fucking no longer can.

Similar themes enliven *Laws of Attraction*, a romantic comedy about two matrimonial lawyers, a premise arguably funnier than the sum of its parts. Julianne Moore and Pierce Brosnan, playing a couple of Hepburn–Tracy wannabes, have sex on their first date, but don't learn to like one another—let alone to love one another—until much, much later.

Jane Campion's harrowing suspense thriller *In the Cut* is in another cinematic league altogether. But the relationship between the film's protagonists follows the same inverted trajectory. The couple in question—Meg Ryan as a tormented urban academic (is there any other kind?) and Mark Ruffalo as the homicide detective she is dying to leave fingerprints on—exchange bodily fluids before so much as exchanging surnames. But it isn't until they experience their first kiss that they become truly intimate.

In the movies, no one ever seems to get bored with sex. That's entertainment, I guess. In real life, the script is different. Take away what I am tempted to call the thrill of the chase (except that it is one of my mother's favourite phrases and so I wouldn't be caught dead) and what you're left with is often a distinct anti-climax. I have one friend whose two teenagers both live at home with their respective partners. All four—ranging in age from fifteen to nineteen—are wonderfully responsible and mature members of the household, he tells me. And they are also precociously passionless. 'I was totally *obsessed* with sex at their age,' he says. 'But these kids are like—hey, we can take it or leave it.' He shakes his head in wonderment. 'Their lack of interest astounds me. I mean, it's almost as if they're married.'

And in one sense, of course, they are. In a sense, indeed, the whole *world* is married, if by 'married' we mean 'having access to a willing sexual partner' (theoretically anyhow). Although it would be a mistake to confuse mature intimacy with a game of erotic hide-and-seek—or a round of essentially trivial pursuit—perhaps it is equally a mistake to insist that the two are unrelated.

It is also possible that the sexual counter-revolution may not represent anything new at all, that it only seems that way in comparison with that unreal little blip of socio-historical space that began with the 'discovery' of sexual intercourse in 1963 and ended (roughly) with the AIDS pandemic of the late '80s to early '90s. Maybe sex was *never* that big a deal—at least post-adolescent, post-reproductive sex. Maybe the first sexual revolution, like an unfaithful suitor, made a whole bunch of promises it couldn't keep, and maybe this is just one of them.

'Boomers are the first generation to imagine that they can have exciting monogamous sex through old age,' US sex and relationship therapist Marty Klein has observed. 'The collision between that expectation and reality is pretty upsetting for most people.' Especially, it may be, for most male people. Though the statistics on desire discrepancy are hardly conclusive, there is some evidence to suggest that females are not really hard-wired to stay interested in sex for life—or at least not as interested as many men are. Maybe they are just honest enough, or powerful enough, to say so now. Come to that, maybe staying on the boil for decade after decade isn't all that natural for guys either. Maybe—just maybe—it's really OK to prefer watching 'Sex in the City' to doing sex in the suburbs.

Another factor that may be rubbing us all up the wrong way is our increasing use of antidepressants and other psycho-pharmaceuticals—given that reduced libido is one of the most common side-effects of the Prozac generation of serotonin re-uptake inhibitors. As a result, the prospect of having one's libido lowered by one drug, only to require a chemical hand-job from another drug, is a very real one. In the US, for example, at least twelve million adults are on antidepressants—and approximately nine out of ten of them are married. That's a lot of long-term relationships at risk of sexual dysfunction for chemical reasons alone. The figures in Australia, the UK and Europe are equally distressing, particularly when seen against the backdrop of the burgeoning trade in Viagra, testosterone sprays, HRT therapies (many of them prescribed specifically as libido fertilisers) and a growing pharmacopeia of other performance and/or attitude enhancers.

A previous generation of feminists asserted the rights of women to be publicly, and unabashedly, sexual. Today, it may be that we are facing a new and even tougher challenge. Perhaps asserting our rights *not* to be sexual—or, more accurately, sexually available—is the ultimate act of moral courage, and cultural subversion, for both sexes.

Historically, argues historian Elizabeth Abbott, celibacy, especially as institutionalised by the church, provided an attractive lifestyle option for women, offering an escape from childbirth perils and marital drudgery and a possible shot at education, status and power. Even today, she writes in *A History of Celibacy*, 'celibacy has major tangible benefits' and following her own, evidently deeply satisfying, divorce Abbott claims to have missed marital sex about as much as she missed hearing 'that infernal question, "Honey, where are my socks?"' I suppose you would expect no less from an author whose original title was *The Kama Sutra of Celibacy*!

The obligation to be sexual on demand is part of the sexwork many women still perform, and resent bitterly, within marriage. On the other hand, as Rebecca Mead observes, 'It's odd to think that the complex connection with another that constitutes sexual love might simply be traded off against sock duty.' Celibacy is one answer—and a legitimate one—to the question of what women want next from sex. But it is hardly a mainstream solution. Most women, as Mead drily observes, would prefer 'to find a balance between sex and socks'.

Before anybody gets too excited about celibacy, it is worth noting that the research shows that it is in general more sex, not less, that makes us happier human beings. Like it or not—and I suspect Elizabeth Abbott would not—the relationship between sex and well-being could not be more direct or more potent. The more sex people have, the happier they report themselves to be. One large-scale study, conducted in 2004 for the US National Bureau of Economic Research and based on a random sample of 16,000 adults, found that people who had sex four or more times a week were the happiest people of any group studied. The study established conclusively that it wasn't a case of happy people having more sex, but of more sex producing greater happiness. And the effect was identical for women and men.

The conclusion that lots of sex is good for us is inescapable. But then so is eating raw wheatgerm and running on a treadmill, and most of us don't do that either. For many women, the suggestion that we might need to motivate ourselves to experience sexual pleasure—just as we may need to motivate ourselves to do exercise or eat enough fibre—seems wrong. Contradictory, even. Surely feeling obliged to experience desire is a bit like forcing yourself to become more spontaneous. Or is it?

Researchers who study the neuro-chemistry of sex have some odd theories about the biological basis for women's sexual happiness. 'Can semen cure the blues?' queried one recent Salon.com article. (I suppose there's no harm in asking.) 'A researcher says male ejaculate may act as an antidepressant,' it continues, 'but other scientists aren't swallowing his theory.'

The original study, published in 2002 in *The Archives of Sexual Behaviour*, showed that women who had sex without condoms were happier than those whose partners used them. Study author Gordon Gallup, a psychologist at SUNY Albany, attributes the effect to some 'unknown chemical' in semen. That's one explanation. A simpler one might be that non-condom users are more likely to be in a serious committed relationship. Possibly the 'unknown chemical' is—dare I say it?—love. Interestingly, there was no discernible difference in depression/happiness scores between those using condoms and those sleeping alone.

So the equation of more sex with greater happiness may turn out to be slightly more complicated than one might wish. It's hard to imagine that four one-night stands per week, for example, would increase *anybody's* wellbeing. Face it. Most people who report having a great deal more sex than the average are likely to be either people in love—or lying.

Then again, love itself is a chemical reaction, albeit a breathtakingly complicated one. Scientists at the University of Edinburgh, for example, confirmed in the lab in 2001 what William Shakespeare suspected four hundred years earlier: that women's brains release a 'love potion' during sex. Its more prosaic name is 'oxytocin'—and if you think you've heard that somewhere before, you're right. It's exactly the same feel-good bonding chemical released during breastfeeding.

How fitting that the drug that keeps nursing women coming back for more despite engorgement, chewed nipples and massive inconvenience should be the same one that bonds us to our male partners! The oxytocin factor not only encourages women to commit, it appears to ensure that the more sex the couple has, the deeper the bond will become. Male brains, in case you were wondering, do not release oxytocin during sex. (No, I didn't think you were wondering.)

Having said all that, the fact remains that semen really is a 'rich chemical brine' of hormones, to use the poetic language of one researcher, including testosterone and oestrogen. And these chemicals really *are* absorbed into a woman's bloodstream through the vagina. In addition to the possible anti depressant effect of this chemical cocktail, researchers are also investigating a rather more likely link: which is to libido itself.

One recent study, for example, looked at the effect of prostaglandin E1—a hormone found in semen—on Sexual Arousal Disorder, aka SAD. Women in this study, reported Salon.com, 'basted their clitoris, labia, and vaginal opening with a prostaglandin liquid, then watched erotic videos for thirty minutes while taking notes on how aroused they became'. In addition to these self-reports, researchers measured genital blood flow. The response was significant. What one wag has termed 'the cum cure' may, believe it or not, have some credibility. I can't help but think, though, that after thirty minutes of visual porn and incredible amounts of interest and attention, women could have 'basted' their genitals with anything from Vaseline to barbecue sauce and have registered the same effect. But maybe I'm just being a hostile presence.

The link between testosterone and libido—for both sexes—is nevertheless well documented. So is the fact that a woman's testosterone levels peak when she is in her twenties, and thereafter decline slowly and steadily with age. There is no doubt at all that hormone 'therapies' that involve high doses of testosterone definitively increase women's sexual interest and pleasure. Unfortunately, they also tend to definitively increase body hair, acne and cholesterol production.

The existence of SAD as a diagnostic category at all—remembering that clever acronyms are made, not born—is itself significant. For women, and quite possibly for men as well, the loss of libido with advancing age is no more a 'disorder' than is the loss of elastin or hair pigment...or patience with the medical establishment. Declining interest in sex may be just another case of women 'doin'' what comes naturally' and being pathologised for it.

Yet let us not commit the equal and opposite fallacy of assuming that mid-life for women is a time of inevitable loss of vitality, sexual or otherwise. *The Jubilee Report*, a British study of women born when the Queen came to the throne, for example, provides compelling evidence that life really does begin at fifty for many women today. (Or, as I prefer to think of it, that fifty is the new thirty.) Sixty-five percent of women said they were happier after menopause than before it, and 66 percent said they were more independent. Even more startling—to anyone who isn't a postmenopausal woman, anyway—was that 64 percent said their sex lives were unchanged or *better*.

Even study author Kate Fox, co-director of the Social Issues Research Centre, admitted being 'taken aback' by these findings. The good news—that virtually every aspect of women's lives, from health and work to sex, energy and happiness—improved after menopause was balanced by the more sobering news that women on Hormone Replacement Therapy had a dramatically better profile than those who weren't.

A mere hundred years ago, the average age of menopause for a British woman was 47 (it is much the same today)—and her life expectancy was 49. No wonder our ignorance of what menopause 'really' means for women appears so fathomless. A large-scale Australian study that followed a group of women for ten years, published in May 2002, for example, reached exactly the opposite conclusion to that of the British study. It found that postmenopausal women experienced a dramatic *loss* of sexual function.

Trisha Posner, author of *This Is Not Your Mother's Menopause*, agrees that women experience a libidinal ebbing at menopause. She argues further that this natural biological fact has created an unnatural commercial opportunity for the pharmaceutical industry. The 2002 Australian study just cited, for example, concluded that women suffering from low libido—and it was definitely assumed they were suffering—should be treated with HRT, to put back the oestrogen their sluggish ovaries were refusing to produce. It seemed like a reasonable assumption at the time. Then, a few months later, the hormones totally hit the fan. Research linking the most widely prescribed hormone prescription in the US to increased risk for blood clots, invasive breast cancer, heart attacks and strokes not only halted the massive Women's Health Initiative study in mid-stream. It spelled a decisive end to the HRT 'miracle'.

Writes Posner, 'Hormones address the mechanical part of it but don't address the complex emotional part of what really makes sex work for us. Hell, we've been giving millions of women HRT for forty years and it doesn't seem to me that many of them are enjoying active sex lives...' (Keep in mind that the fiftysomething women in the *Jubilee Report* who reported feeling no less sexual than they had before menopause may have been starting from a low baseline.)

Personally, Posner found her own sexual desire did return slowly postmenopause. She and many other researchers have noted that women often experience a 'use it or lose it' phenomenon: basically, that *having* regular sex is a precondition for enjoying regular sex. It's not 'just psychological' either. The impact on vaginal lubrication and elasticity is measurable. In fact, it's almost as if, without regular sex, our genitals forget how to respond. 'A critical part was that my partner did not rush me or make me feel bad about my lack of interest,' Posner adds.

If only such men were available over the counter, who'd need nutritional supplements, vitamin E, sarsaparilla and calendula cream?

bewitched, bothered and benumbed

Whenever we presume to ask 'what women want'—whether in relation to sex or softdrink—we need to specify *which* women. As we have seen, sexual activity is a broad predictor of happiness for adult women. For teenage girls, on the other hand, the relationship between sex and wellbeing turns out to be entirely inverse. Sexual activity in teenage girls is associated with less happiness, and significantly more depression, than abstinence is.

According to the 2003 National Longitudinal Survey of Adolescent Health, over a quarter of sexually active teen girls were clinically depressed compared with less than 8 percent of their non-active peers. (Becoming sexually active appears to erode the happiness of boys, too. Male teens who have sex suffer more than twice the rate of depression of boys who don't, although the figures are comparatively much less significant: 8.3 percent versus 3.4 percent.)

No wonder studies show that two-thirds of teenagers who have lost their virginity wish they hadn't. Numbers like these suggest that the drawing power of teen abstinence movements like True Love Waits and The Silver Ring Thing may have as much to do with psychological factors as religious or ethical ones. The 'if it feels good, do it' philosophy evidently cuts both ways, though the notion that *anything* could be better than sex—let alone celibacy—is a radical one for the children of the revolution.

Maybe that's why the abstinence movement is being treated in the media as the latest shock trend since gangsta rap. It can be easy to forget that the abstinence movement was in fact spawned by the 'indulgence movement'—the trend toward young people having much more sex at ever-earlier ages. According to data reported in *A Statistical Report of a Generation*, US women born between 1963 and 1972 were twice as likely to report multiple sex partners by age eighteen as women just ten years older—and six times as likely as their grandmothers (those born between 1943 and 1952). In Australia, where the age of first intercourse has been declining for the past fifty years, the average girl loses her virginity at age sixteen. Oral sex also starts younger today: at about the same time as intercourse, surveys show, if not earlier.

Today, according to Paula Kamen, author of *Her Way: Young Women Remake the Sexual Revolution,* a comprehensive survey of what women born between 1960 and 1979 want from sex, young women's sense of sexual entitlement is unprecedented. By way of evidence, Kamen tracks the rise of the 'superrats', young women whose out-there, super-aggressive sexuality is a point of pride. Like Germaine Greer in the '70s, only minus the politics, or Madonna in the '80s, only minus the pop music, superrats both expect and insist on 'conducting their sex lives on their own terms and with a new degree of openness'.

Superrats have always existed, Kamen concedes (think Mary McCarthy, Simone de Beauvoir, Eve). But what distinguishes today's rats is their 'imperviousness to excessive self-blame'. One of Kamen's informants, Stacie, a 27-year-old Chicago-area social worker, confides that when she first met her present boyfriend 'I thought about him all the time. And, you know, I wanted to get to know him—*in the biblical sense*. I didn't want to know what he thought about or anything. I didn't want to know what was his favourite colour.' Stacie does not see herself as a sexually demanding person, however. 'I don't demand to have an orgasm,' she told Kamen. 'But if I don't have one, nobody's going to sleep that night.'

Stacie has contempt for guys who don't bother to find out what turns her on and dismisses sex with them as little more than male masturbation. 'Whack sex', she calls it. Another superrat, Cat, told Kamen the turning point for her came when she realised she didn't need to use sex as a 'power thing', or 'for love', but simply 'just for pleasure'. Then there's Tasha, who freely admits to the occasional masturbation break in front of friends. ('I've just been like, "Look, I'm really stressed out today. I need to relax."') Such confidence may be seen as liberating and healthy, or simply scary.

The challenge is to avoid morphing straight from sexual subservient to sexual plantation owner, which is the leap of bad faith many teenage girls appear to be taking these days. 'Girls have been told in every part of their lives to go for it,' *CosmoGirl* editor Atoosa Rubenstein observes. 'Their mothers have told them, go for student council, go for the team, go for that job, and that has turned from a message directed toward achievement to being something their whole lives are about. So they apply it to pursuing boys as well.'

A Texas-based sexual health counsellor who sees twenty to thirty teenagers a month agrees. 'The teenage boys I see often say the girls push them for sex and expect them to ask for sex and will bring it up if the boys don't ask.'

'The girls are way more aggressive than the boys,' sixteen-year-old John Bernard told a *New York Times* reporter. 'They have more attitude. They have more power. And they overpower guys more. I mean, it's scary.'

Teen agony aunts, notes Helen Walsh in the *Independent*, 'are no longer inundated with questions such as "How long should I wait?" but rather, "Is it rude to spit or should I swallow?"' Marty Beckerman, nineteen, author of *Generation SLUT* (an acronym that stands for 'sexually liberal urban teenager') believes that girls are trying to transform sex into something as meaningless as it is for boys. If *that's* what women want next, heaven help us. Practices like 'dogging'—a sort of drive-through orgy, carried out in well-lighted parked cars in public parks and laybys—reported to be increasingly common in the UK, hardly give cause for optimism about either gender.

Yet, against all evidence to the contrary, young women are still more likely to attach (if not confuse) love with sex. According to a 1998 study by the UCLA Higher Education Research Institute, 26 percent fewer young women approve of casual sex than do young men. Other recent research has shown that almost half of teenage girls cite 'affection for partner' as the reason they first had sex, compared with only a quarter of males. It's important to keep the superrats thing in perspective. To an extent, a superrat by any other name is simply a normal teenage boy.

What women want from sex within the context of monogamy— assuming they decide to go there at all—is no less contradictory. One study of 106 couples over two years of marriage, for example, showed that wives' sexual interest was related to husbands' satisfaction with the marriage in general. Oddly, though, sexual affection as a whole did not seem to relate directly to either partner's marital happiness. Possibly, researchers have speculated, sex becomes more of a happiness factor in marriage with the passage of time. Another more exhaustive study conducted by Georgia State University sociologist Denise Donnelly found a strong inverse relationship between marital happiness and sexual inactivity.

Donnelly's conclusion that sexually benumbed marriages are not, on the whole, happy or satisfying would seem to be a fairly safe intuitive bet. Except that when it comes to sex in marriage, intuition has nothing to do with it. A third study, this one published in the *Journal of Sex Research* in 1993, also found marital satisfaction and sexual functioning to be closely related. At the same time, researchers found that sexual *dys*function was *un*related to marital satisfaction. Having good sex within marriage is a good predictor of happiness. But the lack of good sex could mean almost anything, these studies suggest (especially, common sense suggests, in cases where two low-libido types have been lucky enough to find each other).

Again, it may well be a phase-of-life thing. Among older adults, for example, the evidence suggests that marriage is a better predictor of sexual activity than of sexual satisfaction. Researchers in one recent study, published by *The Gerontologist* in 1997, found that elderly women were 24 times more likely to report sexual activity if they were married than if they were single. Older married men, by contrast, were only 1.4 times more likely to be having sex. Overall, the greatest predictors of sexual activity for men are age (or youth, really) and educational level. The greatest predictors of sexual satisfaction for both sexes are: 1) being sexually active; and 2) being in good mental health. All of which suggests that the link between marriage and sexual satisfaction is at best indirect.

The differences between male and female sexual responsiveness, some of them clearly biologically based, only complicate the picture. At the risk of oversimplifying the awesome individual diversity out there, men's sex drive appears to be triggered by visual stimuli while for women emotional factors play a larger role. In a Kinsey Institute survey, women nominated 'an overall sense of wellbeing' as their number one precondition for enjoying sex—a finding that suggests we may be left with a classic chicken/ovum dilemma as far as sex and women's happiness is concerned. Do women who have more sex feel happier? Or do women who feel happier have more sex? Or is the relationship a reciprocal one?

It may not be entirely clear what adult women do want from sex. But what they do not want from it is an obligation, 'one more thing on an already long to-do list', in the words of Dr Jan Shifren, director of the Menopause Program at Massachusetts General. One woman tells the story of how her husband used to light a candle in their bedroom as a not-terribly-subtle signal that he was looking forward to having sex that night. 'I used to dread seeing that damned candle,' she confesses. 'I'd go in there and I'd think, "Oh. Please. God. Not the candle."' Kate Reddy, fictional heroine of Allison Pearson's *I Don't Know How She Does It*, confesses 'I take my time brushing my teeth. A count of twenty for each molar. If I stay in the bathroom long enough, Richard will fall asleep and will not try to have sex with me.'

Some evolutionary psychologists maintain that there are compelling biological reasons why the average woman's sex drive, especially in the post-reproductive phase of life, may be lower than the average man's. The Wild Oats Theory of human sexuality, as I like to think of it, postulates that because males can produce a theoretically limitless number of offspring, but females can only conceive, bear and raise a very small number, it is in the evolutionary interests of males to have sex more or less constantly while female interests are best served by being selective in their choice of mates, if not downright picky.

Whether this theory holds true today, or has ever held true, remains a sticky question. But it seems to me that until we eliminate the effects of nurture—the sociocultural forces that shape our sexuality—we have no hope at all of understanding the imperatives (if any) of nature. Personally, I find the argument that women are by nature less interested in sex than men hard to swallow. What I know for certain, on the contrary, is that women are by *nurture* less able to express their sexuality, less likely to be in a position to define what sexuality is, or could be.

The problem of 'desire discrepancy' can work the other way too, of course. Experts estimate that in as many as 20 percent of couples, the woman has the higher sex drive. Cases like these are more likely to be perceived as problematic by both parties—but especially by males.

Yet a women whose sexual joy is compromised by her partner's lack of interest is unlikely to demand her conjugal rights, whether privately or in the consulting room.

The fact is, men's sexual happiness is given a high priority in our culture. Women's sexual happiness, until the past few decades, has not even been an item on the scorecard. Men seek sex therapy more often than women do. And public sex clinics are the only health services that are patronised more heavily by males than by females.

'Women feel that when a man has a problem, everyone rallies around and develops a solution,' notes Brett McCann of the Australian Society of Sex Educators, Researchers and Therapists. 'But when a woman has a problem it's ignored. There's still this cultural stigma: "Well, what do you expect? Are you a whore? You're not supposed to care about sex anyway."'

For me, that's overstating the case. Feminism has made some inroads. And one of them is that, by the end of middle school, relatively few of us are still buying into the whore/Madonna thing. Women are not only 'allowed' to care about sex these days, we are allowed, indeed pressured, to be seen to care about sex. But when push comes to thrust, the assumption that women's sexual pleasure revolves around giving, and only incidentally about receiving, remains quietly pervasive. Sex is now acknowledged to be something women may like. But it is something men *need*. This is a kind of macro desire discrepancy that continues to have significant implications for our sexual politics, both within marriage and outside of it.

The notion that sex is a service women render to men (or wives to husbands, at any rate) was supposed to have gone out with carpet sweepers and steam-powered vibrators. Yet if books like *The Surrendered Wife* and Marabel Morgan's housewife gothic classic *The Total Woman* (re-released in 2000) are any indication, sexwork remains a thriving cottage industry in thousands of marriages today.

Radio relationship guru Dr Laura Schlessinger's coyly titled *The*

Proper Care and Feeding of Husbands (2004) typifies the genre, which casts women in the debased role of sexual service provider and men in the even more debased role of sexual livestock. ('A husband is like a horse,' Schlessinger observes. 'At the end of the day he is usually rode hard and put away sweaty. Like in the movies, if his master drives and beats him, he'll go just so far before bucking and rebelling.') Women need to make sure they give a man what he wants in bed—just as they need to make sure they give him what he wants in his lunchbox—because...because that's what men want. (Further implication: that's *all* men want. Or, as one of Dr Laura's informants so succinctly expressed it: 'Men are simple. If I'm not horny, make me a sandwich.') It seems too obvious to point out—and so I can't resist doing it anyway—that you'll notice no raft of reciprocal bestsellers exhorting men to submit to patterns of female desire 'for the sake of the marriage'.

Psychologist Janet Hyde's research showed that the strongest predictor of diminished sexual desire in women was fatigue—and women who were full-time homemakers reported feeling every bit as much of it as women who worked full time for pay. Australian sex therapist Dr Rosie King has observed that the best sex toy on the market is a vacuum cleaner, skilfully applied. Other women find that the only foreplay they really need is being 'allowed' to sleep in on a Saturday morning. At the same time, Hyde found that career-oriented women—in defiance of the stereotypes—had more sex than anybody. (A case of 'ask a busy person'?)

The problem of unequal libido—like most other forms of domestic inequality—is a topic guaranteed to get the blood pumping. Everybody's got a theory on this one, but my own educated guess is that, yes, Virginia, the majority of adult women *are* less interested in sex than their male partners are, but it's a slim majority (perhaps 60 percent—a highly problematic slice for anybody wishing to make grand gender-based generalisations), and the reasons for the inequality are probably a complex mix of biology, culture and circumstance.

With few but occasionally spectacular exceptions, pregnancy, child-rearing and lactation are for most women the biological equivalent of a cold shower. A cold shower that may last for *years*. Partly, perhaps even mostly, this is the result of fatigue, which is itself the result of the way we divide up both the labour and the leisure (if that's the right word for it) of parenting. But partly too it is simply a case of biological swings and roundabouts. For women, parenting is not just something we do with our minds and hearts. Perhaps pre-eminently, it is something we do with our *bodies*. Men can have babies. But women grow babies. Men may feed their children. But a breastfeeding mother is quite literally consumed by them. And the difference (which to some degree early feminism has taught us to minimise) is a significant one.

But it's not really necessary to drag biology in on a semi-trailer when behaviour alone can take us where we want to go. Full-time care-giving, especially of babies, sets up its own dynamic of needs and gratifications. This is also something we do with both our minds and our bodies, and its impact on our sexuality is direct and profound. Men who care for small children full time generally experience precisely the same waning of sexual desire as do full-time mothers—and precisely the same waxing of the desire for solitude, and for sleep. There is no anatomy/destiny thing going on here. It's not about sex or gender. It's about role. We continue to think of this as a woman's problem only because the role of full-time caregiver (or even default caregiver) remains in the majority of cases the female's portion.

This is not to suggest that childcare supplies no gratifications to the main caregiver. It does—lavishly. Unfortunately, however, the love, the play, the skin-to-skin contact, the sheer delight our children give us back often has the unhappy effect of depressing libido still further. At those times in our life when our children are giving us all that we ever wanted, is it any wonder that we don't go looking for more? On the love thing, we are full up. Our sippy cup runneth over. (And this, inci-dentally, may help explain why women who give up paid work for full-time motherhood in the hope that they will have more energy for their partners, including more sexual energy, are so often disappointed.)

When all the rhetoric is spouted, and all the soapboxes chopped up for kindling, this may be the most compelling argument yet for a more equitable division of parenting labour. In families in which mums and dads participate equally in parenting tasks, participation in all other things—most emphatically including sex—will almost inevitably be more equal as well. In families where they are not, the risk of unequal libido is always going to be high. And this risk, like any other structural impediment to a couple's wellbeing, from a difficult mother-in-law to a difficult mortgage, will need to be managed carefully. Life with young children is pretty much a case of sexual damage control, and the sooner both parties accept it as a temporary reality, the better.

The crunch years of early parenthood last at least until the children are in school full time. That's five years at a minimum. Sooner or later babies grow up, the chaos of infancy and toddlerhood resolves itself, and sleep returns. Yet fatigue may go on and on. Many women find that taking responsibility for the household's unpaid labour, which seemed merely a sensible option when they were home anyway looking after babies, has somewhere along the way hardened into a behavioural ball and chain they drag with them everywhere, even into the full-time workforce.

The impact of this on libido is twofold. First, there's the fatigue. Second, there's the resentment. All work and no play—or even the perception that that's how it is—makes Jill feel as sexy as a pair of polyester bedsocks. Women who are mired in this dynamic don't just get mad, they get even (or think they do). If they can't say 'no' to the demands of domestic life, or to their kids, or to their bosses, or to the social script that directs them to serve or suffer the guilt—they will say 'no' where they feel they can say 'no': in bed.

The irony of course is that by 'getting even'—which does not imply a response that is necessarily conscious, by the way—such women end up even further in the red. They have deprived their partners of the pleasure of sex, sure. But ultimately they have also deprived themselves. Whatever else we may or may not know about libido, it is pretty clear, as we have seen, that over time the less sex one has, the less sex one wants to have. Celibacy breeds celibacy. Although we are used to describing sex as a 'drive' (which sounds unstoppable and thrillingly urgent), in the context of a long-term relationship sex is also a habit. Women who have kicked the habit are arguably less needy, but they are arguably also less fully alive.

Before we can begin to understand what women want next from sex, it may be necessary to do something really kinky: ask them. A report published in the *Journal of the American Medical Association* in 1999 showed that 43 percent of American women are unhappy enough with their sex lives to have officially earned the diagnosis of 'female sexual dysfunction' (yes, FSD). FSD differs from its sister 'disorder' SAD in one crucial respect: FSD is by definition a *self*-diagnosis. A woman who 'has' FSD, in other words, is simply a woman who has decided she could use some help, based on her *own* assessment of her *own* sexual experience (as opposed to her doctor's or her partner's assessment of that experience). The daring idea behind FSD is that women are competent to make such judgments for themselves—a break with tradition as emphatic as the Catholic Church allowing lay people to celebrate mass, or forgive one another's sins.

A woman who is considering a self-diagnosis of FSD, explains *New Yorker* staff writer Rebecca Mead, 'measures her own sex life against what she sees, or imagines, of the sex lives of women around her, and judges whether hers is all she'd like it to be'. Leaving the whole thing to a woman's 'imagination' has got to be preferable to leaving it to her doctor's. Nevertheless, it's important to recognise how drastically such judgments may be mediated by culture and history.

As Carol Groneman reminds us in *Nymphomania: A History*, one woman's healthy libido is another woman's psychosexual pathology. Groneman cites the case of a devoted 24-year-old Victorian wife who sought medical help because she had frequent erotic dreams and fantasies about other men. Her treatment? A bland diet, a horsehair mattress, twice-daily cold baths, a daily cold enema and swabbing her vagina with borax. She was lucky. Other 'patients' endured much more invasive cures, including removal of the ovaries and clitoris.

The American Psychiatric Association did not drop the diagnosis of nymphomania until 1987. Sydney gynaecologist Dr Jules Black, former secretary general of the World Association for Sexology, says he still sees patients who use this label to describe themselves. Often, it's a term that's been applied by a previous partner (especially one the woman may have left for another man). 'Men label women in this derogatory way—"Oh yes, you are a nympho"—just because her drive is somewhat higher than his and the man can't cope,' notes Black.

Before the Victorian age—certainly throughout antiquity and the Middle Ages—the maxim that women take nine-tenths of the pleasure in lovemaking was received wisdom. Even in modern times, the medical profession has regarded women's sexuality as a potentially destructive force—an underground volcano ready to erupt and destroy at the slightest provocation. Some early-twentieth-century doctors even avoided using a speculum—hardly a likely candidate for a sex toy!—or administering anaesthetics during childbirth on these grounds.

Paradoxically, the vibrator—that quintessential symbol of female sexual assertiveness—was originally intended for use by doctors on female patients suffering from 'hysteria' (literally, womb madness). According to historian Rachel P. Maines, author of *The Technology of Orgasm*, prior to the invention of the electrical vibrator in 1902, doctors were forced to treat the symptoms of 'unbridled desire' manually, or through the use of rocking chairs, wind-up 'vulva paddlers' or steam-driven massage apparatus.

Today, all this seems like a nightmare brought on by an overdose of bubblegum-flavoured lubricant. Yet contemporary attempts at 'sexual healing' are arguably no less extreme and, for all their sophistication, only marginally less controlling. True, the medical fraternity today is less concerned with reducing women's 'unbridled desire' than we are with inducing it—as long as the desire in question is for heterosexual intercourse. True too that we are now more likely to manipulate women chemically than mechanically.

Rebecca Mead, among others, worries about the iatrogenic fallout of the intense medical focus on female sexuality, as well as about the 'hypersexualisation of contemporary culture' generally—a return, perhaps, to classical notions of female lasciviousness. It's a conclusion that anybody who reads *Cosmo* or *Cleo* or their teenybopper equivalents would be hard-pressed to refute. ('Six Guys To Do Before You Say "I Do"!' screams the cover of one typical glossy.) Mead also observes the rise of a 'significant subgenre of sex articles' catering for women whose partners want less sex than they do. Under the present circumstances, she suggests, the surprise is not that 43 percent of American women are suffering from sexual dysfunction but that 57 percent aren't.

We've come a long way—too long, some would say—since Freud's bizarre theory that vaginal orgasm was the only psychologically sound way for a woman to come. As a result, 'Women who found that their pleasures were rooted elsewhere,' Groneman reminds us—i.e. virtually all of us—'were considered to be harbouring unconscious, unnatural sexual aggression and hostility toward men.'

We can laugh about it now, but throughout much of the twentieth century, this idea of 'quality climax' was a deadly serious matter. Even a child of the late baby boom, such as myself, did not escape the fall-out of the Great Orgasm Debate. My first lover, admittedly a full generation older than I, informed me early on in the piece that clitoral orgasms were—and I quote—'cheating'. Like the Woody Allen joke about the woman who finally had an orgasm but was told by her the most intense orgasms were of the DIY variety.

To young women who cut their teeth on Ally McBeal re-runs and played oral sex games in middle school, the Great Orgasm Debate must seem as antiquarian as a vulva paddler. The sexual freedoms that their mothers and grandmothers struggled to obtain are taken for granted now. The double standard—like an orchid wrist corsage—is a curiosity from another age. Yet becoming free enough to fuck as men do (or perhaps as men used to do) is only half the battle. What's more, I suspect, it may be the easy half.

The challenge facing feminists a generation ago was to secure a set of sexual rights that would guarantee women freedom of erotic expression. The challenge facing women today is learning how to manage that freedom. It is a developmental task we are a long way from completing. Then again, so are men, and they've had a several-thousand-year head start.

However, a few themes are beginning to emerge with clarity. One of these is that true sexual freedom demands a daunting depth of self-knowledge and self-acceptance. True sexual freedom is perhaps not really a case of saying 'yes' to sex at all, but of something much more confronting: saying 'yes' to oneself. Our mothers and grandmothers felt guilty for having sexual feelings and acting on them. Today, it some-times seems, we haven't so much solved the problem as turned it on its head. Women and girls who feel guilty about being *insufficiently* sexual are still measuring themselves by somebody else's yardstick, probably a male somebody's. This is why true sexual freedom for women must include the freedom to delay having sex, as do members of the absti-nence movement, and the freedom to say no to sex, and to do so without guilt—whether intermittently or as a way or a stage of life. Being free to express and enforce personal sexual limits has got to be part of the deal.

The freedom to transcend limits does too, of course, particularly limits that have been imposed arbitrarily or in ignorance or (which is

therapist it was the wrong kind, this would have been hilarious—if
had not been seventeen, and believed him.

To paraphrase Larkin, 'the clitoris was discovered / in ninetee
fifty-three.' That was the year Alfred C. Kinsey published *Sexu
Behaviour in the Human Female*, the book that did for female sexual
what Copernicus did for the solar system. (Kinsey himself preferred
earthier metaphor. He saw himself as a kind of Christopher Colum
of the Clitoris, likening the belief in female orgasm through pene
tion alone to the conviction that the earth was flat.) Kinsey emplo
the same bizarre research methodology as modern-day adherent
FSD. He actually listened to women. The conclusion he eventu
reached—that what women wanted, sexually speaking, was cli
stimulation—rubbed millions of readers up the wrong way, espec
those in the medical community. (Among Kinsey's other s
findings were that only 50 percent of women were virgi
marriage—yes, only!—and one in four would sooner or later ch
their husbands.)

In response to Freud's dictum that vaginal orgasm was th
'true, mature' sexual response for females, Kinsey argued tha
wasn't any such thing as a vaginal orgasm, but rather 'only one
orgasm' which was 'triggered by clitoral stimulation and in
contractions of all parts of the female body, including the v
Today, the clinical evidence overwhelmingly confirms Kinsey
Though they may differ dramatically in quality, intensity and
from a neurological point of view, all female orgasms are create

Sexologists William Masters and Virginia Johnson pi
where Kinsey left off. Their eleven-year study, *Human Sexual I
published in 1966, was intended as a technical journal but
became an international bestseller. Among other findir
revealed that women experienced 'stronger contractior
and higher rates of heartbeat during orgasm without interco
especially during masturbation'. For many women, in oth

more often the case) as a means of control.

Freud posited a three-stage sequence of sexual development in human beings, beginning with the undifferentiated 'polymorphous perversity' of the infant (associated with orality), progressing through to the anal stage and culminating—triumphally—in the genital stage, in which erotic feeling is localised almost exclusively in penis–vagina intercourse ('insert tab A into slot B').

Yet on the cultural level, over the past forty years, this hierarchy of erotic needs has been largely dismantled. Heterosexual intercourse no longer takes undisputed pride of place at the apex of human sexuality; it is no longer the defining act, the standard-bearer besides which all other couplings must be judged. (Would Clinton's now-infamous disclaimer, 'I did not have sex with that woman!' have sounded as hollow a generation ago? I doubt it.) For women, this diffusion away from what feminist theorists call a 'phallocentric' or penis-centred view of human sexuality, represents a substantial win.

This is not to suggest that oral sex was invented in 1963. Or that anal sex, or B&D, or masturbation were either—let alone any of the hundreds of other variations on the theme we might call 'extra-coital sex'. What is new is the way these practices have become mainstream, middle-class—domesticated, almost. Sex toys, like pet toys, are available at every suburban mall. For young men and women (but especially women) same-sex sexuality has not only lost its stigma, it has acquired a positive patina of glamour. American women in their thirties, for example, are more than twice as likely as women in their fifties to have had a same-sex partner. The postmodern imperative to 'embrace diversity' has put on flesh. In many ways, this represents an extraordinary triumph.

For many women who grew up in the 'sandwich generation' of the '60s and '70s, however, the struggle to define a genuinely woman-centred sexuality remains ongoing. 'Every one of us who grows up in this culture is conditioned to think of "sex" first and foremost as intercourse—which current research shows works brilliantly for men, but more often than not leaves women wondering, "Isn't there supposed to be something more?"' observes Gina Ogden, author of *Women Who Love Sex*. If the aim of the sexual revolution was to get us to lay down our hang-ups—or at least to beat them into ploughshares—then it has succeeded, magnificently. Our sexuality is less repressed than at any other time in human history. That much is certain.

What is less clear is whether our sexual liberation, for all its exponential increase, has genuinely enhanced our sexual happiness…or only our anxiety about obtaining it. The evidence is at best equivocal. Being more open and better informed about sex has undoubtedly increased our awareness and intensified our pleasure. But the impact of all this on our subjective wellbeing appears to have been minimal. As American feminist Anne Roiphe has observed, 'While pleasure is surely pleasurable, it didn't, all that orgasm–erection talk, in the long run make people feel much better about their lives, their marriages, their bodies.'

If there is one answer to the question of what women want next from sex, it would be to go beyond the capacity to control our own sexuality to the much more ambitious task of re-imagining the totality of the sexual enterprise. Not the power to order sex à la carte—but the opportunity to re-write the whole damn menu. As we have seen, our sexual liberation has not even necessarily translated into more sex, let alone into better sex, let alone into better lives. Sex is not, in fact, the answer. And to that extent, the sexual revolutionaries of the '60s and '70s got it wrong.

Traditionally, sex has been a commodity that men demanded and women supplied—or not. For men, sex has been a primary source of pleasure. For women, it has been a primary source of *power*—and, if we're honest with ourselves, still is. Women who choose not to play sexual politics, in their relationships or the wider world, constitute a tiny and subversive elite. They tend to be women who don't give a damn about 'catching and keeping a man', as if he were an interesting bug, usually because they have acquired sufficient economic power to buy themselves out of the game. Like the pop singer Cher, they have become the rich man their mothers wanted them to marry.

Younger women who show us it's possible to have sex for no 'good reason'—not strategically, seeking no advantage or privilege, conferring no obligation or demand—may represent the next stage in our erotic evolution. But whether it will prove the ultimate stage seems doubtful. Like happiness itself, perhaps, 'great sex'—the kind that doesn't momentarily divert us from ordinary life but powerfully transfigures it—is by definition a by-product of a larger, a more ambitious project.

i do and i don't

'Marriage is like a cage,' Montaigne observed. 'One sees the birds outside desperate to get in, and those inside desperate to get out.' Although frankly I've seen few birds desperate to get into a cage—leaving aside my daughter's budgie the day I chased it with the vacuum hose—I think we all know what Montaigne was getting at. And if we appear to have even more mixed feelings about marriage today, maybe it's just that the cage has acquired a revolving door now.

Marriage—like talk-back radio, or smallpox—was supposed to be obsolete by now. Its stubborn popularity in the face of ideological bludgeoning, economic reshuffling and religious retreat is impressive. Eerie almost. Today, we can choose from among a host of seemingly more practicable alternatives (cohabitation, serial monogamy, staying single) without stigma. Yet most of us, assuming we are given the choice, opt in. Some of us, quixotically or just idiotically, again and again.

Who says women are risk averse?

Not even my ten-year-old believes in Cinderella anymore. She was raised on the feminist version, in which a poor but beautiful boy is plucked from obscurity by a powerful princess, and the three evil stepbrothers end up as house-fairies. Sussy loves Snow White, but pities her for her stupidity. ('What kind of a jerk would eat that apple?' she asks for the two-thousandth time. Her brother answers amiably, 'Hey. She lets a squirrel lick the dinner dishes. What do you expect?') The notion that an able-bodied girl would sit around singing to mice and waiting for her prince to come nowadays requires as much suspension of disbelief as any other Disney conceit—from flying elephants on up. This is especially true, I suspect, for a girl raised since the age of six months by a cheerfully serially monogamous single mother.

Having said that, Sussy did go through a seriously wifey phase a few years ago. Visitors to our home were often startled to find her, aged six, gowned in a miniature bridal dress and veil, determinedly vacuuming the front hallway. (Mother was in a de facto relationship at the time and writing *Wifework: What Marriage Really Means for Women*.)

'Shouldn't you…*say* something?' my cousin Felicity hissed. But what could I say? 'You missed a spot'? The Bride remains as potent a cultural icon as Batman or Bo Peep, and children can no more be shielded from such symbols than they can be kept from guns or make-up or processed foods. And when she appeared that Halloween in the bridal get-up accessorised with an Edvard Munch-inspired fright mask—'I'm a horror bride, Mummy!' she cried—I'll admit I felt vindicated.

As the mother of a son, I have had ample opportunity to observe that little boys rarely experience an equivalent urge to impersonate grooms—or, for that matter, to vacuum the front hallway. Bill's dress-up phase set in earlier, at about the age of three. It centred on a moulded plastic Superman mask and a cape, which for several months he wore as faithfully as he did underpants. More faithfully, if truth be known. Bill's identity issues at this phase of life made Clark Kent's look mild-mannered. (If asked his name, he would answer firmly, without the slightest hesitation or irony, 'Superman.') No one suggested, not even Felicity, that I should 'say something' to Bill about this. It never occurred to me to worry that his identification with a super-hero portended anything at all for his later life. Bill's delusions of super-human strength bore about the same relation to reality as Sussy's delusions of sub-human subservience.

Yet the endurance of these cultural caricatures—the fact that they were capable of spontaneous generation in a family environment featuring a veritable textbook case of non-traditional role structure—reminds us how thin is the veneer that separates postfeminist family life from the primordial division of sexual labour: The Caregiver Wife (The Bride Who Vacuums) and The Protector Husband (Whose Identity Issues Are the Whole Point).

Everybody knows these cardboard cut-outs are vestigial figures in the lives of contemporary couples. ('Make Your Own Damn Dinner' reads the caption on my notepad below an image of a radiant '50s housewife gesturing almost lewdly towards a bulging fridge. I love that notepad. I try not to let the irony that I use it mostly to write grocery lists get in the way.) Yet we are continually distressed to discover that between what we know and how we feel—hell, between what we know and how we *act*—there yawns a chasm deeper than the longest crevice tool. Forty years of feminism have succeeded in driving a stake through the heart of Horror Bride. Yet like Glenn Close in the final reel of *Fatal Attraction*, she just keeps coming back for more.

A generation ago, the concept of a 'self-made bride' would have made as much sense as a 'blushing best man'. Marriage, like a game of playground basketball, was something a girl was selected for, or not. No more. Today, we no longer necessarily wait to be picked by our prospective mates, as if we were apples or contestants on reality TV.

When it comes to marriage proposals, we can now give as good as we get—theoretically—and there is no more emphatic reminder of how the balance of power has shifted. Or wavered, at least.

According to a report in the New York *Daily News*, when Britney Spears proposed to her boyfriend Kevin Federline on a flight to New York from Ireland, he said no. 'I was taken by surprise,' the 26-year-old explained to reporters. 'I thought the guy was supposed to ask the girl. So a couple of minutes went by and then I asked her.'

'And I said yes, of course!' Britney purred.

As women, we no longer need marriage to awaken us sexually, to rescue us socially or to provision us financially. With a quarter to a third of babies now being born to single women throughout the English-speaking world, we obviously don't feel we need marriage to have children either. So what *do* we need it for? Or, more to the point, what do we *want* it for? For, make no mistake, women by and large do want to be married—young, never-married women almost universally so.

Bizarrely enough, marriage is sexy again. Of all the unanticipated side-effects of second wave feminism—from the rise of the metrosexual to the decline of the family dog—this one is perhaps the most outrageous. Feminism was supposed to liberate women from the shackles of wedlock, not send them racing headlong for a new set of leg irons.

Yet as journalist Anne Kingston observes in *The Meaning of Wife*, women are snarfing up enough pro-marriage propaganda to make Jane Austen blush, from glossy bridal mags to grisly How To Catch a Man manuals (my personal favourite being *How to Get a Husband after 35 Using What I Learned at Harvard Business School*), from the genuinely witty confections of Bridget Jones-creator Helen Fielding to the downright daft Dr Laura or John T. Molloy, author of the '80s style bible *Dress for Success*, who cut the cloth to fit the zeitgeist in 2003 with the release of *Why Men Marry Some Women and Not Others*. 'If a woman is seriously trying to find a husband,' advises Molloy soberly, 'she should date men who have reached the age of commitment.'

Post-9/11 America is particularly bullish on the wife industry, as Kingston calls it. That's hardly surprising. After all, there's nothing like the threat of imminent Armageddon to send young people scurrying to the security of conservative values. The real shock is that a generation dominated by the children of divorce can use 'marriage' and 'security' in the same sentence.

'I wake up in the morning, look at that ring and think, "Very cool,"' Britney coos. 'I love cleaning, I really do,' she adds (though no one appears to have asked her), and 'I'm learning how to make all my mom's salads.' Kingston cites an article that appeared in *Elle* Canada in 2001 advising young women to seek work in 'glamorous industries' run by rich men. (Wait a minute. Isn't that *every* industry?) 'Marrying well is the best labour-saving device,' *Elle* advised its young readership, 'and ritzy jobs can pave the way.'

In my day, teen idols were too busy having unprotected group sex to worry about making salads. 'Very cool' was to 'marriage' as 'good shit' was to 'Nestle's Quik'—which is to say, not. People still had weddings back then, but they were rather sad people: guys who wore short-sleeved shirts with pen protectors, or girls sporting home perms. The cool folk co-habited or at the very least downplayed the trappings. They got married barefoot, or on the beach, as if marriage was something one did for the hell of it, like going skinny dipping or eating ice cream cones.

Or that was my perception, anyhow. In reality, marriage in those years—the '60s, '70s and '80s—was still the default option. Today, the production figures overall show a sharp downturn in the Wife Industry. Although the aura surrounding the marital enterprise has never been more rose-tinted, fewer and fewer of us are tying ourselves into the marital knot these days. Yet one's sense is that the birds slamming their heads against the outside of the cage door are as numerous as ever.

Our feelings about marriage are, at best, ambivalent. Not so our feelings about weddings. In Australia, for example, where the average bride is now aged 28—which means that among middle-class educated women, thirtysomething is more probably the norm—and up to 40 percent of women are expected never to marry *at all* (though only a fraction of those by choice), the wedding business just keeps getting bigger. Although meringue-shaped frocks and freight-length trains are out, spending up to $5000 for a wedding dress is par for the course, according to Glenn Findlay, founder of Australian Bridal Services. Bridesmaids have been binned, but a host of new bridal accessories have arisen to take their place, from teeth whiteners to silicon implants. 'There are brides who might have some work done,' Findlay admitted coyly to the *Age* in February 2004. After all, 'the day is about them'.

The average Aussie wedding is a bargain at $15,000. In the UK, where couples currently spend twice that, more and more couples are taking out wedding insurance to cover the risk. The financial one, that is. Marks & Spencer has a policy that even provides rebates for family counselling.

At the same time, figures show that increasing numbers of young women are delaying marriage, or avoiding it (or missing out on it—statistics fail to capture the nuance). In the US, where marriage rates are now at their lowest point in history, single female households have increased by a third in the last fifteen years. In Japan, they have increased 50 percent in that time. In the UK, the Office for National Statistics forecasts that by the year 2020, a quarter of all British women will be single (and presumably a quarter of all British men as well, though funnily enough they never phrase it that way). Australia's marriage rate is the lowest it's been in a hundred years. 'Who Needs a Husband?' trumpeted the cover of *Time* magazine in August 2000, below a photo of TV's 'Sex and the City' stars. Four years later—with the apocalyptic revelation that, among others, ubersingle Carrie Bradshaw did—it was beginning to seem that maybe *Time* had asked the wrong question. Maybe it was not a matter of who *needed* a husband but rather who *wanted* one. Like a cosmopolitan, or pair of Manolos.

Observers who prophesied that the institution of marriage would have withered away by now made a compelling case. But they were still wrong. Part of the mistake, we are beginning to understand, was applying additive logic to a non-linear proposition. Assuming that people will marry only under conditions where it made sense to marry is like assuming that people will work only if they can't get food for free.

Marriage has an economic basis, no doubt about it. The theory that monogamy rests on the primordial trade-off of reproductive resources for material ones is correct, as far as it goes. It simply doesn't go far enough. There's an analogy with work that's instructive here. Work is 'about' getting paid, whether in cash or in kind. But people who don't *have to* work, because they have other means of economic support to keep them afloat, do so anyway. And they do so in droves. Partly, it's a question of how much is enough—we all know families that protest that they *have* to work the insane hours they do because otherwise how on earth could they afford that annual trip to Europe / that beachside weekender / those school fees. But it's also partly that work provides other, less tangible rewards. Friends, for example. Stimulation. A sense of accomplishment and purpose. An excuse to wear make-up.

If none of us actually needed to work for pay anymore, we would have an opportunity to see those 'pull factors' much more clearly. We would probably discover that what we once thought of as the fringe benefits may have a far more central place in the experience of our working lives than we ever reckoned.

Something similar is happening with marriage today. Women need marriage less and less. The *Time* magazine article was right on the money in that sense: a woman with a steady income, good health insurance, a pension plan, and access to a sperm bank needs a husband like a fish needs a four-wheel-drive. But the need, it is turning out, was only ever part of the story. After all, suburban soccer dads don't need four-wheel-drives either, and you don't see that stopping them. Now that everything else has been stripped away, it's time to consider whether the fringe benefits of marriage were really so negligible after all. Who knows? Maybe the fringe is the whole point.

Whether owing to delusion, denial or the desire for damage-control, even the world's most empowered women continue to rank marriage, or at least a marriage-like (maritoid?) relationship, right up there on the contemporary wishlist, second only perhaps to happiness itself. Perhaps stranger still, the belief that marriage will bring happiness is not entirely superstitious. Notwithstanding the tempestuous state of the marital union over the last four decades and a divorce rate that hovers between 35 and 50 percent throughout the Western world, research shows that satisfaction with marriage predicts satisfaction with life itself. Having a happy marriage is not a *necessary* component of adult happiness, especially of female adult happiness, as scores of studies documenting the satisfying lives of many single women attest. And it is possible to have a satisfying life even within a deeply flawed marriage, especially for husbands, as we shall see. But where marriages *are* satisfying, the larger lives of the men and women within them seem inevitably, indeed incorrigibly, worth living as well. A good marriage, in other words, is a risk factor for a good life.

In this sense, marriage is distinctly *unlike* snagging a Prada handbag (although having a big blow-out of a wedding may be very similar). Although most of us fail to think so analytically about it till it's too late, getting married and being married are two entirely distinct states. One is all about a rite of passage, which is inherently exciting. The other is all about having passed, which inherently isn't.

We have already observed that most people tend to overestimate the degree of happiness that intense, positive, one-off experiences will yield. This 'focusing illusion' helps explain why weddings are so over-valued, so elaborately planned and choreographed compared to marriage itself, which often remains perilously unexamined. Yet the wedding is not what transforms us, except in the legal sense—and I don't care how good your lingerie is. Getting married cannot bring lasting happiness any more than having a baby or, for that matter, getting divorced can. *Being* married, on the other hand, may.

One cannot read the literature and fail to reflect that happiness, like evil, is a disconcertingly banal affair. Philosopher Hannah Arendt observed long ago that most of the world's misery, far from being the product of some Satanic bolt from the blue, was the result of a multitude of prosaic failures. Evil, she argued, was an anticlimax—perpetrated by the most ordinary of people acting on the most familiar of impulses. Perhaps paradoxically, happiness is too. What makes us truly and lastingly happy is almost disappointingly simple. Eating, drinking, having sex, sleeping and—yes, in many cases—existing in that state that researchers romantically call 'pair bonded', whether in marriage or its moral equivalent.

Social trends that suggest—no, make that holler—that young men and women are finding it more and more difficult to sustain marriage or any other form of committed, intimate relationship need therefore to be taken seriously. It's not the ethics of our collective failure to commit that's at issue, or the impact on somebody's nebulous concept of 'family values'. It's not our mortal souls that are at stake, I would argue, but something far greater. I refer of course to our capacity to enjoy ourselves.

According to a 2002 study conducted by the UK Future Foundation, there are now more single-person and one-parent households than any other family type. Living without a partner, in other words, is now the norm in the UK and close to it throughout the developed world. In Germany, for example, the number of people aged 25 to 45 in single-person households has risen by 500 percent since 1960.

The good news, say some observers, is that young people no longer feel the same pressure to couple. Others—including anyone who has ever spent an evening in the company of two or more single women over the age of 23—beg to differ. They point to the rise of the 'starter marriage', a phenomenon involving a small but growing segment of young middle-class couples who marry in their twenties but divorce after a few years without having children. Starter marriages would not exist in a society that was less afflicted by matrimania, observes Gen X trend analyst Pamela Paul, author of *The Starter Marriage and the Future of Matrimony*. Paul also argues that the starter marriage can equip participants with a skillbase to build on in future marriages—a kind of Little League of the heart, as it were. Unfortunately, the grim divorce statistics for re-marriage—60 percent at last count—do little to support this theory.

Reports of droves of singletons thriving in so-called urban tribes may be something of an urban myth as well. The claim that people now get intimacy and support through friendship networks that replace 'family life' cannot be supported by the research, argues British psychologist and social critic Frank Furedi, author of *The Culture of Fear*.

'Since 1986, the proportion of British singles who see a best friend on a weekly basis has been falling,' Furedi notes, 'and surveys show that thirtysomethings today have about half the number of friends that their counterparts would have had thirty or forty years ago.' It's not just marriage or cohabiting that's putting us off, Furedi suggests. We are increasingly wary of *any* long-term relationship, whether with an employer, a best friend or even a dog.

But one woman's risk aversion is clearly another woman's lifestyle choice. You've got to wonder, though, why news of people who are single and happy about it continues to make headlines. Sasha Cagen was 25, 'terminally single' and—get this!—*satisfied with her life* when she kickstarted Quirkyalones, a grassroots movement comprised of 'people who are saying no to the tyranny of dating'. Yet, as the subtitle of Cagen's book *Quirkyalone: A Manifesto for Uncompromising*

Romantics suggests, quirkyalones have hardly turned their back on the possibilities for pair-bonding bliss. It's not marriage they object to; it's dating—or the dumber side of dating, anyhow. In fact, the aim of the quirkyalone is quite definitely to end up quirkytogether. But in the meantime, they seek ways and means of being single with dignity. Again, the fact that women need grassroots movements to support this lifestyle choice is telling.

In truth, for the vast majority of young women, being single really isn't a lifestyle choice. It's a lifestyle *circumstance*.

This is not to say there aren't groups out there that actively promote single life as an alternative to coupledom. There are plenty, just as there are groups out there that actively promote bog snorkelling and serial self-amputation. The American Association of Single People has declared a holiday for singletons as a kind of Valentine's Day anti-venom. Other lobbyists for the single cause urge women to wear 'right hand' diamond rings as a way of celebrating their solo status—which is a bit like encouraging the child-free to wear Teletubbies pyjamas, or urging non-drinkers to guzzle water out of vodka bottles. There is a thin line between 'celebrating' and 'protesting too much', and many of these groups cross it.

Of course, one could say exactly the same for those groups that insist with equal stridency on the moral superiority of marriage. You can't help but ask yourself: if this lifestyle is so self-evidently stupendous, why are so many spin doctors working overtime to sell it? It is also noteworthy that you don't see books or websites authored by single *males* celebrating the happily-never-after thing. Guys don't need any convincing, and they don't need any instructions either. Most of all, they don't need the PR.

Betsy Israel, author of *Bachelor Girl: The Secret History of Single Women in the Twentieth Century*, notes that single women (as opposed to single guys) are still perceived as a special interest group. Carolyn Dinshaw agrees. Dinshaw, director of the Center for the Study of

Gender and Sexuality at New York University (a city in which, according to census figures, solo females number upwards of two million), told the *New York Times* recently she believed the term 'single woman' was 'outdated' because it 'problematises the single woman as if the standard is the couple, and it seems to me that we have really gone beyond that'. Dinshaw is correct as far as demographics go. But our notions have yet to catch up with our numbers. And even our numbers get rubberier the closer you get to them.

The singleton tsunami notwithstanding, demographers still project that more than 85 percent of American adults will marry at some point in their lives. (Interestingly, the fastest growing group of single people are the *divorced*.) In Australia and the UK, forecasts for marriage proper are less sanguine. But coupledom, in the form of de facto relationships, shows little signs of weakening.

In Australia, for example, while there has been a fivefold growth in the number of men who have never married, the proportion of de facto relationships has more than doubled in the past twenty years. According to 'Men and Women Apart', a Monash University study released in 2004, marriage in Australia is becoming increasingly class-linked, with most of the decline taking place among the less affluent—a pattern that has been evident elsewhere throughout the developed world. In the US, for example, about half of births to early school leavers are out-of-wedlock. Among college graduates, the rate is only 6 percent.

While we're on the subject of births, another trend is that marriage is becoming increasingly *offspring*-linked. (Not that it ever wasn't. Science is clear on the matter, even if Hollywood isn't: the wellbeing of children is the whole point of monogamy. It is only in the last fifty years or so out of the last 500,000 that we've lost sight of that.) In the US, for example, married couples currently comprise only 52 percent of all households—yet of those, 88 percent have at least one child.

The truth is probably not that single life is eclipsing the joint household—especially among the middle class—but that it represents a new and improved (or at least rejigged and elongated) phase of adult development that has been inserted between adolescence and committed coupling. 'With little fanfare,' writes *Urban Tribes* author Ethan Watters, 'we've added a developmental stage to adulthood that comes before marriage—the tribe years.' The key word here is 'before', not 'instead of'.

Australian demographer Bernard Salt suggests an alternative developmental sequence. Increasingly, Salt forecasts, adult life will be divided into three serially monogamous relationship stages: a prenuptial partner, with whom we will pair for 'travelling, fun and sex'; a reproductive partner who will share with us the traditional 'marriage, mortgage and baby' package; and a postnuptial or 'wind-down' partner for the post-secondary, pre-managed-care-facility years. If Salt's predictions turn out to be accurate, monogamous pair bonding—with or without the legal imprimatur of matrimony—will remain a central feature of adult life experience. Marriage is unlikely to wither away, in this view; it will simply diversify.

Personally, I suspect Salt is onto something here—and not only because my own relationship history offers a textbook case of his theory. Projections that huge numbers of the population will remain single for life fail to take into account the so-far unquenchable yearning of human beings to pair bond—males as well as (though arguably not quite as strongly as) females. We are *delaying* the forging of committed unions, not rejecting them. And there's a big difference. In the developed world at least, we seem now to regard monogamy as St Augustine regarded celibacy. 'Give me chastity and continence,' he prayed to the Lord, 'but not yet.'

Remember the population explosion? Projected figures assured us that that was going to happen too. Instead we've got a worldwide fertility crisis. I am old enough to recall similar prognostications about home ownership. 'Your generation will be renters for life,' my mother told me gravely, with just the tiniest hint of schadenfreude. It was something she'd heard on the news. But the news is like that. Reality may not be.

Having a Superfriend—as quirkyalones style the person you trust to feed your cat or move your car to the other side of the street—is self-evidently life-enhancing. But friends do not replace partners any more than they replace children, or grandparents, or family pets. 'My best friend is like my husband,' one satisfied (dare one say 'smug'?) single told the *Observer*'s Liz Hoggard in February 2004. But in a sense, doesn't that prove the point? If being single is so good because it's just like being in a couple—then what's so good about being single? If, on the other hand, the point is that married couples have no monopoly on committed, intimate, adaptive and sustaining unions, there is nothing to argue about. Of *course* there are other ways to connect. Yet even when we reduce marriage to a metaphor—a good friend is like a faithful husband, or (as one of my girlfriends, a single mother, noted recently) 'my mum is my wife, really'—we italicise its persistence as an ideal.

No one in their right mind would argue that marriage 'makes' anybody happy. Except that people do argue this all the time—even researchers who, despite their academic credentials, really ought to know better. Statistics do show a clear, cross-cultural relationship between marriage and subjective wellbeing overall. But then they also show a clear relationship between marriage and divorce, so what does that prove?

The devil—and the depression also, as it happens—is in the detail. For instance, it is well known that rates of depression are in general much higher for both genders among the separated and divorced. Yet the marital mental health picture is very different for women than it is for men. Weirdly, marriage seems to protect men from depression regardless of the quality of the relationship. Then again, maybe that's not so weird. More on this in a moment.

For women, by contrast, marital status per se tells us very little.

For us, relationship *quality* is where the action is. According to figures from the US National Institute of Mental Health, unhappily married women have the highest rates of depression of *all* groups, male or female, partnered, separated, divorced or never married. As we have observed elsewhere, rates of depression are normally twice as high for females as they are for males. But when it comes to unhappy marriages, wives are three times more likely than husbands to be depressed, according to statistics from the American Psychological Association. Men, on the other hand, are more likely to become depressed when a relationship breaks down or when a spouse dies.

Linda Waite and Maggie Gallagher, authors of *The Case for Marriage: Why Married People Are Happier, Healthier, and Better Off Financially*—not that they have a point of view or anything—believe that 'the reason getting a wife boosts your health more than acquiring a husband is not that marriage warps women, but that single men lead such warped lives.' They have a point. There is little doubt that, on the whole, men embark on marriage from a much lower wellbeing base-line, notwithstanding the collective hysteria about desperate and dateless single women pondering the possibility of being eaten by Alsatians.

Other research has found that marriage enhances wellbeing most dramatically among men and women who were demonstrably miserable as singles. People who were more or less happy as singles will continue to be more or less happy once married. A recent study by University of Texas psychologist Ted Huston found that happily married couples had dated for an average of 25 months. So-called 'early exiters'—those who divorced after two to seven years—had actually dated for longer (about three years), though not exclusively. Huston found the early exiters were far more likely to have had an 'unpredictable romance' and to approach marriage as a solution to relationship problems.

Perhaps that's understandable, given the power of the pro-marriage propaganda machine that's been reassuring us for decades that well-being and marriage go together like the proverbial horse and carriage. Yet the latest research suggests that we may have been putting the carriage before the horse—and overlooked the fact that married people are happier because happy people are more likely to get married in the first place.

'Misery may love company,' observes psychologist David G. Myers, author of *The Pursuit of Happiness*, 'but research on the social consequences of depression reveals that company does not love misery.'

A fifteen-year study published in 2003 in the *Journal of Personality and Social Psychology* found happiness spiked for partners both before and (interestingly) after marriage, but the increase was minimal, about one-tenth of a point on an eleven-point scale. Study author Richard Lucas, a psychologist at Michigan State University, interpreted these findings as a confirmation of the 'set point' theory of happiness: that individuals have a pre-set personal satisfaction barometer that regulates wellbeing over the long term, regardless of peaks and troughs encountered along the way. These findings suggest that previous research that seemed to demonstrate otherwise—i.e. that marriage 'created' happiness—was the result of what researchers call a selection bias. If married couples report being slightly happier than the non-married, Lucas's research suggests, it may be because those who marry represent a self-selected group of slightly happier people.

The study, which tracked the relationship ups and downs of more than 24,000 participants, also found that people who were already satisfied with their lives before marriage were more likely to stay married. Specifically, the study asked people to rate how happy they were on a scale of zero to ten. Most scored between 5.5 and 8. But people who eventually got married scored an average quarter point higher. In the year prior to marriage (think falling in love and tons of sex), these same lucky folks experienced a happiness rise of another fifth of a point. Immediately after the wedding (think presents and tons of sex), the same thing happened. All of that adds up to two-thirds of a point—considerable, when you consider that most of us rate our happiness within a 2.5 range. So the slightly happier were more likely to marry. And the sequence of events leading up to marriage—courtship, wedding and honeymoon—consolidated that advantage.

But wait. There's more. After two years of marriage, couples' happiness levels dropped back to exactly where they were as singles.

Having said that, Lucas also found there were plenty of people whose happiness levels changed dramatically, and permanently, with marriage. But those for whom marriage proved an ecstatic experience were balanced out by those who were traumatised—for a cumulative effect of zero. Another unexpected finding was that those people who enjoyed a big boost within the first three years of marriage were likely to go from strength to strength in the years to come. According to Lucas, 'the three years after your marriage are going to predict how happy you are in the three, four, five years after that'—a finding that he believes would apply equally to marriage-like relationships among cohabitors and gay couples.

But what about marital satisfaction over the longer term? Researchers formerly assumed that marital happiness, tracked over a couple's lifetime, would assume a U-shaped curve: starting out on a high, dipping during the crunch years of career- and family-building, and rising again at the empty nest phase and beyond. The most recent longitudinal studies, unfortunately, suggest a pattern that looks less like a U than a set of steps—descending downwards.

'We find declines in marital happiness at all marital durations,' concluded the authors of a seventeen-year national study published in *Social Forces* in June 2001, 'and no support for an upturn in marital happiness in later years.' This study, the most comprehensive of its kind, found that on average the steepest declines in satisfaction occurred during the earliest years of the relationship, and the latest years.

One nearly unanimous finding over several decades of research is that married couples who have children report lower marital quality than those who don't. Kids may add immeasurably to women's lives, but they also show a very measurable tendency to do to adult relationships what childbirth does to our pelvic floors. And no amount of restumping will ever quite restore them.

Psychologist Lawrence Kurdek of Wright State University, author of a recent study confirming (yet again) the erosive effect of children on marital quality, notes that, 'Caring for children may result in time taken away from the marriage.'

And giving birth to children *may* result in discomfort, too.

ambivalently ever after

Is there such a thing as living happily ever after in marriage? It's a hard question. It's also, almost certainly, the wrong one.

Marital happiness and personal happiness are two different measures—highly correlated, to be sure, but different. We also need to keep in mind that no one ever studies 'singleton happiness', or satisfaction with remaining *un*partnered. It is difficult to imagine that most people growing old alone would experience greater happiness (or lesser unhappiness) than those who have pair-bonded. And anyhow, whoever said that marriage was supposed to make you happy (apart from your mother, Walt Disney, the church, the Bush administration, the Brothers Grimm, Dr Laura…)? 'Marriage is not supposed to make you happy,' growls Atlanta psychiatrist Frank Pittman, author of *Grow Up*. 'It's supposed to make you married.'

Pittman, among many other observers, argues that naïve expectations of marital bliss actively erode couples' wellbeing. In the full glare of 50 percent divorce rates, you'd think we'd have sussed that by now. If anything, in fact, you'd predict the main problem facing couples today to be a surfeit of cynicism. But you'd be wrong, according to *Starter Marriage* author Pamela Paul. Paul observes that the children of divorce, herself included, far from having a more clear-eyed take on relationship risks and realities, may actually be at special risk of marital myopia. As adults, such people may feel driven to heal the wounds left from childhood. 'We want the kinds of marriages that we've always fantasised about but have never actually seen,' she says.

Has *anyone* actually seen one?

Put it this way, there have been sightings. Lots of them, in fact. In the US—the country with the highest divorce rate in the world—two-thirds of all couples describe their marriage as 'very happy'. Significantly fewer, however, describe *themselves* that way. According to National Opinion Research Center figures over the past thirty years, 40 percent of married men and women say they are personally 'very happy'. That's still a figure that blows singletons out of the water, mind. Only a quarter of single people report being this happy.

On the other hand—and I think we've got about four of them so far—we need to remember that singletons ain't necessarily singletons, as a longitudinal study of 14,000 men and women conducted by Australian economists Michael Shields and Mark Wooden in 2003 reminds us. One obvious problem is that people who are married have chosen their relationship status. People who are single may or may not have. Shields and Wooden found that people who were single by virtue of separation or divorce were the least satisfied of all groups—especially if they were female. But they also found that, by the time divorce was finalised, satisfaction levels recovered, and these people were as happy as other singles. Which is to say, still rather less happy than either married or cohabiting couples.

You might think that today's higher divorce figures would result in a 'survival of the happiest' scenario, with the truly miserable having been weeded out. Yet a closer look at the figures over time reveals exactly the opposite. If anything, the halo effect of marriage on perceived happiness has lost some of its shimmer in recent years. It couldn't really be otherwise, given the enormous added weight that marriages today have been asked to bear: from growing economic inequality to increased work–family conflict to precipitous shifts in gender roles.

Recent research based on the vast General Social Survey data-set shows a gradual decline in the percentage of people reporting 'very happy' marriages from 1973 to 1988. Another study that compared marriages in two generations of respondents, identical in age at the times the data was collected, found that the younger couples reported less inter-action, more conflict and more problems overall in their relationships. On a brighter note, researchers say the decline in marital happiness, evident in the 1980s, appeared to have levelled off in the '90s (which makes me wonder if my second divorce had anything to do with it).

One study that appeared in the *Journal of Marriage and the Family* in 2003 found that between 1980 and 2000, marital happiness and divorce proneness changed little, but the quality of marital interacting declined 'significantly'. Those declines were associated with—not 'caused by', there's a big difference—premarital cohabiting, wives' long hours of employment and wives' job demands. Changes over that period that enhanced marital quality included extra income—presum-ably also the result of 'wives' long hours of employment'—more decision-making equality and non-traditional gender attitudes.

This study also found that, while marital satisfaction overall had remained constant, wives were feeling slightly happier and husbands slightly less happy about the state of their unions. The study authors speculated that housework was the reason for both changes. 'Increases in husbands' share of housework appeared to depress marital quality among husbands,' they observed with a straight face, 'but to improve marital quality among wives.' A 1995 CBS Newspoll appeared to confirm this interpretation. It found that 63 percent of women, but only

49 percent of men, believed their marriages were better than those of their parents.

In marriage, as in any other dimension of our lives, happiness can be operationally expressed as the ratio of expectation to eventuality. (I know, I know. If I've told you that once, I've told you that a thousand times.) There are two implications here. This first is that, if we want to be happy in our relationships, we need to keep our expectations, if not realistic—because there is enough stagnation in the world—then at least realistic-ish. The second is that we need to devote considerable energy to examining the realities of marriage before those same realities start examining us. Otherwise, we can't possibly know what 'realistic' looks like.

Matters aren't helped by the fact that falling in love inevitably fosters the delusion that 'you and I aren't like that, darling'. The conviction that one's own partnership constitutes a unique and transcendent exception to life's rules is not, alas, the best place to begin a reality check. For most of us, falling in love is the easy part. (It is also the single greatest source of positive emotion that human beings can experience, bar none. Not even shoe shopping comes close.) The real bitch is the expectation that we will *stay* in love, aka The Passion Fallacy.

Research conducted by Ellen Berscheid of the University of Minnesota showed exactly the same thing that my first marriage showed: that 'the failure to appreciate the limited half-life of passionate love can doom a relationship'. Frank Pittman believes that 'nothing has produced more unhappiness' in contemporary relationships 'than the concept of the soul mate'. Psychologist Joshua Coleman agrees. Coleman is the author of *Imperfect Harmony*, a spirited defence of the 'good enough' marriage. 'It's a recent historical event that people expect to get so much from individual partners,' Coleman insists.

As we have also had repeated occasion to observe, happiness is a relative construct—and who, or what, a woman chooses to compare herself to can be as salient for her wellbeing as any objective criterion.

When one considers the hugely inflated hopes women have for their marriages today compared to those of a generation or two past, it would be astounding if we didn't feel a sense of anticlimax (at best) or bitterness (at worst). 'A man's reach should exceed his grasp, or what's a heaven for?' wrote Robert Browning. But he was talking about poetry, not the prosaic business of partnering for life. I would argue that when a woman's reach is *chronically* short of her grasp, as it is so often in marriages today, the result feels more like purgatory. For most married men, on the other hand, the reach/grasp differential is smaller and evidently less problematic.

Sociologist Ken Dempsey's research among an educated, middle-class sample of white Australians, published in 2001, suggested 'strongly' that 'men generally were more satisfied than women with their marriages'. Dempsey found that seven out of ten married men wanted their marriages to go on the same as they had in the past, compared with only four out ten women. The women in this study were not necessarily unhappy. And there was certainly no indication that they longed to be single. But they did have complaints about marriage. Lots of them. One woman made 28 separate complaints about her partner, and several made more than ten, Dempsey found.

All the usual suspects were represented: from the way housework and childcare were divided to the way intimacy needs were being met (or failing to be met). Significantly, however, complaints about 'who does what' were much more common when women felt short-changed emotionally by their partners. Among those who reported high levels of companionship and intimacy, and sufficient emotional support from their men, housework was less of an issue.

Overall, two-thirds of the women Dempsey studied made at least three complaints about their partners, compared to only a quarter of the men who did. The most popular items on the shitlist for women were: participation in housework and childcare; participation in leisure activities; level of intimacy; quality of communication; willingness of partner to listen to personal problems. Wives complained further of husbands being too busy with their own interests, failing to take initiative in organising joint activities, making too many demands for housework, and off-loading kids rather than taking responsibility for them. When women were asked whether they thought the division of childcare in their marriages was fair, only 4 percent said yes.

Guys, on the other hand, were less likely to want to press for future change, Dempsey found. And they were also less likely to report anger or annoyance about the present state of their unions. In fact, there was only one area in which husbands were less satisfied than wives, and you get no points whatsoever for guessing what it was. That's right: one out of every three husbands reported being troubled by their partners' 'insufficient interest in physical love-making'.

Of course, there were wives who made the same complaint. Two out of a hundred, to be precise. Sex aside (which is exactly where many wives seemed to want it), an impressive 75 percent of husbands agreed with the statement, 'Every new thing I learn about my partner pleases me.' Yet only 47 percent of wives returned the compliment. When women were asked which they found the most rewarding: caring for kids, doing housework or performing wifework (i.e. caring for their partner), a mere 12 percent chose the latter.

Dempsey found that husbands were much more likely to be 'very happy' about being married (67 percent versus 47 percent of wives). But, perhaps more to the point, he also found a majority of *both* sexes reported that they were happy with their marriages. For most married women, then, the desire for change needs to be understood within this context. It's not that marriage is a bad deal for women, or that wifework today isn't an improvement on wifework a generation ago. It's more a case of women wanting even more, and even better. Maybe even as much as men have. These days, it would be hard to find a man who objected to that (publicly at least). But it would also be hard to find one so passionately committed to the goal of equity that he'd compromise his own wellbeing to make sure it was achieved.

As women, we need to stop expecting otherwise, and figure out how sisters can start doing this—yes, this too, I'm afraid—for ourselves. It may be the winners who write the history, but it's the losers who amend the constitution, culturally speaking. Which is probably the wrong metaphor too. As we have seen, women do not by and large *lose* from marriage. They just don't gain as much as a) they would like to, or b) men do. Wanting change—even wanting it passionately—is not the same thing as wanting out.

The psychotherapeutic truism that a person can only change herself (not others) is wildly unfair—and outrageously true. 'Getting men to take responsibility for themselves' is a bit like telling an insomniac to sleep it off—or forcing sleeping tablets down his throat and imagining you've cured him. You can't 'get' people to be independent any more than you can program them to be spontaneous.

If you are still in charge of the duty roster…guess what? You're still in charge. Protesting that 'if I didn't do it, it wouldn't get done' doesn't cut it either, I'm afraid. If you stop contributing and nobody notices, you have learned one of two things. Either what you were doing was unnecessary; or it was necessary, but only to you. In which case, if you choose to go on doing it, it is for your *own* good and no one else's.

Harsh? Perhaps. But then the truth—like a hangnail—always hurts.

My own personal epiphany about all this came about in the painful aftermath of a 'marriage-like' relationship. All in all, it was a pretty typical blended family scenario. We both worked for pay (though he worked slightly longer hours and earned a great deal more money). Apart from what we outsourced, I did pretty much all of the cleaning, 100 percent of the laundry, three-quarters of the shopping and cooking and maybe 80 percent of the childcare. He fed the pets. When I reminded him.

All right, I think you're getting the picture. Needless to say, struggles about who did what ranked high on our to-do list as a couple. (Well, on my to-do list anyhow; I'm not sure he actually had a to-do list—which, when you stop to think about it, was half the problem.)

Eventually, probably inevitably, we separated. And don't let my flippant tone fool you: I was devastated. So was he—only not in the way I'd predicted.

I'd assumed—not unreasonably, I think—that he would miss 'what I did for him'. In fact, I had some pretty vivid fantasies about it. About how neglected he'd feel as the house slid from everyday, blended-family untidiness to certifiable health hazard. About the despair he'd feel to look into the top drawer of the tallboy on Monday morning and know with a sickening certainty that the socks-and-jocks fairy would never come again. In brief, I indulged myself in what I now think of as the Big Yellow Taxi Delusion: that once I'd gone, taking the Miele vacuum and the Enjo cloths with me, he'd be left, sobbing and slightly soiled, bereft among the dust bunnies.

To my astonishment and annoyance, none of this came to pass. The break-up was very difficult for him, and I think it's fair to say he missed me. But what he did not miss were the services I had rendered. Not greatly. Maybe not even at all. As predicted, the house did degenerate swiftly into an entropic stir-fry of sporting equipment, take-out wrappers and overdue DVDs. So far, so good. The problem was, he didn't seem to care. In truth, I'm not entirely sure he even noticed.

Eventually of course he did. I think it was the day the cats started confusing the bedclothes with their litter tray. But when he did finally notice, he didn't fall on the floor frothing at the mouth with remorse for the woman he'd never fully appreciated. He picked up the phone and hired some cleaners. Food was similar. The fixation with the family meal was something I'd introduced, like an invasive species. When I departed, he simply went back to buying takeaway when he didn't feel like cooking. You know, like a normal person. Laundry may have been more difficult. I wasn't intimate enough with the household to find out, and I certainly wasn't going to ask (though I was dying to). I suspected his mother was ironing his shirts again, as she'd been doing when I first met him. ('But she *wants* to,' he'd protested with a shrug. The awful part was it was true.) There was no satisfaction in that either. Just a spasm of jealousy, really.

OK. You're probably thinking that was comeuppance enough. I know I did. But as time wore on, it just kept on comeupping. Another thing I hadn't anticipated was how my own attitude toward housework would change. Basically, once we separated, I did everything I had been doing before and then some—because after all, even a man who is stuck at the 'helping out' stage of development contributes *something*. There was only one big difference: I didn't resent it. I knew absolutely that I was doing what I was doing for 'me' (a pronoun that should always go in inverted commas when used by the mother of three school-aged children), either because I wanted to, or because I felt I really ought to—but indisputably because I *chose* to.

I cared about the whiteness of the whites—a little bit, anyhow. *I* cared about making the beds, and tidying the toys, and doing a big grocery shopping every week. *I* cared about making lunchtime 'interesting' and alphabetising the spices (just kidding!). He didn't. My wishing that he did was understandable. But I now saw that it was also unproductive. Self-sabotaging, even.

Keeping house the way I wanted it kept—which pretty much translated into the way my mother, a full-time homemaker, had kept hers—really *was* a job bigger than I could manage on my own. But that wasn't his problem anymore. In fact, it never should have been. My options were suddenly, painfully clear. I could lower my standards, or

I could get some help. In the end, I did both, and am the happy woman you behold today.

Of course, I am also single.

A happy marriage is not necessarily a peaceful marriage, it needs to be said—especially from a woman's perspective. In fact, the evidence suggests that, for women, anger and wellbeing are often linked. Observes psychologist Lesley Brody, 'Women who do express anger in marriages by initiating conflicts with their spouses report greater marital satisfaction when reassessed three years after the initial data collection than women who do not express their anger.' Wives who feel they are *allowed* or perhaps *entitled* to get mad, in other words, enjoy marriage more than women who don't. In highly dysfunctional marriages, on the other hand, wives' expression of anger often acts as a trigger for abuse—much more so than either sadness or distress.

What else makes women happy in marriage? Research published in the *Journal of Happiness Studies* in 2002 found that a positive age gap between husband and wife increased life satisfaction for both partners. When the man is older, in other words, couples are happier. I hate that. I also hope it is a period effect—in other words, something that will change with changes in the wider social sphere. A generation ago, a woman who mated with a man even slightly younger than herself was a cultural anomaly. (My own mother, for example, a mere three months older than my dad, is still embarrassed about being a 'cradle snatcher' even after fifty years of marriage.) Today, more and more, the snagging of a younger guy is seen as a feather in a girl's cap, or on her g-string, or *somewhere*, anyhow.

But recreational sex is one thing, and marriage quite another, and I suspect many young women remain reluctant to go tadpoling for a future husband. For good or ill, a man who qualifies as 'partner material' still tends to conform to the ancient dictates of hypergamy (literally, marrying up): that is, slightly older, slightly wealthier, and, yes, slightly taller. And we wonder why equality is so elusive!

Nevertheless, the so-called Iron Law of Marriageability, once thought to be as inexorable as gravity, is showing signs of rust these days. The same study, for example, showed that wives' life satisfaction was inversely related to the size of the education gap between partners: translation, that couples whose qualifications were more equally matched had the best chance of happiness. A generation ago, the reverse would more likely have been true. This is good news for women at the top of the occupational food chain who, under conditions of strict hypergamy, would have a hard time finding anybody to marry up *to*. And while we're on the subject, the oft-repeated statistic that university-educated women have lower marriage rates than any other group is completely unfounded. A woman's qualifications will delay her entry into marriage, for obvious reasons. But they will also decrease significantly the odds of her remaining single for life.

Up until now, we've been making generalisations that tend to lump together marriage and marriage-like relationships. In fact, there are important differences. One of them is that rates of cohabitation have surged astonishingly over the last thirty or so years. In the US, for example, the number of cohabiting couples has increased fivefold since 1970. In 1978, when my sister moved to Florida to 'live in sin' with her boyfriend (whom she later married), my parents stopped short of pinning a letter A to her chest, but only just. A decade later—like so much else that happened in the '70s—it was all over bar the shouting. People learned to say 'partner' instead of 'lover', thank God, and got on with it. (I am old enough to remember my parents referring to somebody as a 'common-law wife'—and, even more thrillingly, to discover they meant my great-grandmother.)

Today, cohabitation is no longer a moral issue. But questions about how living together stacks up qualitatively to marriage are more relevant than ever. The basic answer seems to be that, for women generally, and mothers especially, the wellbeing advantages of marriage over cohabitation are significant. It's been replicated many times over in the research: overall, cohabitors are a little bit happier than singles, and a little bit less happy than marrieds.

That's interesting on a number of levels—especially because in many ways cohabiting females appear to get the best value out of their men. For instance, research published in 2003 by Australian sociologists Janeen Baxter and Edith Gray found that men in de facto relationships did considerably more housework than husbands (40 percent versus 26 percent), although slightly less outdoor work. Compared with cohabiting women, married women spent an additional *six hours a week* on housework—almost the equivalent of a full day's work—regardless of the presence of children, gender-role attitudes, education or any other variable. Other research, paradoxically, has shown that cohabiting men's contributions to the housework are greatest among those with 'marital intentions', and weakest among those with no plans to marry.

British research published in 2004 in the *Journal of Epidemiology and Community Health*, based on responses of 4500 adults, found that cohabiting was beneficial for men's mental health—especially as a re-partnering option—but less so for women's. Specifically, researchers found that while long-term relationships were better for the mental health of both sexes, men's emotional wellbeing was more likely to be enhanced by cohabitation and women's by marriage: an effect that, if true, seems to constitute a veritable connubial catch-22.

Of all those surveyed in this report, women who remained alone after divorce or de facto break-up reported the worst mental health. (Although I can't help thinking that the word 'reported' may be significant here.) These findings prompted one observer, Dr David Katz, an associate clinical professor of public health at Yale University, to proclaim that 'biologically, men do well with a series of female partners over time at the level of propagating their genes' while women 'are best served by long-lasting, stable relationships'. Oh please. And I suppose biology also explains why, according to the UK Office for National Statistics, 40 percent of divorced women over 65 are poor enough to qualify for income support. The research in question clearly showed that *both* sexes are best served by long-lasting, stable relationships—and so have a host of other studies. (It showed also, incidentally, that women who stayed single for life had an excellent mental health profile—especially when compared to single men.)

Other research has consistently found that cohabiting couples—men and women alike—report lesser levels of contentment than married folk. But it also shows that the gap is narrowing. Australian research published in 2004 by Mariah Evans and Jonathan Kelley of Melbourne University showed the mean life satisfaction score for married men and women was 74, compared to 71 for cohabitors. That's a difference of 4 percent. Small, yes. Dwindling, certainly. But still significant.

The question is: what does it mean? Obviously, cohabitation offers less security than marriage—a fact which most researchers concede is especially salient for women, for a combination of biological (i.e. repro-ductive), economic and social factors. When a relationship breaks down, women are left holding the baby in every sense of the word. In the present high-divorce climate, described by Princeton family histo-rian Lawrence Stone as utterly without historical precedent, marriage may be a slender reed on which to hang one's happiness. But cohabi-tation is more like the Psalmist's flower: the wind passeth over it, and it is gone. And it's a strong wind. Compared to marriage, the failure rate for de facto relationships is up to three times as high.

Although most cohabiting couples will eventually marry—and most couples marrying today have at one time cohabited—living together does not increase the odds of either marital happiness or marital stability. Just the opposite, in fact. Penn State researcher Claire

Kamp recently looked at two groups of de facto couples who later married: early adopters, who had lived together thirty years or more ago (at a time when only one in ten couples 'shacked up') and couples who cohabited in the past twenty years. Her findings, published in the *Journal of Marriage and the Family* in 2003, showed that both groups reported less marital happiness and more conflict than couples who lived separately prior to marriage. It's hard to understand why that would be so, and the oft-cited theory that 'bad habits formed during cohabitation may carry on into married life' seems singularly unconvincing.

Findings like these are often trotted out by pro-marriage interest groups, like the Catholic Church and my mother. Yet recent research suggests the difference between the happiness of cohabitors and that of their wedlocked counterparts has little to do with 'the piece of paper'. To an extent, it's not what marriage or cohabitation does to couples that makes the difference, but rather the differences that couples bring to those relationships.

Social researcher Ruth Weston and colleagues at the Australian Institute of Family Studies, whose large-scale study 'Premarital Cohabitation and Marital Stability' was published in 2003, found that couples who cohabited before marriage tended to self-select for more of the characteristics that predispose to divorce. In other words, these couples were more likely to have parents who had themselves divorced, to be less religious, less educated and to be English speakers. And if you think that's a profile that fits the vast majority of people you know, maybe you won't be surprised to learn that in Australia presently only 27 percent of marrying couples have *not* lived together first! (In the US, the figure is closer to 50 percent.)

Cohabitation per se does not put couples at risk of relationship breakdown; the pre-existing conditions that are associated with cohabitation do. Once those conditions were controlled for, there were no differences at all between the survival rates of 'direct' and 'indirect' marriages eight years on.

On the other hand, de facto couples for whom 'keeping the options open' is an avowed priority, happiness and stability are likely to be precarious for both partners. Again, it feels like cultural heresy to say this, but options operate a bit like fridge doors: when they are kept open indefinitely, things get spoiled. As sociologist Bernard Farber noted almost two decades ago, the trend toward 'permanent availability' on the partnership market practically guarantees permanent dissatisfaction. And not even marriage offers much protection.

When 'all adults, whether married or not, remain on the marriage market', observes University of Texas sociologist Norval D. Glenn, 'and married persons can be lured out of their marriages if they can attract a more desirable spouse', the 'piece of paper' becomes just that. And marriage itself is just another form of shacking up.

Glenn believes young men and women—but particularly young women—still yearn to be married. He cites statistics showing that, for example, 83 percent of college women agree with the statement, 'Being married is a very important goal for me.' There is even evidence that young people regard marriage more highly now than they did in the '70s or '80s. One recent poll of young Americans showed that 80 percent agreed with the statement, 'Unless a couple is prepared to stay together for life, they should not get married.'

Yet there is evidence, too, Glenn argues, that young women tend increasingly to view marriage as 'just a special kind of close relationship rather than a social institution'. On the basis of in-depth interviews, Glenn classified college women according to their 'approaches to happiness in relationships' as either hedonistic, individualistic or altruistic in orientation.

The vast majority, he found, were individualistic, with altruists and hedonists about equally represented at around 10 percent of the sample. Glenn takes this is as an ominous portent for the relationship future of these young women, on the assumption that it is altruism—

the putting of the needs of others before personal desires—that most conduces to harmonious marriages.

Maybe he's right. Maybe the desire of women to please themselves really *is* an alarming trend. To me, however, this research seems to be saying that young women want to be married; they just don't want to be wives. And who could blame them for that? After all, it is doubtful that young men want to be wives either.

The desire of women to be served by their relationships, rather than to serve within them, will inevitably disrupt established patterns of marital interaction. Or continue to disrupt them, I should say. (Women, remember, initiate two-thirds of all divorce.) Neoconservative critics who point sourly to the rise of the 'self' in contemporary culture forget that, for women, this is the good news—the redressing of an ancient imbalance. True altruism is possible only where one can choose to be otherwise. Under any other conditions, it is a form of extortion.

Having said all that, the desire of women to find self-actualisation in marriage, or through marriage, is problematic to the point of delusion. Monogamy is not an arrangement predicated on sentiment, but on survival—reproductive survival especially. (Not surprisingly, the 'more people view self-actualisation rather than child-rearing as the purpose of partnership, the more likely they are to divorce', observes psychologist David G. Myers.) Happiness, to the extent that it enters into the equation at all, is more in the nature of a side effect. And in this I agree entirely with Norval Glenn's observation that young women today know what they want yet 'lack the age-old insight that a direct, self-interested pursuit of happiness is not the best way to achieve it'. This is as true in marriage as in any other area of endeavour. When happiness comes—if it comes—it sneaks in through the back door. Looking to marriage for personal fulfilment, perhaps, is a bit like looking to motherhood for serenity. It sounds so logical till you try it.

It's important to distinguish between what a relationship can 'do' for us, and what may be accomplished within the context of a relationship. Personally, I don't believe that any relationship, no matter how supportive or empowering, can manufacture a sense of self where none existed before. Nor however do I believe that marriage and 'self-actualisation' or 'individuation' are mutually exclusive goals.

The view that marriage 'insists upon the merging of identity—of both husband and wife—if it is to be sustained', as Danielle Crittenden puts it in *What Our Mothers Didn't Tell Us*, is to my mind both bleak and unimaginative. And I am in good company. Psychiatrist David Schnarch, author of *Passionate Marriage*, argues that the merging of identity is precisely what *prevents* marriages today from flourishing. And so too, even more famously, did Arabic poet Kahlil Gibran. 'Fill each other's cup but drink not from one cup,' Gibran advised intending marriage partners in *The Prophet*.

> *Give one another of your bread but eat not from the same loaf.*
> *Sing and dance together and be joyous, but let each one of you be alone.*
> *Even as the strings of a lute are alone though they quiver with the same music.*

OK, OK, I'll take off my flares now.

Marriage can make people very, very happy for precisely the same reason that it can make us very, very afraid: because it seals closed the exits. At the risk of oversimplifying—but hey, you've got to go with your strengths—it's a commitment thing. Mariah Evans and Jonathan Kelley's research, which looked specifically at the effect of family structure on life satisfaction, confirmed this hunch very strongly. It also found, somewhat counter-intuitively, that the familiar Frying Pan–Fire sequence—divorce followed swiftly by a second marriage—was more likely to maintain lifetime happiness than to erode it.

As a marital recidivist myself, I can sort of understand this. The advantage of marriage over living together is simply that it implies a deeper, more public and more visible commitment. I said 'implies'—not 'is'. But in the happiness game, isn't perception three-quarters of the battle? That Ever-After illusion, even within a culture where first marriages are seemingly as disposable as nappies (and as unlikely to biodegrade), is especially salient for women, for whom security needs tend to be keyed just that little bit higher. If men were left holding the babies and women the super fund, this might be different. But not at this point in our social evolution.

There was a time, not so very long ago, when what women wanted from marriage was simply to be married. In truth, there are a fair number who still do, if the rash of recent Monogamy for Dummies manuals is any indication—though I continue to hope that most women read them, as I do, for comic relief.

By and large, the days when a woman had to say 'I do' before she could say 'I am' are as much a relic of our social history as kidney-shaped coffee tables and harvest gold appliances—and about as sorely missed. Whatever it is women want next from marriage it is not identity, readymade like a box of biscuits. Most of us come to marriage with that already now: thanks to education, work, travel and a host of prior relationships, meaningful or otherwise.

Little more than a decade ago—if the polls by women's magazines like *McCall's* and *New Woman* are to be believed—a majority of women believed, or perhaps feared, that 'wives submerge a vital part of themselves'. That 'you give up part of your true self when you marry'. We are no longer content to settle for that. What women want next from marriage—or from any other long-term, committed relationship—is to find ways of becoming *more* of who we are, not less. And if that's a tall order...so be it. That's what happens when you've got standards.

never satisfied

'You can never get enough of what you don't need
to make you happy.'
Eric Hoffer

When I was a teenager, I thought love would solve everything. In my early twenties, I thought sex would solve everything. By my late twenties, I thought a career would solve everything. At age thirty, I thought marriage would solve everything, and then—when it didn't—I was sure that motherhood would. By my late thirties, following a brief period of certainty that therapy would solve everything, I became convinced that divorce would solve everything. At forty, I was sure an extension would solve everything (and, frankly, the ensuite came damn close). Now, edging fifty, imagine my surprise to find that I am as fucked up as ever.

But seriously, folks.

A few years ago it hit me that the only solution left was to stop looking for one. I'm not entirely certain whether this means I have mellowed or just given up. Maybe the difference has been exaggerated.

At Christmastime last year, I was struck by the number of catalogues and commercials hawking gifts as 'solutions'. I was further struck by how apt the metaphor really was. For so many women—and God knows, for me—holiday time is a little like a gaily decorated obstacle course. The most joyous season of the year, so-called, is so often a matter of clearing hurdles, of gaining ground. Of 'nailing it', as, to my horror, I found myself saying to a salesgirl as she rang up my last purchase of the season. Who was nailing whom? I wondered afterwards. It was a weird mix of religious metaphors: Mummy on the cross.

The quest to 'solve' Christmas, like the quest to 'solve' the riddle of what women really want, is doomed by definition to failure. When it comes to female happiness—or any other kind of happiness, for that matter—there *is* no 'solution'. No Grand Unified Theory. No Holy Grail. No Magic Interval which, if only it could be calculated, might suspend in perfect tension the essential elements of a woman's life— the allied and opposing forces of love and sex, marriage and motherhood, friends and family, career and chocolate.

Creating a life of fulfilment and meaning is within the grasp of almost all of us. But to insist upon some monolithic solution only gets in the way of achieving it. To frame our lives as a multiple choice exam to which the answer key has been perversely withheld by the powers that be—whether men, or money, or our mothers—is not simply mistaken. It is tragic.

We are accustomed to chattering on about 'choice', as if the sheer multiplicity of options was what mattered most of all. We are only just discovering how shallow a goal this is. As postfeminist women in an affluent age, we have been practically bludgeoned by choice, seduced into believing that She Who Dies with the Most Options Wins.

'Only she who says she did not choose is the loser in the end,' wrote the great feminist thinker Adrienne Rich. Yet freedom of choice, we are learning, is only the beginning. That's what women wanted then—and we, their daughters, are the living beneficiaries of that largely granted wish. What women want next is the courage to choose fearlessly, and the wisdom to choose well.

'But we are not *really* free!' some women will continue to protest. 'We cannot *really* choose!' To an extent, of course, this is correct. There are circumstances that constrain our freedoms, even still. There probably always will be. Heaven knows there are for men.

This is no longer what you'd call 'oppression'. More what you'd call 'life'.

From a distance, it looked like men had it all. Love and work, sex and sleep, family time and leisure time. These were not mutually exclusive for guys, so why did they have to be for the rest of us? 'Work or family is a choice no man ever has to make,' we observed bitterly.

Now, we have looked closer and we see that, in fact, it is a choice every man always has to make. They just make it differently. They certainly make it more automatically, with less angst and ambivalence. There are a million exceptions, but it is still the rule that men by and large choose to privilege work over family and women choose to privilege family over work. Among other things, that means that men get to 'have' families but not necessarily to 'hold' them. Sure, they get to have full-on careers and be Daddies. What they don't get, any more than the rest of us, is to have full-on careers and be Mummies. That was one of those little details we overlooked.

And yes, I am aware that by phrasing things this way I am perpetuating gender stereotypes. I should be more disciplined. I should say, Full-Charge Parent and 2IC—because that's what I really mean. Numerically, gender still predicts the distribution of those roles. In qualitative terms, it is almost entirely irrelevant. My best male friend is a full-charge single parent who refers to his ex-wife as Auntie Mum. In other families, it's a case of Uncle Dad. For most of us, the roles do not divide up so definitively, thank heavens. Cases that are this lopsided are only slightly less rare than cases of truly shared parenting.

And while we're on the subject of anomalies, most estimates put genuine co-parenting families at no more than 10 to 20 percent of the total. I used to wonder that the number was so negligible. More and more, I wonder that it looms so large.

For one thing, people less often choose partners that mirror them than they do partners that complete them. My need for security matches up with your need to protect. Your ability to nurture complements my capacity to drive myself. Your virtuosity with the vacuum matches the crap under my couch. Couples in which both partners are good at making money but bad at making dinner can also work beautifully, thanks to the miracle of take-out. But for the most part, we tend to gravitate to partners who can do, and maybe even like to do, the stuff we can't or don't. That's not unfair. That's fortunate.

Specialisation within a relationship may or may not be equitable. But the failure to specialise is almost inevitably inefficient. The time and energy spent negotiating who does what may be more than most couples have to spare, especially when kids are added to the to-do list. It's no secret why so (relatively) few families ever achieve the egalitarian dream: frankly, there's too much tossing and turning.

Having said all that, what some women want next really are relationships that are mathematically equal, and to achieve this will require both a canny selection of partner and a willingness to keep putting energy into the system—probably, in cases where partners become parents, in perpetuity. Women who insist on marrying 'up'—seeking taller, older, wealthier, higher-status males—will fight an uphill battle and quite possibly an unwinnable war. Think about the 10–20 percent of truly equal relationships in your social set. In how many of them does the woman earn more money, or have superior qualifications, or a higher-status job, or at the very least a wealthier or more socially prominent family? In how many is she just a tiny bit taller, or just that little bit older? Let's see now…All of them?

What about women who change their name to that of their male partner—and the practice is still common (in the US, the trend of brides keeping their own names is now reversing itself, researchers tell us)—and then complain that their husband still thinks he's boss? I've got news for you, girls. If you let him stamp his name on you, he *is* boss. It's easy to forget that these are choices women make, too.

Another reason, probably *the* reason, the egalitarian dream has yet to materialise is simply that most of us, in our heart of hearts, don't really want it. The drive to remain differentiated—once dismissed as 'chauvinism' or, more charitably, insufficiently raised consciousness—has turned out to be so much stronger than we ever anticipated. What makes a woman a woman and a man a man is not as salient as what unites us as human beings, and all that jazz. But the differences, however we choose to re-frame or re-shuffle them, still matter. In fact, they matter intensely. Androgyny, a bit like socialism or on-demand breastfeeding, looked so much more appealing at arm's length.

Perhaps that explains why women today speak almost apologetically about the yearning to find a 'real man', as if masculinity were a vice they haven't fully conquered, like a weakness for milkshakes. That does not make a nonsense of feminism, as the dimmer-witted among our conservative critics have tried to argue. But it does suggest the need for a re-fit. Maybe learning how to live as equals, not necessarily equivalents, is the riddle men and women must grapple with next.

In a recent radio survey, British women were asked to nominate the book they felt had had the greatest influence on the lives of twenty-first-century women. Six out of ten of the shortlisted books were classic love stories, including *Jane Eyre*, *Pride and Prejudice*, *Middlemarch*, *Little Women* and *Tess of the D'Urbervilles*. To be sure, Marilyn French's *The Women's Room* and Margaret Atwood's *The Handmaid's Tale* also made it onto the list. Then again, so did *Bridget Jones's Diary*! (Personally, I found those results confusing and contradictory. The fact that they mirrored my own literary tastes made it that much worse.)

Professor Lisa Jardine, speaking on the BBC's Women's Hour, noted that many of the novels women cited centred on 'the struggle between self-realisation and the domestic, between wanting to fulfil yourself and knowing that the ultimate goal of your life is a husband and a family and a home.'

Putting 'ultimate goal' and 'husband' in the same sentence is enough to make my flesh creep. Yet I would be lying—though maybe dreaming is a better word—if I denied that the man–child–house package remained at the top of most women's wishlists. For most of us, career has joined this triumvirate, not usurped it.

In Australia, the overwhelming majority of young people— 90 percent—intend to have children, according to recent research by University of Adelaide sociologist Barbara Pocock (despite demographic projections that suggest only 75 percent will actually do so). Most of the ten- to eighteen-year-olds surveyed, male and female alike, assumed they would live in dual-earner couple households and share childcare. But when researchers dug deeper, they found clear gender differences. Young women tended to anticipate working *around* their care responsibilities. Young men expected to do the opposite. For them—as for their fathers—work came first, and 'life' trailed after.

Pocock found little evidence for the emergence of a New Australian Wife—a born-again cocooner intent on finding a rich husband and hunkering down at home with the kids. Nor, however, did young women buy into the Having it All mystique. Their expectations of their male partners were, if anything, low—i.e. realistic. (Their expectations of their mothers, by contrast, were downright romantic, especially with regard to providing free and universal childcare for grandchildren.)

When asked how they envisioned the domestic division of labour in their future households, the young women Pocock spoke to were equally resigned—i.e. realistic. Although working-class girls employed 'a more assertive discourse of fairness', their more affluent sisters harboured few illusions—perhaps 'standards' is a better word—about who would be doing what, and for whom.

It's as if these young women are wanting exactly the lives their mothers have had, minus the angst and stripped of the idealism. Nice work if you can get it, I guess. One can't help but feel a sense of anticlimax about all this—as if all of feminism's hard work has ended not with a bang or even a whimper but a smug, slightly Stepfordian smile. On the other hand, if we are to believe the research showing life satisfaction to be a direct result of realistic expectations, then the prognosis for the rising generation is clearly a positive one.

As a woman who came of age during the heyday of '70s feminism, I must confess that I struggle with the notion of an achievable goal. It seems almost ignoble to aim so low. Remember that Browning quote? A woman's reach should exceed her grasp, or what's a heaven for? If I had to embroider a motto to hang over my bed—assuming I had a clue how to embroider anything which, thankfully for all of us, I don't—that would be it. Yet to be constantly reaching for life, and never actually getting there, is a fair vision of hell. What women want next lies somewhere in between, I suspect: enough striving to make life meaningful and enough repose to make it pleasurable.

Pleasure is one of those concepts, like fulfilment and—dare I say it?—gratitude, we rarely associate with mainstream feminism. If we expect to have any constituency left at all, that's something that will have to change radically. It is happening already in some ways, thanks to our Gen X sisters who have reminded us that our bodies have a right to be as genuinely liberated as our minds are—that they are more than just inconvenient sacks of protoplasm we must haul around after us.

Human happiness, as we have already observed, is hinged inextricably to our human bodies. Using those bodies, not just sexually but in sport and play, is a such a vital, such an obvious way of expressing and creating wellbeing. Yet by the time most of us reach adulthood, it is as if our bodies have become like our cars: our best hope is that they will get us from A to B with minimal servicing.

One of my very favourite findings in all the happiness literature is the one about dancing: that dancing not only makes people happier than money, or marriage, or moving to California. It makes people happier than *anything*. I think of all the hours I spent dutifully dragging my kids around to Toddler Tunes and Junior Jazzercise and Mahler for Midgets, or whatever the heck they called it. What our family really needed was a music and movement class for Mummy. Not a 'workout'—with three preschoolers, trust me, I had plenty of that—but a bliss-out: ballroom dancing, say, or salsa.

Today, if I had to do it over again, I'd say enough with the postnatal pilates. I'm going bellydancing.

Eating is of course another of life's most basic bodily pleasures that women deny themselves. When it comes to food, we are classic facilitators: enabling others to experience the enjoyment and getting our thrills symbiotically, at second hand. Providing proper meals is an obsession for many of us; actually tasting those meals—let alone savouring them—is beside the point. Women who become diet obsessed (and frankly that's almost a redundancy these days) not only deny themselves nutritionally but sensually, hedonically.

Nothing makes me more pessimistic about the future of womankind than watching my fourteen-year-old daughter's friends pick self-consciously at their sad little salads and yoghurts, or grabbing their stick-thin thighs in mock dismay at 'all that fat!' A couple of years ago, they'd descend on our kitchen after school like a plague of locusts. Now it's like a tea party for stick insects. My own daughters, thankfully, have been genetically loaded to plough into their food like peasants.

I pray it may be ever thus. Being a true domestic goddess is an act of creation *and* consumption. Heaven knows it's not about serving food to others. That's being a domestic *waitress*. There's a big difference.

A person who denies herself the pleasure of food cannot possibly experience long-lasting happiness, and I don't care how much of a buzz it is to wear size eight knickers. A person who is denied the pleasure of sleep is in for an equally rude awakening. In fact, recent research has shown that, for women, poor sleep erodes day-to-day happiness more than any other factor, except tight work deadlines. In a study published in the journal *Science* in 2004, the mood states of 900 US women were tracked using the Day Reconstruction Method— basically, a log of everything they did during the day, which was then 're-lived' the next day and rated using twelve mood scales ranging from 'worried' to 'hassled' to 'friendly and happy'. The least pleasant moment-to-moment activities for most women, researchers found, were commuting, housework and facing the boss. The most pleasant were sex, socialising with friends and relaxing. Interestingly it also found that divorcees were slightly more cheerful during the day than married women…but I think I'm getting off the point. Ahem.

What I really wanted to focus on was the sleep finding: that women who slept poorly the night before reported little enjoyment in that day's activities—even stuff they normally found gratifying, like watching TV or (and this is really extreme) shopping.

On a very basic level, what women want is *sleep*. Yet, for many, many women sleep is exactly what they are most deprived of— especially during the crunch years of family-building, when pregnancy, lactation and the sleep habits (or lack thereof) of young children make a good night's rest as hard to come by as a nanny who irons—or even flies, for that matter. How often does sheer exhaustion masquerade as depression—or even trigger psychosis—among young mothers? Wheeling a sleep-deprived woman off for couples counselling for low libido is a bit like treating an alcoholic for bad breath. And in a world which drives women harder and further than ever before, the decline in our quality of sleep is reaching nightmarish proportions. They say Margaret Thatcher could get by with only five hours sleep, but let's face it: doesn't that prove my point?

For the rest of us, sleep is not a luxury we can get by without, like

Belgian chocolate or simultaneous orgasm. It is a bedrock necessity. Questions about whether marriage makes women happy, or children do, or work does are extravagantly beside the point when you're not getting enough oxygen to your brain.

It amazes me how much we take our bodies for granted—and then we wonder why everybody else seems to as well. But there are other obvious sources of women's wellbeing that we routinely overlook. The first and most important of these is other women.

The question of what women want from each other—as mothers, daughters, sisters and friends—is an issue so rarely addressed. Yet, for my money, it is a topic every bit as confronting as the more usual questions about what men can give us. The last five years has seen an explosion of popular and scholarly interest in what one author calls 'woman's inhumanity to woman', and the rest of us call sheer bitchiness.

It's hardly news that women are capable of making each other miserable. Back-biting, innuendo, exclusion, gossip: our virtuosity in the arts and sciences of nastiness is the dark underbelly, or perhaps the pale cellulite, of our oft-celebrated capacity for caring and nurture. And it also ranks among the most stubborn obstacles to women's wholeness and wellbeing.

Women are the nurturers of the world, and this is a source of enormous emotional strength. Yet our capacity for self-nurture, and our willingness to receive nurture from our sisters, has arguably never been less developed—or more urgently required. Despite our obsessions with our partners (or lack thereof) and our children (or lack thereof), the research tells us that most women derive their greatest happiness from their *friendships*. Men come and go. Children grow up. But a woman's friends, if she is lucky, endureth forever.

'All men are brothers,' the poet reminds us. (It was Rilke—a guy, just in case you were wondering.) If only all women were girlfriends…what a wonderful world it would be. Yet in the present climate of gender role confusion, maintaining woman-to-woman friendships poses special challenges. Perhaps inevitably, the more life options we have to choose from, the greater our insecurity that the ones we have chosen are the 'right' ones, the 'best' ones. Maintaining an attitude of openness towards those who have made other choices can be difficult, especially when it seems to serve as a reminder of what-might-have-been for us.

The consequences of all this for our female friendships—potentially such a source of strength and support—can be cruelly damaging. Instead of celebrating our differences, and learning from them, we are more likely than ever, it seems, to close ranks and play it safe. In a risky world, it is understandable that we will seek social safety wherever we may find it, becoming risk-averse even in our friendships—sticking with the PLUs—the People Like Us—and dismissing the rest. It's understandable—but it is also, ultimately, self-defeating.

Women need other women for their emotional sustenance. Our friendships one to another are not some sort of psychological snack-food but rather (as they say on the cereal ads) part of a balanced diet. Taking those relationships as seriously as we do the ones our society more usually foregrounds—the ones we have with sexual partners, and members of our biological family—deserves a place of its own on the postfeminist wishlist.

The imperative to connect is a human drive women appear to experience with particular intensity. (Why is it we hear so much about the 'fight or flight' impulse, and so little about the equal and opposite urge to 'mend and tend'?) Perhaps that helps to explain the role spirituality and religion can play in enhancing our wellbeing. In virtually every happiness study that's ever been conducted, religious affiliation and subjective wellbeing are surprisingly closely correlated. As a former

Anglican clergy wife (don't ask), who has flirted with Buddhism, dated Judaism and gone all the way with Wicca, I find this fascinating.

One recent survey of 163,000 people in fourteen European countries found that 84 percent of regular worshippers said they were very satisfied with life, compared with 77 percent of non-churchgoers. Other research has found that having firm beliefs, whether they are religious or not, has the same effect. It is not faith per se that makes the difference, this research suggests, but rather 'existential certainty'—basically, believing that you are right about things!

Other observers incline to the view that churchgoers are happier for the same reason that people who belong to sporting clubs or pet-breeding associations or porcelain-painters' support groups are: because the affiliation provides them with extra social support and a clear sense that they belong—perhaps especially within those traditions where the concept of the 'chosen people' looms large. We like to think of ourselves as special, and religion helps us do this. (My friend Chris claims she turned away from the Presbyterian faith when she was taught in Sunday school that Jesus loved all little children equally. 'Doesn't He have *any* standards?' she wondered scornfully.)

Equally obvious, it seems to me, religious people—whatever else may divide them—are united in the belief that life fundamentally makes sense, or at least has a point. Perhaps having all the answers isn't the main thing at all. Maybe it's simply the conviction that there *are* answers—or even the capacity to harbour a reasonable doubt that there might be.

Finally, although religious observance generally connects us to a community, it also means making time for solitude and reflection. 'Both the need to be alone and to engage others are essential to human happiness and survival, with equally provocative claims,' writes psychologist Ester Bucholz, author of *The Call of Solitude*. In a secular society, observes Bucholz, we run the risk of dismissing 'time outs' as unproductive intermissions. But from a spiritual perspective, opportunities for reflection are an essential part of the action.

For far too many of us, reflective states that last longer than a yellow light are rare, and the closest we ever get to a spiritual perspective is praying for a cleaning lady to appear. Too often we nourish our spirits exactly as we nourish our bodies: carelessly and on the run. Bucholz notes that, in her therapeutic practice, she is often struck by women's expressions of gratitude for time out: 'like prisoners who are granted parole before they deserve it'.

As women, we experience an insistent drive to connect and to relate. But the need to dis-connect is real, too. A life without pauses and stillnesses, like a paragraph with no punctuation, leaves you short of breath and gasping for coherence.

We have learned about 'me' time in recent years, and the glossy magazines are full of fatuous advice about it—as if a bubble-bath and an exfoliating glove were all the maintenance our immortal souls required. Don't get me wrong—I believe the world would be a better place if we all indulged religiously in an hour-long full-body massage each week. Yet the Day Spa Spirituality thing can take us only so far. If the research on women and wellbeing is to be believed, we need more than 'me' time. We need 'Thou' time—the space to get *beyond* self.

For feminists, gratitude hasn't exactly been a forte. Well, why should it be? Gratitude is hardly the recommended emotional response when you want to generate change, which probably explains why one encounters so few grateful union bosses, or environmental activists, or human rights advocates—accentuating the positive is the best political strategy ever devised to preserve the status quo. Challenging it requires exactly the opposite take.

It's no secret why the notion of a 'grateful feminist' sounds like the punchline of some off-colour joke. I am old enough to remember '60s TV debates (and their dinner-table equivalents in our dining room, featuring a stellar cast of aunts and uncles) that might have been subtitled 'You Women Have No Idea How Good You Have It'. How ignorant and unjust an accusation it was—and what a red herring!

Yet I suppose I am young enough and, thanks to my feminist foremothers, powerful enough, to want to return to the idea of gratitude. To in some way reclaim it.

The research is clear that gratitude is a key component of wellbeing. Studies show that people who, for whatever reason, lack the capacity—or is it a habit?—to feel thankful, or blessed, or just plain lucky suffer more anxiety and stress, and enjoy lower vitality and optimism, than the population as a whole. Experiments have found that college students who keep 'gratitude journals', for example, enjoy better physical health, are more optimistic, exercise more regularly and report feeling generally happier than those who don't.

(Not to depress you or anything, but researchers often use 'frequency of exercise' as a reliable marker of wellbeing. Statistically, working out three times or more a week virtually guarantees a happy individual. Combine that with having sex four or more times a week, and you are practically delirious. But I digress.)

The effects of this kind of gratitude cultivation are so unexpectedly large—and so bizarrely concrete—they have spawned a virtual gratitude industry, both research-based and otherwise. If you don't believe me, just visit www.gratefulness.org—and don't forget to light a cyber-candle of thanks.

Previously, psychologists 'tended to look down their nose at gratitude as little more than a question of having good manners and remembering to say thank you', observes Northwestern University psychologist Dan McAdams.

Today, it is increasingly clear that being grateful gives you more to be grateful about—including documentably better outcomes in career and relationships. Robert Emmons, a psychology professor at the University of California (Davis) and a leading gratitude guru, observes that, though most people think of gratitude as the result of positive events, it is may also be linked directly to tragedy and misfortune. A study by University of Michigan researcher Barbara Frederickson, for example, was able to compare people's emotions before and after 9/11. (She happened to be in mid-study at the time of the attacks.) Although the tragedy inspired pain and fear and outrage, for many people it was also associated with positive emotions: gratitude especially.

Even more interestingly, gratitude is not necessarily a function of naïvete, or denial. On the contrary, notes *The Progress Paradox* author Gregg Easterbrook,

> People who score highly on various indicators of gratefulness also report strong awareness of the bad in their own lives and in society. In fact, some research finds that grateful people may be slightly more likely to be cynical than the population as a whole. But they may achieve the ability to be wary of life's problems and yet thankful for the ways in which the actions of others lighten their burdens.

As something of a career cynic myself, I was grateful to learn that. As a feminist, I felt positively liberated. (My generation has been so hedged about by guilt, one practically needs a permission slip to feel good about something.)

What women want next may be to learn to cultivate our gratitude at least as assiduously as we collect our grievances—not out of smugness or superficiality but because it feels good. And because feeling good makes us more of who we are. Having said that, I'm not convinced that keeping a 'gratitude journal' is really my style, but I am definitely considering a 'gratitude list'. I'm good at lists. They're so lovely and…short.

In real life, where even the sequels have sequels, things are messier. In real life, every time a spell is broken, another spell moves up in the queue. As my son tells me about playing Gameboy, 'You never really win. You just move up a level.'

Winona LaDuke is right, too, when she observes that at this point in our evolution, women don't just want a bigger slice of the pie, but a different pie. If anything, she doesn't go far enough. Some of us, in fact, would prefer the cheese platter. Or the Death by Chocolate. Others the spinach salad, or the lamb shanks and garlic mash with extra gravy. Some may decide they want to have it all, and be happy to pay the price. Others would sooner stick a finger down their throat. The point is, feminism has led us to the banquet table, but the meal we make of it is up to us.

What women have always wanted is what women now have: the power to shape their own destinies. What women want next is the wisdom to use that power, without guilt or blaming, to compose richer, more satisfying lives. Sure, wreaking vengeance for the injustices of the past was kinda fun while it lasted. But we're over that now.

Living well, my dear, really is the best revenge—because it makes revenge unnecessary. What's the point of justice in the first place, if it doesn't bring joy?

select references

Abbott, Elizabeth. *A History of Celibacy*. Cambridge, MA: Da Capo Press. 2001.

Amato, Paul *et al*. 'Continuity and Change in Marital Quality between 1980 and 2000'. *Journal of Marriage and the Family*. Feb 2003, v65 i1 p1.

Baxter, Janeen and Edith Gray. 'For Richer or Poorer: Women, Men and Marriage'. Australian Institute of Family Studies Conference. Melbourne 2003.

Belkin, Lisa. 'The Opt-Out Revolution'. *New York Times Magazine* 26 Oct. 2003.

Belsky, Jay. 'Developmental Risks (Still) Associated with Early Child Care'. Emanual Miller Lecture. *Journal of Child Psychology and Psychiatry*. 2001, v42 n7 pp845–59.

Benjamin, Jessica. *The Bonds of Love: Psychoanalysis, Feminism and the Problem of Domination*. London: Virago. 1990.

Bianchi, Suzanne M. *et al*. 'Is Anyone Doing the Housework? Trends in the Gender Division of Household Labor'. *Social Forces*. Sept. 2000, v79 i1 p191.

Bolton, Michele Kremen. *The Third Shift*. San Francisco: Jossey-Bass. 2000.

Brody, Leslie. 'Gender and Emotion: Beyond Stereotypes'. *Journal of Social Issues*. Summer 1997, v53 n2 p369.

Brody, Leslie. *Gender, Emotion and the Family*. Cambridge, MA: Harvard University Press. 1999.

Bstan-'dzin-rgya-mtsho. Dalai Lama XIV and Howard C. Cutler. *The Art of Happiness*. Sydney: Hodder Headline. 1998.

Bucholz, Ester. *The Call of Solitude*. New York: Simon & Schuster. 1999.

Bunting, Madeleine. 'Life's Uneven Rewards'. *Guardian*. 10 Oct. 2003.

Cagen, Sasha. *Quirkyalone: A Manifesto for Uncompromising Romantics*. New York: HarperCollins. 2004.

Cannold, Leslie. *What, No Baby?* Fremantle: Curtin University Books. 2005.

Coleman, Joshua and Julia Lewis. *Imperfect Harmony*. New York: St. Martin's Press. 2003.

Conlin, Michele. 'The New Debate over Working Moms'. *Businessweek Online*. 18 Sept. 2000.

Cowan, Carolyn Pape and Philip A. Cowan. *When Partners Become Parents*. New York: Basic Books. 1992.

Crittenden, Ann. *The Price of Motherhood*. New York: Metropolitan Books. 2001.

Crittenden, Danielle. *What Our Mothers Didn't Tell Us: Why Happiness Eludes the Modern Woman*. New York: Simon & Schuster. 1999.

'Cuddles "More Important than Sex"'. *BBC News*. 7 June 2001.

Cusk, Rachel. *A Life's Work: On Becoming a Mother*. New York: Picador. 2003.

Davis, Michele Weiner. *The Sex-Starved Marriage*. New York: Simon & Schuster. 2003.

Declercq, Eugene R. *et al*. 'Listening to Mothers: Report of the First National US Survey of Women's Childbearing Experiences'. New York: Maternity Center Association. Oct. 2002.

De Marneffe, Daphne. *Maternal Desire*. New York: Little, Brown and Co. 2004.

Dempsey, Ken. 'Women's and Men's Consciousness of Shortcomings in Marital Relations, and of the Need for Change'. *Family Matters* Autumn 2001, p58.

Diener, Ed, *et al*. 'Similarity of the Relations between Marital Status and Subjective Well-Being across Cultures'. *Journal of Cross-Cultural Psychology*. July 2000, v31 i4 p419.

Douglas, Susan J. and Meredith W. Michaels. *The Mommy Myth*. New York: Free Press. 2004.

Doyle, Laura. *The Surrendered Wife*. New York: Simon & Schuster. 2001.

Drago, Robert and Yi-Ping Tseng. 'Family Structure, Usual and Preferred Working Hours, and Egalitarianism'. University of Melbourne. HILDA Conference, March 2003.

Driscoll, Margarette. 'Motherhood's New Spin'. *Australian*. 15 Sept. 2003.

Easterbrook, Gregg. *The Progress Paradox*. New York: Random House. 2003.

Efthim, Paul *et al*. 'Gender Role Stress in Relation to Shame, Guilt and Externalization'. *Journal of Counselling and Development*. Fall 2001, v79 i4 p430.

Elliott, Carl. *Better than Well: American Medicine Meets the American Dream*. New York: WW Norton & Co. 2003.

Evans, M. D. R. and Jonathan Kelley. 'Effect of Family Structure on Life Satisfaction: Australian Evidence'. *Social Indicators Research* 69(3): 303–53.

Ferguson, Tamara, Heidi Eyre and Michael Ashbaker. 'Unwanted Identities: A Key Variable in Shame–Anger Links and Gender Differences in Shame'. *Sex Roles* v42 n3/4 2000.

Firestone, Shulamith. *The Dialectic of Sex*. New York: Farrar, Straus & Giroux. 2003.

Fisher, A. H. (ed.). *Gender and Emotion: Social Psychological Perspectives*. Cambridge: Cambridge University Press. 2000.

Flanagan, Caitlin. 'Housewife Confidential'. *Atlantic Monthly*. Sept. 2003.

Fox, Bonnie. 'The Formative Years: How Parenthood Creates Gender'. *Canadian Review of Sociology and Anthropology*. Nov. 2001, v38 i4 p373(18).

Fox, Faulkner. *Dispatches from a Not-So-Perfect Life*. New York: Harmony Books. 2003.

Friedan, Betty. *The Feminine Mystique*. New York: WW Norton & Co. 2001.

Freud, Sigmund. *Civilization and Its Discontents*. New York: WW Norton & Co. 1962.

Furedi, Frank. *The Culture of Fear*. London: Continuum International. 2002.

——. 'Singleton Society'. *Spiked*. 11 Oct. 2002.

Galinsky, Ellen and James T. Bond and Dana E. Friedman. 'The Role of Employers in Addressing the Journal of Social Issues'. *Journal of Social Issues* Fall 1996, v52 n3 p111.

Gilligan, Carol. *The Birth of Pleasure*. New York: Alfred A. Knopf. 2002.

Gittins, Ross. 'Why Happiness Won't Last'. *Sydney Morning Herald* 4 Sept. 2002.

Glenn, Norval D. 'Young Americans' Neotraditional Views of Marriage'. *World Family Policy Forum*. 2001.

Golden, Stephanie. *Slaying the Mermaid: Women and the Culture of Sacrifice*. New York: Three Rivers Press. 1998.

Graglia, F. Carolyn. *Domestic Tranquillity: A Brief against Feminism*. Dallas, TX: Spence Publishing. 1998.

Greer, Germaine. *The Change*. New York: Ballantine Books. 1993.

Greer, Germaine. *The Female Eunuch*. New York: Farrar, Straus & Giroux. 2002.

Groneman, Carol. *Nymphomania: A History*. New York: WW Norton & Co. 2001.

Groot, Wim and Henriette Maassen Van Den Brink. 'Age and Education Differences in Marriages and their Effects on Life Satisfaction'. *Journal of Happiness Studies* 2002, v3 i2 p153.

Hakim, Catherine. *Work/Life Choices in the 20th Century: Preference Theory*. Oxford: Oxford University Press. 2001.

Hamermesh, Daniel S. and Jungmin Lee. 'Stress Out on Four Continents: Time Crunch or Yuppie Kvetch?' National Bureau of Economic Research. NBER Working Papers 10186.

Hanauer, Cathi (ed.). *The Bitch in the House*. New York: William Morrow. 2002.

Hayt, Elizabeth. 'Admitting to Mixed Feelings about Motherhood'. *New York Times*. 12 May 2002.

Hewlett, Sylvia Ann. *Creating a Life: Professional Women and the Quest for Children* (titled *Baby Hunger: The New Battle for Motherhood* in 2003 UK edition, Atlantic Books). New York: Hyperion. 2002.

Hill, Amelia. 'Teenage Girls Just Want to Marry and Stay Home'. *Observer*. 19 Oct. 2003.

Hochschild, Arlie Russell, with Anne Machung. *The Second Shift*. East Rutherford, NJ: Penguin. 2003 (first edition 1989).

Hochschild, Arlie Russell. *The Time Bind: When Work Becomes Home and Home Becomes Work*. New York: Henry Holt & Co. 2000.

Hoffman, Merle. 'Happiness and the Feminist Mind'. *On the Issues*. 22 Oct. 1996.

Israel, Betsy. *Bachelor Girl: The Secret History of Single Women in the Twentieth Century*. New York: HarperCollins. 2003.

Jackman, Christine. 'Two Careers Crushing Relationships'. *Australian*. 9 Dec. 2003, p5.

Jones, Heather Grace and Maggie Kirkman (eds). *Sperm Wars: The Rights and Wrongs of Reproduction*. Sydney: ABC Books. 2005.

Kahnemann, Daniel, Ed Diener and Norbert Schwartz (eds). *Well-Being: The Foundations of Hedonic Psychology*. Russell Sage Foundation. 1998.

Kamen, Paula. *Her Way: Young Women Remake the Sexual Revolution*. New York: Broadway Books. 2002.

Kaufman, Joanne. 'Good Guilt, Bad Guilt'. *Good Housekeeping*. Sept. 2001, v233 i3 p88.

Kenny, Mary. 'The Strange Rebirth of the Family'. *Guardian*. 27 Jan. 2004.

Kingston, Anne. *The Meaning of Wife*. New York: Farrar, Straus and Giroux. 2004.

Kingwell, Mark. *In Pursuit of Happiness*. New York: Crown Publishers. 1998.

Kolbert, Elizabeth. 'Mother Courage: Kids, Careers and Culture'. *New Yorker*. 8 March 2004.

Kuczynski, Alex. 'She's Got to Be a Macho Girl'. *New York Times*. 3 Nov. 2002.

Kushner, Harold S. *How Good Do You Have to Be?* Thomson Gale. 2004.

Laumann, Edward O. *The Sexual Organization of the City*. Chicago: University of Chicago Press. 2003.

Lawson, Nigella. *How to Be a Domestic Goddess*. New York: Hyperion. 2001.

Learner, Tobsha. 'The Economics of Intimacy'. *Weekend Review (Australian Financial Review)*. 16 April 2004.

Lucas, Richard E. *et al.* 'Reexaming Adaptation and the Set Point Model of Happiness: Reactions to Changes in Marital Status'. *Journal of Personality and Social Psychology* v84 n3.

Luo Lu. 'Gender and Conjugal Differences in Happiness'. *Journal of Social Psychology* Feb. 2000, v140, i1, p132.

Lutwak, Nita, *et al.* 'Shame and Guilt and Their Relationship to Positive Expectations and Anger Expressiveness'. Adolescence. Winter 2001, v36 i144 p641.

Magnet, Myron (ed.). *Modern Sex: Liberation and Its Discontents*. Chicago: Ivan R. Dee. 2001.

Maines, Rachel P. *The Technology of Orgasm*. Baltimore, MD: Johns Hopkins University Press. 2001.

Marcus, Amy Dockser. '3–5 Years between Babies May Be Best for Mom, Child'. *Wall Street Journal*. 8 Feb. 2004.

Maushart, Susan. *The Mask of Motherhood*. Sydney: Random House. 1997.

——. *Wifework*. Melbourne: Text Publishing. 2001.

Meager, David and Declan Murray. 'Depression'. *The Lancet* 1 March 1997, v349, n902.

Milkie, Melissa *et al.* 'Gendered Division of Childrearing: Ideals, Realities and the Relationship to Parental Well Being'. *Sex Roles* July 2002, p21.

Molloy, John T. *Why Men Marry Some Women and Not Others*. New York: Warner Books. 2004.

Mookherjee, H. H. 'Marital Status, Gender and Perception of Well-being'. The *Journal of Social Psychology* 137, p95–105.

National Institute of Mental Health. 'Depression: What Every Woman Should Know'. NIH Publication 00-4779 August 2000.

Nolen-Hoeksema, Susan and Cheryl Rusting. 'Gender Differences in Well-Being,' in Kahneman, Daniel (ed.) *Well-Being: The Foundations of Hedonic Psychology*.

Noor, Noraini M. 'Some Demographic, Personality, and Role Variables as Correlates of Women's Well-Being'. *Sex Roles: A Journal of Research*. May 1996, v34 n9–10 p603(18).

O'Keeffe, Alice. 'It's a Tough Call: Should You Have to Make It?' *Observer*. 11 January 2004.

Ogden, Gina. *Women Who Love Sex*. Cambridge, MA: Womanspirit Press. 2000.

'Older Mothers Push Up US Infant Mortality Rate'. *Chicago Sun-Times*. 12 Feb. 2004.

Orenstein, Peggy. *Flux: Women on Sex, Work, Love, Kids and Life in a Half-Changed World*. New York: Anchor. 2001.

Orrange, Robert. 'The Emerging Mutable Self: Gender Dynamics and Creative Adaptations in Defining Work, Family and the Future'. *Social Forces* Sept. 2003, v82, i1.

Pan, Cindy. 'The Chromosome Factor'. *Sunday Telegraph*. 26 Sept. 2004.

Paul, Pamela. *The Starter Marriage and the Future of Matrimony*. New York: Random House. 2002.

Perera, Sylvia Brinton. *Scapegoat Complex: Toward a Mythology of Shadow and Guilt*. Toronto: Inner City Books. 1985.

Peters Joan K. *Not Your Mother's Life*. Cambridge, MA: Perseus Publishing. 2001.

Pirani, Clara. 'Middle-Age Soon No Baby Barrier'. *Australian*. 27 Oct. 2004.

Pittman, Frank. *Grow Up*. New York: St. Martin's Press. 1999.

Pocock, Barbara. 'Having a Life: Work, Family and Community in 2000'. Adelaide: Centre for Labour Research. 2000.

——. *Work and Family Futures. How Young Australians Plan to Work and Care*, The Australia Institute, Canberra, Discussion Paper 66. 2004.

Posner, Trisha. *This Is Not Your Mother's Menopause*. New York: Random House. 2000.

Roberts, Yvonne. 'Having a Child at 46 Acts on Your Life like Alka Seltzer in Water'. *Daily Mail*. 20 Oct. 2003.

Rogers, Stacy and Paul Amato. 'Have Changes in Gender Relations Affected Marital Quality?' *Social Forces*. Dec. 2000, v79 i2 p731.

Roiphe, Anne. *Married: A Fine Predicament*. London: Bloomsbury. 2004.

Ryan, R. M. and E. L. Deci. 'On Happiness and Human Potentials: A Review of Research on Hedonic and Eudaemonic Well Being'. *Annual Review of Psychology* 2001, p141.

——. 'Self-determination theory and the facilitation of intrinsic motivation, social development and well being'. *American Psychologist* 55, 68–78. 2000.

Sack, Steven and J. Ross Eshleman. 'Marital Status & Happiness: A 17-Nation Study'. *Journal of Marriage and Family*. May 1998, 527–36.

Sandholtz, Kurt, *et al. Beyond Juggling*. San Francisco: Berrett-Koehler Publishers, Inc. 2002.

Schlessinger, Laura C. *The Proper Care and Feeding of Husbands*. New York: HarperCollins. 2003.

Schnarch, David. *Passionate Marriage*. New York: Henry Holt & Co. 1998.

Schwartz, Pepper. *Everything You Know about Love and Sex Is Wrong*. E. Rutherford, NJ: Perigee/Penguin. 2001.

Sen, Amartya. *Development as Freedom*. New York: Knopf Publishing Group. 2000.

Shields, Michael and Mark Wooden. 'Marriage, Children and Subjective Well-Being'. Australian Institute of Family Studies Conference, Melbourne. Feb. 2003.

Shulman, Polly. 'Great Expectations'. *Psychology Today*. Apr/May 2004.

Smith, Margaret and Patricia Michalka. *Is It Me or My Hormones?* Leederville, WA: Caring for Women Publications. 2003.

Schwartz, Barry. *The Paradox of Choice: Why Less Is More*. New York: HarperCollins. 2004.

Seligman, Martin E. P. *Authentic Happiness*. New York: Random House. 2002.

'Sex a Turn-off for Many UK Women'. *BBC News*. 26 June 2001.

Smith, Roger W. (ed.). *Guilt: Man and Society*. New York: Anchor Books. 1971.

Summers, Anne. *The End of Equality*. Sydney: Random House Australia. 2003.

Talbot, Margaret. 'Supermom Fictions'. *New York Times Magazine*. 27 Oct. 2002.

Tischler, Linda. 'Why Men Work Harder than Women'. *Financial Review BOSS*. March 2004.

Trinca, Helen and Catherine Fox. *Better than Sex: How a Whole Generation Got Hooked on Work*. Sydney: Random House Australia. 2004.

Van Laningham, Jody *et al.* 'Marital Happiness, Marital Duration, and the U-Shaped Curve: Evidence from a Five-Wave Panel Study'. *Social Forces*. June 2001, v79 i4.

Waite, Linda and Maggie Gallagher. *The Case for Marriage: Why Married People Are Happier, Healthier, and Better Off Financially*. New York: Broadway Books. 2001.

Warren, Elizabeth and Amelia Warren. *The Two-Income Trap: Why Middle-class Parents are Going Broke*. New York: Basic Books. 2003.

Watters, Ethan. *Urban Tribes: Are Friends the New Family?* New York: Bloomsbury. 2004.

Whitehead, Barbara Dafoe and David Popenoe. 'The State of Our Unions: The Social Health of Marriage in America'. The National Marriage Project. 2004.

Williams, Marjorie. 'A Working Mom's Comedy'. *Washington Post*. 2 Oct. 2002.

Wolf, Naomi. *Misconceptions*. New York: Doubleday. 2001.

a note on the author

Susan Maushart was born in New York and has lived in Australia since 1985. She is a senior research associate at Curtin University and a columnist for the *Australian Magazine*. She lives in Perth with her three children.